PRAISE FOR

The Passport Project

"*The Passport Project* is an enticing global travelogue led by teenagers ..."

— *FOREWORD REVIEWS*

"[B]rilliantly captures the awkward hilarity of teen/family travel while highlighting the gift of a global worldview ... sprinkled with humor, moments of discovery, and appreciation for diversity and cultural awareness. This kind of perspective is ... so essential right now. [P]eople of all ages will read and take to heart."

— RACHEL MACY STAFFORD, *NEW YORK TIMES*
BESTSELLING AUTHOR AND CERTIFIED SPECIAL EDUCATION
TEACHER

"I laughed. I cried. I was scared. As a history teacher, I like to think I know it all, but this book taught me so much. Geography, culture, religions, and customs I never knew existed."

— J. ISBELL, SIXTH GRADE SOCIAL STUDIES TEACHER

"This book changed my family's life."

"As a teacher, I am always looking for books to help students open their eyes to different points of view. The narration through the sisters makes it as engaging as it is educational."

THIS BOOK!! Inspiring. Fun. Educational. Page Turner. Memorable. VERY entertaining and relatable.... [R]eaders are transported around the world, all from the comfort of our own homes and classrooms.

"[P]acked with harrowing travel tales and hilarious anecdotes ... full of cultural information. [It's] a very important read for middle grade children ... that will inspire teens and tweens to see the world from a different perspective."

"LOVED this book!!!! I want to go on a global family field trip now!!!"

THE PASSPORT PROJECT

THE PASSPORT PROJECT

Two Sisters Ditch Middle School
for a Life-Changing Journey
Around the World

Kellie McIntyre

Contributors:
Delaney McIntyre and Riley McIntyre

SHAMROCK
HOUSE

SHAMROCK
HOUSE

Publisher's Cataloging-in-Publication data

Names: McIntyre, Kellie, author. | McIntyre, Delaney, contributor. | McIntyre, Riley, contributor.
Title: The passport project : two sisters ditch middle school for a life-changing journey around the world/ by
Kellie McIntyre ; contributors: Delaney McIntyre and Riley McIntyre.
Description: Includes bibliographical references. | Birmingham, AL: Shamrock House, 2022. |
Summary: When sisters Delaney (14) and Riley (12) trade middle school for a global family journey, they
discover new countries, cultures, customs, and ultimately, themselves.
Identifiers: LCCN: 2021919097 | ISBN: 978-1-7377438-2-8 (hardcover) | 978-1-7377438-1-1 (b&w
paperback) | 978-1-7377438-3-5 (color paperback) | 978-1-7377438-0-4 (ebook)
Subjects: LCSH McIntyre family--Travel--Juvenile literature. | McIntyre, Kellie--Travel--Juvenile literature. |
McIntyre, Delaney--Travel--Juvenile literature. | McIntyre, Riley--Travel--Juvenile literature. |
Families--Travel--Juvenile literature. | Voyages around the world--Juvenile literature. | Voyages and travels-
-Anecdotes. | BISAC TRAVEL / Essays & Travelogues | TRAVEL / Special Interest / Family |
JUVENILE NONFICTION / Travel | JUVENILE NONFICTION / People & Places / General |
JUVENILE NONFICTION / Family / Siblings
Classification: LCC G465 .M35 2022 | DDC 910.4/1--dc23

For bulk sales, permission requests, and corrections, please visit:
ThePassportProjectBook.com

Published by Shamrock House, Birmingham, Alabama
1 3 5 7 9 10 8 6 4 2

For Dale, my champion, encourager, and trusty travel companion.

For Delaney and Riley, exploring the world with you has been the greatest joy of my life. Thank you for allowing me to share our story.

And for everyone who has dreamed about the world beyond their bubble.

Author's Note

The idea for this book emerged during the Dumpster-fire summer of 2020. While the nation and world imploded, I felt compelled to create something—anything—that would unify rather than divide. But what could I do? Like everyone else, I was trapped at home trying to figure out how to navigate our new normal.

Then it hit me.

People always say to write what you know, and I know two things: One, there is no better way to learn tolerance and an appreciation for diversity than through travel. And two, anyone who survives 24/7 family time while hopscotching across the globe has a story to tell.

And so it began.

However, instead of writing another 'round-the-world memoir for adults, I thought it would be far more entertaining to share our story from my (then) 14- and 12-year-old daughters' perspectives. While conversations have been reconstructed to the best of my ability, the spirit of the dialogue is accurate.

In addition to the dramatic and traumatic moments seared into my grey matter, Delaney and Riley's old blog posts and personal journals proved invaluable in stitching together our story. They have assured me that I've accurately and painfully portrayed their characters—awkward moments, (pre)teenage anxiety, and all.

All events are true, especially the ones we wish weren't. In a few cases, timelines have been adjusted for storytelling purposes. Some names have been changed to protect the innocent or guilty.

I hope you learn a little, laugh a lot, and fall in love with the world along the way.

ITINERARY

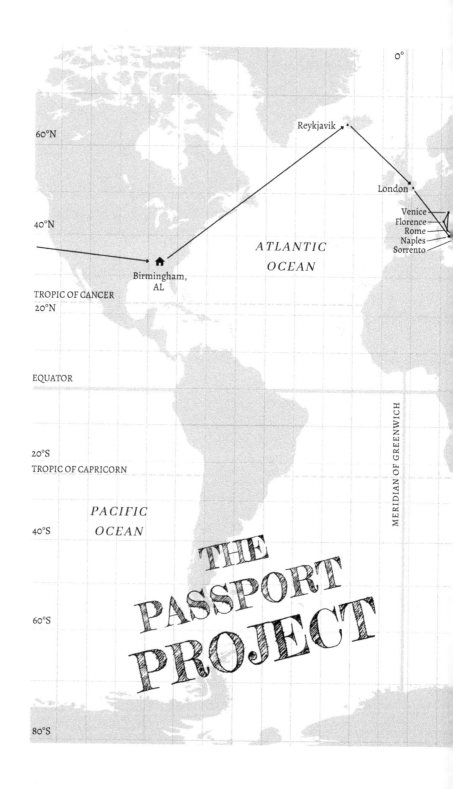

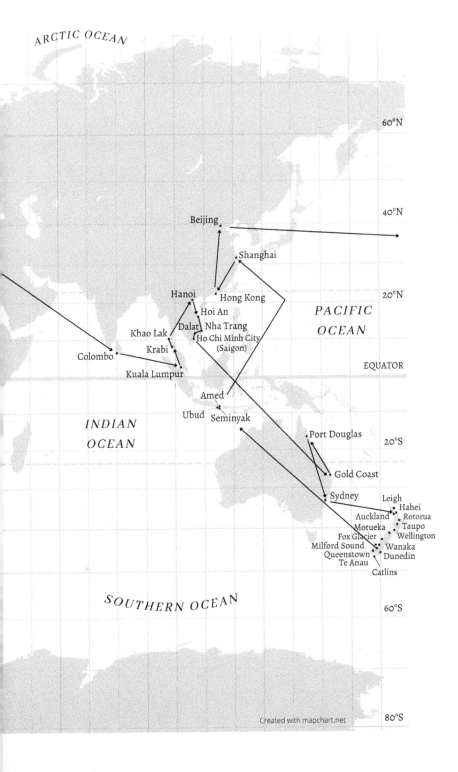

Introduction

Hey y'all,
What would you do if your parents said:

> We've come up with a brilliant idea! We're going on a global adventure. You won't go to school, see your friends, play your favorite sport, or go to any parties or dances for five months. You can only take one suitcase, three pairs of shoes, and you have to pack for hot and cold weather. And as a bonus? You get to spend 24/7 *with your parents.*

Would you squeal with delight? Or squall with dread?
Would you hug them? Or hate them?
That is exactly what our parents did. This is our story.

 Delaney (14) and Riley (12) McIntyre

I. The Bubble

bubble
noun bub·ble | \ 'bə-bəl \

: an enclosed or isolated sphere of experience or activity in which the like-minded members of a homogeneous community support and reinforce their shared opinions.

Merriam-Webster.com. 2022.

1.

Tryouts

Fall of Seventh Grade

Why fit in when you were born to stand out?

— Dr. Seuss

Delaney, 13

How am I supposed to choke this down? It's taco night, which I normally love. But I'm too nervous to eat—or play the High-Low game.

"My high was winning the coffee-grinder dance contest in gym. I even beat the boys." Riley wipes taco juice from her grin. "My low was spilling my yogurt at lunch, so I looked like I had barf on my shirt all day."

"My low was that a contract fell through for some clients I've been working with for months. My high is having dinner with my girls." Typical Dad always says something mushy.

It's almost my turn. If I don't come up with something quick, my parents will start grilling me. Not about homework or chores —like normal parents—but about the world.

"If you could go anywhere in the world, where would it be?" Mom will ask.

"Name the top five places on your bucket list," Dad will follow.

Our answers are always the same—French Polynesia for Riley and London for me.

Then we'll turn it around and ask them, which is what they really want us to do. Because they always have a long list of places to rattle off. Sometimes they'll name some random country we've never heard of. Asking "where is that?" is a huge mistake. It always results in a one-way ticket to the Wall of Dreams for a geography lesson.

I glance at the microwave clock again. 6:33 p.m. In less than thirty minutes, I'll have my High-Low answer. The new girls' basketball team roster for Liberty Park Middle School will be posted on the gym door at seven o'clock. I might throw up.

I'd much rather spend Friday night with my cat, Jingles, in my lap and a Harry Potter book in my hands. It doesn't matter which one. I've read them all. Multiple times. I wish reading could be a sport. I'd be captain of that team for sure.

At 6:50 p.m., my mom and I make the quick two-mile drive to my middle school ... which sits right next door to my elementary school ... which is just one mile down the road from my preschool ... which is why I love my neighborhood. I've lived in Vestavia my entire life. And I've been friends with these kids since we were pooping in our pants.

Drizzle falls as we pull into the school parking lot. I'm the first one here. Yay. I want to be alone for this. I hate getting bad news in front of people, especially my friends.

"Wait here," I say, jumping out of the car.

"Good luck," Mom says as the passenger door closes behind me.

I race through the rain to the gym doors. Another girl, Caroline, runs up beside me. Even though she's nice, we aren't in the same friend group. Don't ask me why. Our eyes and fingers quickly scan the newly hung roster. Bad news for both of us.

Before I can stop them, hot tears begin streaming down my face. Tears roll down Caroline's face too. We share an awkward moment and then dash through the rain back to our parents' cars.

"I'm sor—" Mom starts.

"I made it!" I blurt out, tears gushing now.

"Wait. What?"

"I didn't want to make it!" I sob, using my sleeves as tissue to wipe my eyes and nose.

"But why?"

"Because I don't *like* basketball, Mom!"

And that's the problem with middle school. We do things we don't even like because we're trying to fit in.

Somewhere.

Anywhere.

I can't wait 'til next year. Eighth grade is going to be the Best. Year. Ever.

2.

Riley Reinvention Project

Fall of Sixth Grade

Isn't it amazing that we are all made in God's image, and yet there is so much diversity among his people?

— Archbishop Desmond Tutu

Riley, 11

Even though my Riley Reinvention Project (RRP) is only halfway complete, middle school is off to a good start. I don't have hatchet hair anymore.

I cut my hair when I was little, so I would look like Nanaw. Everyone was always telling my sister, mom, and Nanaw that they look like three-generation triplets. Supposedly, I take after my other grandmother, but she died before I was born. So no one tells me I look like anyone. I thought I could change all that with a pair of scissors. Wrong! I hid under a smelly beach towel in a laundry basket until my parents found me.

Sadly, the only way to fix my hair was to get a pixie cut. "Pixie" is code for a boy's haircut on a girl. Some girls can totally rock a pixie. But I wasn't rockin' anything. It was tragic. To make things even worse, my mom wouldn't let me grow it out because she thought it was "adorable." Wrong again! More like a-dork-able. To make up for it, Mom let me get my ears pierced. That didn't help either, and I have proof.

One day, I stopped by the lake in our neighborhood to feed the ducks. A boy and his dad were fishing on the pier. When the little brat saw me skipping in a tie-dye skirt and pink halter, he looked at his dad and yelled, "WHY DOES THAT BOY HAVE HIS EARS PIERCED?" Double tragic!!

Fortunately, the bad-hair phase of my life is over. Unfortunately, my body is stuck in elementary school. If it weren't for my long hair, I'd still get mistaken for a boy. Why do I have to take after the super-pale-late-bloomer side of the family??? But besides being small, I pretty much blend in. Which is the number one goal of every middle schooler on the planet.

"Time to go. It's my week to drive," Mom calls up the stairs. "You've got a snack in the car."

"Coming." I finish changing into my hip-hop outfit and stuff my leo and dance shoes into a bag.

Even though it's my first year, my friends have been dancing forever. By sixth grade, most girls are either girly girls, sporty girls, or artsy girls. I'm none of them. Even though I'm into adventures more than activities, my parents always make me sign up for something. Last year was figure skating. Before that was diving, gymnastics, drama, swimming, softball (the worst), karate, piano, harmonica, art, and even fencing. They're all fun for a few months, but who wants to do that stuff all the time? Boring!

My favorite activity ever was French Camp. I loved the two women who ran it, an artist and a teacher. We made crêpes, learned French, and painted the Eiffel Tower on canvases. On the last day, Ms. Tricia told us to paint whatever we wanted. So I did.

When Mom picked us up, the teachers couldn't wait to show her my painting.

"Riley made this." Ms. Tricia held up my canvas like a trophy.

"She came up with it *all by herself*," Ms. Katie gushed.

Pride and shock flashed across Mom's face like I'd just scored the winning point in a championship game. Which has never happened. Stick people holding hands stretched across my painted globe. At one end of the canvas, the skin color was tan, at the other end, almost black. And in the middle were different shades of beige. I'd scrawled across the canvas in bright red paint:

> EVERYBODY IS THE SAME WHEREVER THEY GO.
> IN THEIR HEART THEY ARE THE SAME.

That was my seven-year-old home run. Mom loved the painting so much that I made another one just like it. I gave it to Ms. Katie, and she hung it in her ESL classroom.

If only I could come up with a way to fast-track the completion of the RRP 2.0 upgrade, then my life would be perfect. Riley 1.0 had boy hair and a boy body. Riley 1.5 has girl hair and a boy body.

And that is where I'm stuck.

3.

Thanks for Ruining My Life

March 15

If you're always trying to be normal, you will never know how amazing you can be.

— MAYA ANGELOU, *RAINBOW IN THE CLOUD*

Delaney, 13

olly barks, jumps off my bed, and runs downstairs. My parents must be back. A few weeks ago, Ri and I took our usual Sunday-morning-church seats between our parental bookends. That week's sermon was about not living a life of "accumulating regrets." Next thing you know, my parents have booked a trip to Chicago and I get to spend two school nights with my BFF.

"Hey, girls. Dinnertime," Mom yells up the stairs.

"What are we having?" I yell back.

"Tazikis."

"Bummer," Riley says, leaning against my door. "I was hoping for Surin's coconut soup."

"Same." Tazikis is Mom's go-to dinner when she doesn't

want to cook, which is basically every night. Most moms have a specialty dish their kids love, like Ms. Diana's spaghetti or Ms. Erin's chicken. My mom's specialty is YO-YO. As in, you're on your own. "I'm curious to hear about this meeting they went to."

"Did you see how they looked at each other when Pastor Wade said 'accumulating regrets?' And for the rest of the service, they kept having an invisible conversation with their eyes."

"Yup. They're up to something," I say. "Time to find out what."

We head to the kitchen and fill our plates from the carry-out cartons lined across the counter. We take our usual seats at the kitchen table.

"Tell us about the meeting. Was it fun?" Riley starts the conversation.

"It was *so* much fun. It was full of travel junkies. Everyone in the room wore a name tag that listed the last place they'd been and the next place they were going," Mom says.

"Sounds like your kinda thing," Riley says.

There's nothing my parents like to talk about more than travel. Nothing.

"What'd y'all do besides stand around and talk?" I ask.

"Well, they had a panel of people who had taken gap years or traveled around the world. So people asked them questions about how they did it. Tips they could share. That sort of thing. Most of the people on the panel were single or young couples. But there was one family who had biked all the way from Alaska to South America *with kids*."

"No way. I would die," I say.

"Whoa. That's sooo cool. Did you pick somewhere for us to go next?" Riley asks.

My parents give each other the same look they did in church a few weeks back.

"Well, sort of ..." Mom grins. "We're going on a global family field trip!"

"What?!" Riley squeals.

"What?" I repeat, stopping my fork mid-air. "What does *that* even mean?"

"It's like taking a gap year after college to travel, but we'll do it as a family and only for half the year. Here's what we're thinking so far," Mom begins. "We'll leave in the fall. That way you can start school like normal. Then when your dad's business slows for the season, we'll take off. We'll leave in October when your cross-country season ends and come back in the spring. And then you can finish the school year with your friends."

Are they crazy?! I drop my fork and inhale deeply, trying to slow my racing heart. I can't miss eighth grade—or the Halloween, Christmas, and New Year's Eve parties, Dirty Santa, bonfires, sleepovers, the Valentine's dance, football games, basketball games and so much more. I'd become that weirdo kid who doesn't fit in. My social life would never recover.

"Why can't we just go in the summer? That would make way more sense," I pivot, offering a more teenage-friendly option.

"You know I can't be gone in the spring or summer. That's the busy season for real estate. But if we travel in the winter like we normally do, then it won't be as big of a financial hit," Dad explains.

For the past few years, we've taken a big trip over winter break. Sometimes we miss an extra week of school, which is fun. But this is a whole different deal. They've obviously lost their minds. This must be a mid-life crisis. We have a cat, a dog, and a house. Not to mention they have jobs. I've *got* to remind them of their responsibilities. Riley and I take turns firing questions at our parents, like boys with spitballs at a substitute teacher.

"What about Jingles?"

"And Molly?"

"And school?"

"And our house?"

"And remember,"—I bare my teeth—"I have *braces* which require regular orthodontist visits."

My mom is super hyped, like she's had too many Diet Cokes. Dad's pumped too. This is not looking good. I hold my breath as Mom lays out the plan.

"I've already called Dr. Sarver, and it's no problem to skip your adjustments for a while. You'll just have to keep your braces on a bit longer. He can hook us up with someone if a wire breaks or a bracket pops off. He knows orthos all over the world. We'll find foster families for the pets. That's the tricky part, but we'll figure it out.

"As for school, you'll homeschool while we're gone and then go back to regular school when we return. Seventh and eighth grades are our last window to do this. After next year, you'll be in high school, then college. If we're gonna do something big, now is the time. We want to experience so many places with you, and there isn't enough time to do it over two-week winter breaks. Besides, the most expensive part of traveling is getting there. If we're gonna go halfway around the world, we should stay a while," Mom says.

Dad continues, "So we'll go back to Southeast Asia and explore more of that area. Then we'll go to Australia and New Zealand. Since it's the southern hemisphere, it'll be summer there. The timing is perfect. We want to focus on the really far away stuff now, and when you're older, you can explore Europe on your own. What do you think?"

"Are you serious?! This is AMAZING!! I'm dying to bungee jump in New Zealand." Riley jumps up and down, clapping and squealing. Then she busts into one of her cringey dance moves. "Are the Baums going with us?"

Great question. My head jerks toward my parents. The Baums are our family travel buddies from California. They have kids our ages. Taylor and Sydney coming along is the only way to keep this idea from being a total train wreck.

"No. Just us." My parents lock eyes with me and ask, "Delaney, what do you think?"

Arms crossed, I give them a long, hard stare. I slowly reply, "I'm not missing eighth grade. I'm. Not. Going." Then, for extra effect, I march upstairs to my room and slam the door.

THREE SOFT KNOCKS on my door. I know the knocks. They are my mom's.

"May I come in?"

Silence. I lie in bed, staring at the ceiling while she sits next to me. My mind scrambles for the words to convince her to get off this crazy train.

"I know you don't want to go," she starts, "but this is the opportunity of a lifetime."

"You don't understand! You don't remember what it's like to be thirteen. Eighth grade is the best year of middle school. We're finally the oldest ones. It's not fair to make me miss eighth, and Riley gets to miss seventh. Seventh grade is the worst. Everyone knows that."

"I know you think eighth grade is going to be the greatest year ever, but you're lacking one thing. Perspective. I have perspective. And I can promise you, you will be glad we did this when it's over."

"This is *your* dream. Not mine! It's not fair to make me miss school for this. Why can't we just be a normal family?!"

"Number one, why in the world would you want to be normal? Normal is overrated. Number two, you're right. This is my dream. To see the world *with you*. So here's the deal: we're doing this. We will regret it if we don't, and we'll never have this opportunity again. So you can choose to be mad, or you can choose to embrace it. But either way—you're going."

Mom stands and walks toward the door. "And one more

thing …" She reaches for the knob and turns around. "I love you."

"THANKS FOR RUINING MY LIFE!" I sob as I pull the covers over my face.

4.

Three Conditions

March 22

I have found out that there ain't no surer way to find out whether you like people or hate them than to travel with them.

— MARK TWAIN, *TOM SAWYER ABROAD*

Riley, 11

It's been a week, and Delaney is still giving my parents the silent treatment. She's so dramatic.

I pour brownie batter into the pan, then run my finger around the bowl. "I promise I won't act like that when I'm thirteen." I lick the goopy-chocolate-goodness from my finger.

"Well, that's good to hear. I'll be sure to remind you of that when the time comes," Mom says, closing the oven.

The trip timing is perfecto. The completion of the Riley Reinvention 2.0 upgrade is moving slowly. So even if the RRP isn't finished by the time we leave in October, a new-and-improved Riley will definitely return next spring. That's a whole year away.

Out of nowhere, Delaney appears. She stands next to the stairs—arms crossed and hip popped to one side. In her bossy-big-sister voice, Delaney announces, "I'll go under three conditions: One, we go to Europe. Two, we are back by spring break. And three, no naked people."

"Ew. No. I hate Europe." Why would any kid want to go to Europe?

"Why would you say that, Riley?" Dad walks into the kitchen sniffing the air like Molly. "You've never even been to Europe."

"It's just a bunch of old cathedrals and museums. B-O-R-I-N-G. Asia's the bomb. There are elephants and beaches and good food and fun markets. And the people are sooo nice."

"I want to go to the Harry Potter set in London," Delaney says.

"I can't promise when we'll be back, and Europe's not really in the plan," Mom says.

"Let's go to the Wall of Dreams. Let me explain why," Dad says.

Oh, yay. Time for another geography lesson brought to you by my dad. We file to the basement and line up in front of the floor-to-ceiling world map. Colorful pins stick out of the Wall of Dreams like lollipops. Different colored pins mean different things. Blue pins show where my dad's been. Yellow is just my mom. Black pins mark the places my parents went before Delaney and I came along. And red pins show the places we've been as a family.

A dozen tiny red balls stick out of North America, South America, and Asia. The Wall of Dreams tracks the progress on our family goal: to explore every continent, except Antarctica, before we finish high school.

Finger pointed, my dad draws an invisible circle around the Southeast Asia/Australia/New Zealand part of the world. "We're planning to go here. See. And London is way over here." He takes the other hand and draws an air circle around London.

"That just doesn't make sense. We would literally circle the globe."

"It's not fair! Everyone gets to go where they want except me. You picked New Zealand, Mom picked Sydney and Southeast Asia, and Riley picked the Gili Islands." She pauses, then announces, "I. Pick. London."

My mom twitches her mouth back and forth. Dad lets out one of his "hmm" grunts like he does when he's considering something. They are having another one of their eye conversations.

Mom studies the map again, then turns to us. "It's official. We're going around the world!"

"Oh yeah, oh yeah." I bust into my best moves until Delaney Downer interrupts my happy dance.

"And what about naked people?"

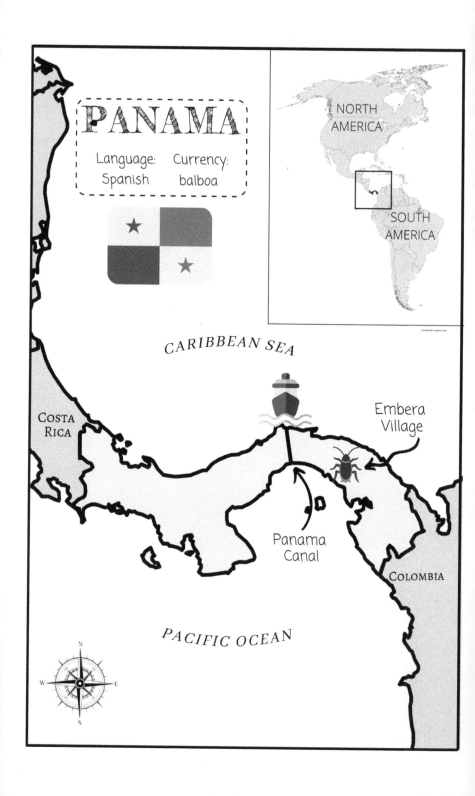

5.

Cockroaches in Paradise

Three years ago

Toto, I've a feeling we're not in Kansas anymore.

— DOROTHY, *THE WIZARD OF OZ*

Delaney, 13

Cockroaches and naked people are not a winning combination for most family vacations. But our vacations aren't like most. We don't do campgrounds or cruises. Oh no. My parents insist we get "out of the bubble."

When I was ten years old, we went to Panama (the country, not the beach town in Florida like everyone else) for spring break. The only reason we went there is because Mom found a cheap flight. That's how most of our trips begin.

Panama is the super skinny country at the bottom of Central America that connects North America and South America, like a tiny paper clip connecting two giant continents. Panama is famous for its canal that allows ships to sail directly from the Caribbean Sea to the Pacific Ocean. Before the canal was built, ships had to make the long, dangerous journey around the bottom tip of South America. Most people who visit Panama go to watch the massive ships squeeze through the narrow canal. But don't confuse popular for exciting. Have you ever watched paint dry? Welcome to the Panama Canal.

After checking off this boring engineering miracle, we headed to the jungle. My stomach started hurting the minute our guide, Diego, picked us up from our hotel. I'd been to Belize's jungle and was not a fan. I don't like bugs, or snakes, or spiders. And the jungle is full of them. But this time would be even scarier—because we were spending the night with a real jungle tribe.

Diego drove us to a little shack next to a river to wait for our boat. The Emberá Puru Indian village sits deep in the jungle and can only be reached by the river. Chickens and pigs ran freely along the river bank. While we waited, Ri and I tried to catch squealing piglets. It's a lot harder—and louder—than you'd think.

The "boat" was actually a dugout canoe made from a hollowed-out tree trunk. A man and a teenage boy—each with a bright red piece of fabric dangling in front of their "parts"— stood in the canoe paddling toward us. In the back, an even skinnier red slice covered their cracks, but not their buns. That flimsy material was the only thing they wore.

"We're not in Vestavia anymore," I whispered to Riley, after silently begging Mother Nature for a wind-free journey.

We paddled down the Rio San Juan de Pequeni for forty-five minutes until beating drums interrupted chirping birds and howling monkeys. By the side of the river, six more practically naked men greeted us under a handmade wooden sign with the words Emberá Puru painted on it. We climbed out of the canoe and up the steep dirt bank into the village.

"The Emberá people are the indigenous people of Panama and Colombia, where North America and South America meet,"

Diego explained. "Besides Spanish, they speak their tribal language, also known as Emberá."

EMBERA PURU VILLAGE, PANAMA–MARCH 2010:
Village men wait for visitors to arrive by dugout canoe.

Diego said a lot of other stuff, but I was too busy checking out this fascinating new world to listen. The Emberá people looked like something straight out of my social studies textbook. Scratch that. My book wouldn't have shown the actual pictures, because these women were topless! All the women and girls were dressed (or not-dressed) the same: they each wore a bright, patterned skirt and a necklace made of coins or beads.

Nothing else.

It was every middle-school girl's locker-room nightmare—baring her ta-tas for all the world to see. Which is why every American girl learns at least one magic trick in her life: the bra-out-the-sleeve trick. All females between ten and seventy can pull that trick quicker than you can ditch your parents at a school function. But not the Emberá. Whether they had big boobs, small boobs, or no boobs, they weren't embarrassed at all. Not even the girls my age. I don't know how they do it.

But I know this: if I had to be naked in front of strangers, I. Would. Die.

DIEGO LED US to our hut to get settled. Our room-on-stilts stood in the middle of the dirt village. I followed Diego up the tree trunk ladder into our hut. There was no furniture, only five striped hammocks hanging from the rafters. Since these jungle cabanas had no walls, we could watch the Emberá families in their huts, and they could watch us in ours.

"Where's the bathroom?" I asked.

"You'll take a bath in the river, and there's a toilet that way." Diego pointed toward a dirt path.

I wondered how long I could hold it.

We gathered in the community center, which was really just a super-sized hut without the stilts. We plopped down on the long wooden bench that ran the length of the dirt floor. Soon a parade of dark-haired women with medium-brown skin filed in and formed a circle. In addition to the patterned skirts, many of them had patterned skin too. Blue-black geometric tattoos covered some or most of their bodies. For the next thirty minutes, we watched a patterned-rainbow-dance-train of clapping hands, stomping feet, and swinging boobies.

After the performance, we followed a barefoot *shaman* through the jungle. He is the town doctor, and the jungle is his pharmacy. Diego translated everything he said. The medicine man pointed out different plants explaining which ones we could eat, which ones would kill us, and which ones would heal us. The headache plant was different from the diarrhea plant, and so on.

"That one,"—the shaman chuckled and pointed to a vine—"fixes older men."

Both of my parents laughed extra hard at that.

We returned to our hut after the hike. As Riley and I sat, swinging our legs from the edge, a group of young kids huddled below. They waved and pointed to the river.

"They want you to go swimming," Diego said.

"Let's go!" Riley and I jumped up and scampered down the tree trunk ladder.

Fortunately, we already had our swimsuits on under our clothes. We followed the village kids to the river bank. The girls peeled off their skirts and jumped in the river, wearing only their underwear. The boys took off the loincloth-thingy they wore around their waists—which didn't cover much anyway—and skinny-dipped. Wearing our neon Target swimsuits, Riley and I joined them.

"Hey Ri, are you gonna skinny dip?" I asked.

"No way, José!"

"Why not? You always do at home." I snapped the back of her swimsuit.

"But that's only when no one else is around!" She popped my swimsuit back.

We spent the next two hours playing river games with our new friends. We panned for gold, played catch with a lizard, and swung from a rope swing. Even though we didn't speak the same language, our laughter said it all.

"Do you want to get tattoos?" Diego hollered from the river bank. "The ink comes from a plant, so it's only temporary."

"I'm not su—," I said.

"Yes!" Riley squealed. "That would be sooo cool to go back to school with a tattoo."

"Alright," I agreed, "but I wanna go first."

We dried off and followed Diego to Rosa's hut. She's the best tattoo artist in the village. While I got situated on the bamboo floor, the Ink Queen asked me a question.

EMBERA PURU VILLAGE, PANAMA–MARCH 2010:
Embera woman paints tribal tattoo around Delaney's wrist.

"What do you want?" Diego translated. "They typically paint the tattoos anywhere on the upper body."

"Just here," I said, using my finger to draw an invisible bracelet around my wrist.

Rosa dipped a stick into a wooden bowl. She painted the juice of a jagua fruit on my skin. The liquid is clear at first, but then turns into a blue-black ink. A few minutes later, a real tribal bracelet circled my wrist.

I smiled at Rosa. "Thank you. I love it."

I couldn't wait to show my friends. I hoped it would last that long.

I got up, and Riley plopped down in my place next to Rosa. Riley's pale skin looked more ghostly than usual next to Rosa's smooth brown complexion.

With her goofy grin and high-pitched voice, Riley said, "I want it to go from here,"—pointing at her wrist—"to here"—running her finger all the way up her arm to her shoulder.

Ugh. Riley always has to outdo me.

EMBERA PURU VILLAGE, PANAMA–MARCH 2010:
Riley shows off her tribal body art with Embera woman.

After a long day of jungle fun, my stomach growled louder than the howler monkeys. While we sat on the floor, two Emberá women cooked our dinner over a three-log fire. Although I'm usually a picky eater, I knew there wouldn't be any other options. I was nervous about eating because there wasn't a real kitchen anywhere in the village. There was no running water. I hadn't seen a fridge. And the only oven was made out of clay and sat in the middle of the village. My expectations were low. Surely, I wouldn't starve to death overnight.

Karina and Maria, the jungle's top chefs, handed each of us a palm leaf bowl filled with fish and rice. Using my hand as a fork, I took my first bite. So good! I devoured it and asked for more.

"Mom, you never make anything that tastes this good." Riley licked her fingers.

"For real," I said, picking the last fish morsel from the leaf bowl.

"Careful y'all," Dad warned, as if we might offend Mom. But she knows her cooking is terrible.

As we laughed and talked about the day, a giant cockroach snuck out of the shadows and raced toward my rainforest feast. My dad grabbed the nearest flip-flop and pounded it, showering my arm with roach juice. Ew! So. Nasty. Another roach darted toward us, and he smashed it too. Soon *cucarachas grandes* scurried at us from every direction. Our shrieks filled the hut. We jumped up and started hopping around, simultaneously trying to kill and avoid the most disgusting creatures on the planet. Laughing at our First World freak-out, Karina and Maria ran to our rescue. They stomped on the roaches, kicking them aside with their bare feet. I thought I would die right there.

No longer hungry, we climbed the tree up to our hut to get ready for bed. After avoiding it all day, the dreaded moment had arrived.

"Mom, I need to go to the bathroom. I peed in the river while we were swimming, but I need to go again."

"I need to go, too. Let's do this," she said.

We followed the faint glow of our cheap flashlight down a dirt path to the potty—a rustic outhouse with a toilet seat mounted on a concrete pedestal. I shined the flashlight into the stall, bracing for the worst. Monster-sized cockroaches were running laps around the toilet seat. It looked like a track meet. Our matching mother-daughter screams pierced the jungle.

"I'm not sitting on that!" I cried.

"Just squat in the dirt outside." Mom backed away from the outhouse.

"I'm not doing that either!" I shrieked.

"Then what are you gonna do?!" Mom shrieked back.

"I need you to hold me over the toilet."

I pulled down my pants and bent my knees like I was sitting in an invisible chair. My mom held me suspended mid-air over the hole. I finally relaxed enough to go number one.

"So, where are you gonna go?" I asked, pulling up my pants.

"Nowhere. I just wet my pants." Then she added, "Remember, what happens in Panama, stays in Panama."

"Pinky promise." We hooked pinkies in the darkness.

Wow. And I thought my freak-out was bad. Back in the hut, I dug my rain jacket out of my backpack.

"Why do you want *that*?" Riley asked. The baby hairs curled around her glistening forehead.

"To keep the roaches off. Duh." I pulled the hood over my head, yanking the cord as tight as I could. Then zipped the jacket to my neck.

Armed with flip-flops, Dad and Ri played whack-a-roach from the safety of their hammocks. Riley screamed, "Die, sucker!" right before she smashed each one. I climbed into my hammock and spread a towel over my legs. I folded the hammock around me, forming a human burrito. The only exposed skin was the circle of my face peeking from the cinched hood. Two beady eyes stared at me from the beam above my head. I squeezed my eyes and started whispering Bible verses to myself. I knew I would die that night. What I didn't know: would I be the first ten-year-old to die of a cockroach-induced heart attack?

Somehow, I survived. Back at school the following week, my teacher gave our class a writing assignment:

My Spring Break

While kids from normal families wrote about the beach or mountains or grandma's house, I had to figure out how to write about naked people and cockroaches without ending up in foster care.

Trust me. This epic adventure is going to be an epic disaster.

6.

Packing Problems

September 15

He who would travel happily must travel light.

— Antoine de Saint Exupéry

Riley, 12

"How am I supposed to pack in *that*?"

We are one month from blastoff, and things are getting real. I stare at the not-very-big purple suitcase. Surely this is one of my mom's pranks. Like when she wraps a humongous box at Christmas. And we think it's gonna be the surprise of the century, and we unwrap it and find a smaller wrapped box inside, and then another and another, until we finally end up with something dinky in the end. But then she always makes up for the joke by giving us something good. So I keep waiting for her to say, "Just kidding! Here's the real suitcase you'll take," and bring out something at least twice the size. But the joke's on me, 'cause this is the suitcase that has to hold everything I'll need for five months.

"There's no way that'll work! The stuff I pack for a week at the beach wouldn't fit in there. And that's just hot weather. How am I supposed to fit enough clothes for hot and cold weather for five months in that tiny suitcase?!"

"The trick is to pack a little bit of everything, but not much of anything. You can take three pairs of shoes. You'll wear one and pack two. You need athletic shoes, sandals, and then a nice shoe, like a flat. Don't pack cotton underwear because you'll sometimes have to wash them in the sink, so a quick-drying material is better. You can use packing cubes to keep all your stuff organized," Mom explains.

"Are you gonna get some Chacos, Mom? You really need some. They're the best sport sandals," I say.

"Nah. I'm good. I've got some sandals that'll work. I don't need to buy anything else for this trip. Delaney, you need to pack enough monthly supplies to last the entire time. Different cultures have different ways of dealing with periods. Since we don't know exactly where we're going, it's best to be prepared."

"Seriously? Ugh. That's gonna take up even more room in my suitcase," Delaney says.

That's when I have the most terrifying thought that a twelve-year-old girl can have: What if *that* happens for the first time in some random country that uses weird girl products?!?! And what if Delaney won't share her stash with me? Surely my mom would make her. Maybe I should pack some things just in case. But I don't want to take up valuable suitcase space for that.

I go to my mirror and pull my shirt snug. I twist and turn, inspecting myself from every angle. Nope. My chest and back still look exactly the same. For once, I'm glad to be a late bloomer. I'm not packing anything. Worst-case scenario, I'll just be extra nice to Delaney.

Delaney continues, "Looks like I'm gonna be wearing the same two outfits in all of our pictures. But I can tell you what I won't be wearing—zip-off pants. You made me wear them in Panama and Peru even though I. Hate. Them. I refuse to wear them ever again."

"I'm with Del. No dorky zip-offs. And you really should get some Chacos, Mom. You're gonna regret it."

"That's because we went to the jungle in those places. But that's fine. No zip-offs. And my sandals are fine, but thanks for your concern. You'll also need to take your school backpack. You'll each carry a laptop in it, along with any other school supplies or electronics stuff you need," says Mom.

"You mean we're getting another MacBook Air?" That would be amazing. I hate sharing ours.

"No, I found the old laptop in the attic. Remember? The blue one? I restored it to factory settings. It's good as new," Mom says.

Sorry, Charlie. New was never good.

Have you ever gotten something new, loved it for a month, then despised it? That's the story of the blue laptop. It was Christmas morning when I was in second grade. Delaney and I were opening our last present. "It's for y'all to share," Mom told us, like it was going to be a pot of gold.

We ripped open the box and found a small blue laptop. I squealed and turned it on. Ten minutes later, the browser loaded. This computer wasn't a Mac, so I didn't expect lightning speed, but ten minutes is ridiculous.

A month later, it was even worse. But I had a routine by then. As the computer was loading, I would sprint around every room in our house—upstairs, main level, and basement—hoping it would be loaded by the time I got back. I always finished first. So the only good thing about bringing the blue laptop along is that we don't have to worry about anyone stealing it. And if we're lucky, someone will.

Now instead of arguing about whose turn it is to ride in the front seat, Delaney and I get to fight about whose turn it is with the MacBook Air. It's gonna be a long five months.

Is it too late to change my mind about this?

7.
One-Way Ticket

October 10–15

Life is either a daring adventure or nothing [at all].

— Helen Keller, *Let Us Have Faith*

Delaney, 14

I cannot believe this is actually happening. I'm sick of grown-ups telling me how "fortunate" I am. Not seeing your friends for five months while spending 24/7 with your parents and annoying sister is called being grounded. This is a million times worse than the time I got Fuggs (fake UGGs) for Christmas when everyone else got the real ones. But my parents think it's dumb to spend a lot of money on things. Mom's always saying, "Stuff goes out of style, but experiences last forever." And Dad says, "Don't spend a lot of money on things that depreciate." So my parents give us lots of experiences, but not much stuff.

Sometimes I'd like the stuff.

The past month has been a blur of packing and last-minute details—like getting shots. I bet the patients in the waiting room thought Riley was getting her legs amputated without anesthesia. And she thinks I'm dramatic?!

While Dad wraps up his business, Mom has been creating our website (4WornPassports.com) and stalking the blogs of other long-term-travel families. There is one family of six—two parents and four older kids/teens—who traveled around the world for a year. You know what I don't understand? Why didn't those kids just commit mutiny and demand to go home? The kids outnumbered the grown-ups two-to-one.

But I have to admit their adventures are pretty cool. They have a video of the oldest daughter kicking a soccer ball from country to country that Riley wants to copy with a baton. Riley even took a few baton lessons (her extracurricular-flavor-of-the-month), so she can make a video twirling around the world. My parents make us watch the soccer video every morning before school. I know what they're up to. They're trying to hype me up about their mid-life crisis.

"Y'all come to the living room," Mom yells up the stairs.

I spit out my toothpaste and yell back, "What's up?"

"We're doing a video call with the Grazianos from Colorado. They have two middle-school daughters and are doing a gap year right now. I thought it would be fun for us to talk."

How does she find these people??? This is all part of Mom's strategy to normalize this ridiculous idea. She's trying to convince me that other kids are perfectly happy leaving their friends to spend 24/7 with their families.

We gather in our living room around Mom's computer.

"Sawasdee from Thailand!" The other parents wave as soon as the video connects.

Whoa. I can see the ocean through the windows of their beach hut. The daughters are working at a paper-and-pen-covered table behind their parents. They glance up briefly and smile. After quick introductions, they go back to their school work. They grab markers, manically working on their project. This is a good sign. The girls look completely normal—and happy. Mom was right. This was a good idea. While the four parents are making family-travel small talk, their daughters tiptoe behind them and hold up a sign. In bold letters, the hostages had scrawled:

SAVE US!

My mom's plan just backfired.

MY DREAD GROWS with each item Mom checks off her list. The homeschool plan has been approved. Riley and I have to write blog posts for English and social studies, and we'll do online programs for science and math. And we have a bunch of books to read depending on which countries we visit. Jingles has gone to live with my grandparents, and neighborhood friends are fostering Molly. Will they even remember us when we return?

"Can't I just stay home? It's my last Saturday night," I say.

"No, we've got a few more errands to run, and you need to come along," Dad says.

Ugh. I'm literally about to spend every *minute* of every *hour* of every *day* with them. Why can't they just give me a little space?

"Will y'all run around back and grab my blue rain jacket. I left it on a table," Mom says when we pull into the church parking lot. "I need to run inside for a sec."

When Riley and I round the corner, voices scream, "SURPRISE!" Dozens of my friends and classmates are gathered around the firepit and scattered throughout the yard. We spend the next couple of hours celebrating an event that I dread. We eat pizza, laugh, and take gazillions of goodbye pictures. I love every second of it. And while roasting marshmallows, my last hope of stopping this crazy train goes up in flames.

It's D-Day (as in departure). Four suitcases stand like dominos by the front door. A pile of four backpacks sits next to them. My dad has shut off the water. The beds are made, but I don't know why. Only burglars will see the inside of our house. Who cares if they think it's neat? My stomach lurches when Mom's friend, Kristi, pulls up in her white minivan. We grab our backpacks and roll our suitcases out the front door.

"Will you take a picture of us with our bags?" Mom asks her friend.

"Of course. Why don't you get the rest of your stuff first?"

"This is everything."

Kristi's eyes get big. "Wow. Impressive."

She has no idea.

Three hours later, our plane departs the Birmingham International Airport. It ascends through the clouds and heads east. *Gone, Gone, Gone* by Phillip Phillips streams through my ear buds. When the tears finally spill over, I don't try to stop them. Holding a one-way ticket, I watch my old life disappear from the window seat.

II. The World

If you reject the food, ignore the customs, fear the religion, and avoid the people, you might better stay home.

— JAMES MICHENER, AMERICAN AUTHOR

ICELAND

Language: Icelandic Currency: krona

EUROPE

GREENLAND SEA

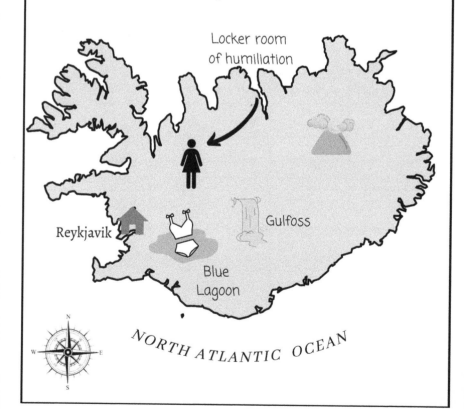

Locker room
of humiliation

Reykjavik

Blue
Lagoon

Gulfoss

NORTH ATLANTIC OCEAN

8.

Naked and Afraid

October 17–19

"Þetta reddast." *It will all work out in the end.*

— ICELANDIC EXPRESSION

Riley, 12

On most Thursdays at 6:00 a.m., I've still got another hour of snoozing. But this isn't most Thursdays. Instead of waking to my alarm clock, the bounce of our plane landing in Iceland wakes me. I can't believe I dozed off.

Delaney always manages to sleep on planes. I don't know how she does it. She can sleep anywhere. When we went to Thailand a couple of years ago, we took a sixteen-hour flight from Atlanta to Seoul, South Korea. Delaney sat sandwiched between my mom and me. Del watched a couple of movies, then conked out for the rest of the flight. Her chin rested on her chest, while her head bobbed from side to side. She was drooling and everything. When her head landed on my shoulder, I shoved her toward my mom. Moms are used to kids slobbering on them.

Meanwhile, I sat trapped next to the window for the entire flight. I survived on an endless supply of airplane movies and snacks. It's fun at the time, but then you're extra miserable when you finally arrive.

Del stirs next to me. "Ugh. I wanna keep sleeping," she groans. "What time is it?"

"Almost six," Dad says from the row behind us.

"What about body time?" I ask.

"One in the morning," he says.

"Time zones are so confusing," Delaney mumbles.

My body didn't get the message about the time change. I hope we can check in early and take a nap. Overnight flights are the worst.

Iceland wasn't originally part of the plan. That changed when Delaney threw a teen-girl tantrum about going to London. It turns out that if you fly on Icelandair from the U.S. to London, then you can visit Iceland for free. Your hotel and food aren't free, but you don't have to pay extra for your flights if you only stay a few days. So you get to visit two countries for the cost of one plane ticket. Since my mom likes free stuff, especially free countries, she added the Iceland stopover to our itinerary. Bonus passport stamp!

Walking through the airport to the car rental place, I try to read the signs. Most of the Icelandic letters look like English, so you might think it'd be kind of easy to figure out some words. Wrong. First example: Reykjavik (RAKE-ya-veek), Iceland's capital city. Doesn't that remind you of a preschooler's made-up word? Like when little kids learn their letters and jumble them all together and think they're writing? That's what Icelandic looks like.

Observation number two: the Vikings were two-time liars. In school, we learned that when the Vikings discovered Iceland and Greenland, they intentionally switched up their descriptions to keep other explorers from crashing their new land. So Greenland is actually icy, and Iceland is green. Everyone knows about that trick. So here's the second lie: Iceland is brown, not green. I guess they didn't think "Welcome to Brownland" would be as catchy.

Downtown Reykjavik is full of brightly colored cottages similar to the red and green Monopoly pieces. Except the houses are all different colors, not just red and green. Our sunshine yellow house for two nights, actually named Our House, sits smack in the middle of downtown.

Our House's owner used to live there with her family, but they moved to a new house in the 'burbs. Now visitors can stay in their downtown house. They rent out each bedroom separately, so you never know who you'll be sharing the house (and bathrooms—*eek!*) with. I hope our instant family of complete strangers is bald. Other people's hair in the bathroom is so gross.

Bedda, the owner, and her gigantic smile greet us at the door. "You made it! Welcome to Iceland. You're the musician, right?"

I love the way her accent makes her sound super happy when she talks. Icelanders love music, and Bedda offers a discount to musicians. Not just famous musicians, but anyone who can play an instrument. My dad plays guitar, so *bam!*, she gave us a ten percent discount. My parents loved that.

I drag my bag into our first home abroad. But this is not a house. It's a time capsule. The living room furniture screams *Brady Bunch*, a 1970s TV show about a family with six kids and a live-in housekeeper that Del and I used to binge watch.

Everything in Our House is retro, but not in a my-grandma's-place-is-so-outdated sort of way, but in a super-funky-vibe kind of way. Music posters from the 1970s hang on the walls, and an old turntable stands in the corner. Bedda's record album collection is even bigger than my dad's. In the opposite corner stands a gumball machine. But instead of gumballs, it's filled with rainbow-colored earplugs. You don't even need a quarter. Just turn the knob and out drop earplugs.

Next to the earplug-gumball machine hangs an organizer filled with hairdryers, chargers, and a bunch of different adapters to fit any sort of plug. This is a major traveler bonus. If you forget to bring an adapter, you can't charge your electronics in other countries. Across the room, a bulletin board hangs on the wall. The sign above it says:

WHO IS STAYING IN OUR HOUSE

"These guests have just checked out." Bedda points to the instant photos pinned to the board. "Let's take your picture, so everyone knows who you are."

Bedda's the hostess-with-the-mostest. She snaps our picture, and we scribble our names and *Alabama, USA* below it. We follow Bedda up the wooden stairs to a room with a queen bed and bunks. Score! I hate sharing a bed with Delaney. She's such a cover hog. We are too tired to argue over the top bunk. It's almost 9:00 a.m., but it's still dark out. We climb into bed and fall asleep.

WE WAKE at noon Iceland time, which is seven back home. Muffled voices come from the kitchen, but we can't figure out what they are saying. I hope there are six *Brady Bunch* kids staying here. I would love to play with three boys and three girls. And what if a housekeeper like Alice showed up to cook us dinner? Even better! We brush our teeth in the bathroom down the hall. Time to meet our roomies.

"You're the family from Alabama," the shortest man says with a smile.

Our new family members are Pai-han and Hui-chun, and Kuan-lin and Chia-hua. Instead of six kids, our housemates are two couples from Taiwan. No wonder we couldn't understand what they were saying. They speak Mandarin. Fortunately, they switched to English when they saw us. It would be so cool to know a language that others don't understand. My BFF and I made up our own language when we were in third grade, but I don't remember much of it anymore.

After making small talk with the new fam, it's time for our first day of world school. Our House is just steps from Skolavordustigur Street, the main street in Reykjavik.

REYKJAVIK, ICELAND–Hallgrimskirkja Lutheran Church

The most famous building in Reykjavik—the Hallgrimskirkja Lutheran church—sits at the top of the long street. The rocketship-shaped building juts straight out of the ground toward the sky, like a sci-fi novel dropped a church into a town of Monopoly-block cottages. A statue of "Lucky" Leif Erikson stands in front of this bizarre landmark. *Who's that?* you ask.

Unless you've seen the "Bubble Buddy" episode of *SpongeBob SquarePants*, you probably haven't heard of him. He's the Viking explorer who discovered the Americas five hundred years *before* Columbus. So technically, he's the first European to bump into America, but Columbus gets all the credit. What a rip-off. Just another fun fact left out of my social studies book. Kids should use this golden nugget to prove that *SpongeBob* is educational.

History lesson: check.

"This is gonna be sooo boring," I say, as we walk to the location of today's Earth science field trip.

"You can't come to Iceland and not learn about volcanoes." Mom stops to read a menu hanging in a window.

The Volcano House is a museum/movie theater that shows documentaries of Iceland's geologic and volcanic history. We buy tickets for the English version and take our seats in the dark theater. We are the only four people here (proving it's gonna be boring). For one hour, we watch video footage from volcano eruptions that drowned the Monopoly houses and town in ash. Imagine the worst blizzard you've ever seen, except the snow is ash, which means it won't just melt away.

Earth science fun fact #1:

The most recent major eruption was Eyjafjallajokull (!!) in April 2010. It spewed so much volcanic ash into the air that it shut down all flights between North America and Europe for almost a week!

Even though it was pretty interesting for a documentary,

Delaney and Dad slept through the entire thing. Science lesson: check (for me). Delaney gets a zero for class participation.

––––

THE SMELL HITS US the second we open the front door. Our roomies have been cooking. The odor is strong and strange. Not really good and not really bad, just different. Mainly, it reminds us that we are hungry and pooped.

"Who's ready for dinner?" Mom asks.

"I'm starving, but I don't feel like going anywhere. Besides, I'm not feeling any of the restaurants we saw," Delaney says.

We looked at tons of restaurant menus while walking around town, and Iceland definitely wins the award (so far) for the weirdest food. The menus listed things like shark, fish jerky, sheep's head, sheep's head jelly, and pork tongue. Ew. Ew. Ew! Supposedly, the shark tastes like pee, because sharks urinate through their skin. How would someone know if it tastes like pee unless they've actually tried it?

"I'd be down for a frozen mac-n-cheese from the market on the corner," Delaney says.

"Sounds good to me. I don't really feel like going out either." My dad plops onto the retro sofa.

Mom and I head to the corner market to buy everyone's favorite frozen dinner. We're hoping to see the Northern Lights along the way. I learned about the *aurora borealis* last year. People come to Iceland just to see nature's psychedelic lava lamp in the sky. We hope to see them too, even though it's October. We buy our dinners and walk back, scanning the sky the entire time.

"Hey, let's tell Dad and Delaney that we saw them. They'll freak out that they missed it."

"Yes! Like when we missed the floating lanterns on New Year's Eve in Chiang Mai? I can't believe they didn't wake us up. I'm still annoyed about that," Mom says.

I open the front door screaming, "You missed it! We saw them! We saw the Northern Lights!"

"No, you didn't." Delaney doesn't look up from her book.

Bummer. She didn't bite. The microwave timer is counting down when Hui-chun and Pai-han join us in the kitchen.

"You're eating frozen dinners?" Hui-chun wrinkles her nose.

"I know it's lame, but we don't have the energy to go out or cook," Mom says.

"We have plenty of extra food. Please, help yourself."

My frozen dinner looks pathetic next to whatever is in the skillet. I scoop the noodle concoction onto my plate. It smells weird, but it tastes great. After eating dinner, the eight of us hang out in the small living room. We squish together on the sectional like my friends and I do for movie nights. Four Americans and four Taiwanese watching *Shark Tank* in our shared living room in Iceland.

Our bubble has popped!

 Earth science fun fact #2:
The best places for viewing the aurora borealis are Iceland, Norway, Alaska, and the Arctic Circle, between November and March.

Delaney, 14

"HEY GIRLS, what kind of cars do people in Iceland drive?" Dad asks.

"I don't know…"

"Fjords!" he says.

"Dad, stop. You're gonna make my ears bleed," Riley says.

"Really, Ri? Your jokes are as bad as his," Mom says.

True. Riley inherited my dad's knack for telling the world's worst jokes. Only their dance moves are worse. I was hoping the dorky dad jokes would get stuck in immigration. But there's no escaping them, no matter where I go.

When we get in the car, Mom asks, "Did anyone grab the guidebook off the coffee table?"

"I did."

"Awesome, Delaney. Then you get to be our tour guide today. Why don't you tell us some interesting tidbits about Iceland."

I skim the book for some fun facts to share.

"Did you know that Iceland's motto is 'Þetta reddast?' It means things will all work out in the end." I continue, "Here's another fun fact: Iceland is known as The Land of Fire and Ice due to all the volcanoes and glaciers. Plus, it has geysers, mud baths, hot springs, thermal pools, and waterfalls. And this geology theme park is all because Iceland sits on top of two tectonic plates."

According to the guidebook, The Golden Circle and Blue Lagoon are the best places to experience this Earth-science-goodness on a quick visit. I'm hyped about the Blue Lagoon tomorrow. The pictures are insane. But today is our road trip around The Golden Circle.

 A four-hour loop to the three most scenic places in Iceland:
1. Strokkur Geysir
2. Gullfoss waterfall
3. Þingvellir National Park

It takes longer than normal to reach Þingvellir—the letter "Þ" is pronounced like *Th*, so it sounds like Thingvellir—because we keep stopping to take pictures of the funny road signs. The best part of Þingvellir National Park, though, is the gift shop.

"Hey, Ri, check out this can of Fresh Iceland Mountain Air."

"Do you think anyone is dumb enough to buy a can of air?" Riley takes a can from the pyramid tower stacked on a display shelf.

"Probably. Why else would they be selling it?"

The gift shop is full of quirky souvenirs, but my favorite is a T-shirt that says:

WHAT PART OF
EYJAFJALLAJÖKULL
DON'T YOU UNDERSTAND?

At least they have a sense of humor. When we finish our hot chocolate, we head to the next stop on the loop: Strokkur Geysir. I've never seen a geyser in real life, so I'm not sure what to expect. I put on both layers of my "coat"—a fleece with my rain jacket on top—and trek across the brown rocky landscape to reach the pool. The geyser eruption cycle goes like this: the water starts out calm, then gurgles, then bubbles, then explodes.

"Whoa! It's like someone dumped a million pounds of Mentos into a million gallons of Coke," Riley says, wiping spray from her face after the blast.

ICELAND: The Strokker Geysir erupts every five-to-ten minutes.

The water shoots up to 130 feet high. Then it starts all over again. The geyser erupts every five-to-ten minutes. Old Faithful at Yellowstone is the most famous geyser in the United States. But it only spews every sixty-to-ninety minutes. I'm glad we don't have to wait that long between blasts.

After spending an hour watching the Mentos show, it's time to find Iceland's most Insta-famous waterfall: Gullfoss. Ten minutes later, we pull into the Gullfoss parking lot. The bitter wind smacks me in the face when I open the car door.

"Yikes! It's freezing!" I clench my rain jacket around me.

"This is crazy. How can it be so much colder here?" Dad rubs his hands together.

We pull our hoods around our heads and tighten the straps.

"This better be worth it!" Mom screams into the wind as we begin our hike to the waterfall.

The coldest person of all, though, is Riley. She's only wearing a thin pink athletic pullover and a hot pink rain jacket. But she can't complain, or my parents will kill her. That's because she didn't pack her fleece. It isn't pink. If the rest of Europe is this cold, she's in big trouble.

ICELAND: Gulfoss waterfall

"THE GOLDEN CIRCLE tour is complete. Don't forget to tip the driver," Dad announces as we arrive back in Reykjavik.

"Who wants to go swimming?" Mom's been flipping through the guidebook looking for something to do. "There are outdoor geothermal swimming pools here. It's like swimming in a hot tub," she adds.

"Me!" Riley says.

"Me too! Is it like the Blue Lagoon?" I ask.

"No, that's a tourist attraction. This is just a community swimming pool where the locals go."

Riley and I are pumped. Swimming outdoors at night in hot water sounds magical. We swing by the house and grab our swimsuits. The pool we're going to even has water slides. This is going to be awesome! Once we're back in the car, Mom continues reading about Iceland's pool rules. Since the water is from a hot spring and not chlorinated, they are very strict about their hygiene rules. My palms sweat and my stomach swirls when she reads the instructions aloud. It's a middle-school-locker-room nightmare that isn't a nightmare. It's real life. The rules go like this:

1. Leave your shoes outside the locker room to keep the floor clean. (In America, we wear our shoes in locker rooms, so we don't pick up someone else's toe jam.)
2. Strip down to your birthday suit. Stash your towel and swimsuit near the open showers. (I want to puke.)
3. Wash the *specified* areas with soap. Then, put your swimsuit on.
4. After swimming, wash off again. This time you can leave your swimsuit on.

"Mom! You promised no naked people!" Now what am I supposed to do about this "authentic" Iceland experience? Is it worth trading my dignity to go swimming?

We arrive at the Laugardalslaug pool and pay 2,060 krona (about $15) for the four of us. A life-sized poster of a naked cartoon figure stands next to the ladies' locker room door. Pink areas show which body parts must be washed—the head, feet, armpits, and private parts. My stomach churns. I do not want to go through that door. But that locker room is the only thing standing between me and geothermal-swimming paradise.

I take a deep breath and push open the door with my sweaty palms. My handprints on the door disappear as my anxiety grows. I enter, trying to stare straight ahead. It's hard to find a locker in the sea of jiggling booties and boobies. My hands sweat more. But none of these Icelanders is the least bit concerned about her body—or anyone else's. We need to ask someone what to do, but everyone is naked. Who's gonna strike up a conversation like that? Talk about awkward!

I spot a clothes-wearing attendant across the room. She smiles and tells us to strip, put our clothes in a locker, and shower.

We quickly undress and hide behind our towels. A gigantic open stall, with shower heads evenly spaced, fills the middle of the locker room. Are we at a swimming pool? Or a prison?! How can this be happening to me? I very clearly stated one of my conditions was "NO naked people." I didn't want to *see* them, much less *be* them! I want to go back to my country with shower curtains. A rollercoaster of anxiety races through my body. How long does it take to die from humiliation?

Then I spot them—three vacant shower stalls on the left side of the room. There are no doors or curtains, but at least we'll have a wall. Dressed in our birthday suits, the three of us bolt for the individual stalls like *Hunger Games* tributes racing for the cornucopia.

Smirks creep across the local women's faces. They struggle not to laugh at our American-sized modesty. The more we don't want to be noticed, the more obvious we become. I flashback to the Emberá village when the topless women laughed at our cockroach freak-out. Are Americans the only ones who like to keep their private-parts private?

I set a new record for the World's Fastest Shower, then make a ding-dong-ditch dash for my swimsuit. I slip it over my still-wet body, exhaling as I pull the straps over my shoulders. Hallelujah. I did it. I'm gonna need professional counseling later to get over this. But right now, I'm headed for the pool.

As Riley and I race down the disco-light water slides under Iceland's stars, I yell, "It's a good thing we don't live here."

"Why's that?"

"Because I'd never go swimming again!"

ICELAND: Steam rises from the Blue Lagoon.

YOU CAN SEE the steam rising from the Blue Lagoon long before you reach it. Set in the middle of a brown jagged lava field, the Blue Lagoon looks like a desert oasis on Mars. The vivid, milky-blue water seems out of place next to the barren landscape that surrounds it. Since the Blue Lagoon sits between Reykjavik and the airport, it is a popular place to visit before leaving the country. Which is exactly what we plan to do. After yesterday's traumatic locker room experience at the local swimming pool, I'm a little nervous about what to expect.

"At fifty dollars a person, they better have doors on the shower stalls," Mom says. "American tourists will not plunk down that kind of money to be naked in front of anyone."

Fortunately, the Blue Lagoon is not your typical hot springs experience. It is the fanciest of all the geothermal spas in Iceland. Even the guy who works at the swim-up snack bar is wearing a black vest and bow tie. It's that fancy.

We enter the upscale locker room and quickly complete the pre-swimming cleansing routine, with plenty of privacy this time. We can't wait to get in the milky-blue mineral water that is great for your skin but terrible for your hair. Before getting in, Riley and I wet our hair and lather gobs of conditioner through it. Then we wrap our hair in buns on top of our heads. If you forget to put conditioner in your hair before getting in, you won't be able to get a brush through it when you get out.

ICELAND: Delaney and Riley relax in the Blue Lagoon

This is the most luxurious swimming experience of my life. Natural mud from the bottom of the lagoon fills containers located around the pool. We slather our faces and bodies with nature's mud mask and float around the warm pool. Every once in a while, someone yells "Ow!" when we accidentally drift into a hotspot. The occasional owie is totally worth it.

After relaxing for a few hours in this lava-field spa, it's time to head to the airport. Next stop, London. Harry Potter movie set, here I come.

As we drive to the airport, Dad asks, "So girls, what did we do in Iceland?"

I don't hesitate. "We froze our butts off and endured naked public humiliation!" I keep my eyes on the steamy lava field in the distance. "But the Blue Lagoon was worth it."

"What did you say Iceland's motto is?" Mom asks.

"Þetta reddast. It will all work out in the end."

PASSPORT LESSON #1:
You won't die from humiliation if you
try something new when you leave your bubble.

ICELAND
High-Low Report Card

	☺	☹
Delaney	Blue Lagoon	Locker room
Riley	Blue Lagoon	Drive around the Golden Circle
Mom	Blue Lagoon	Locker room
Dad	Blue Lagoon	Not going inside Hallgrimskirkja church

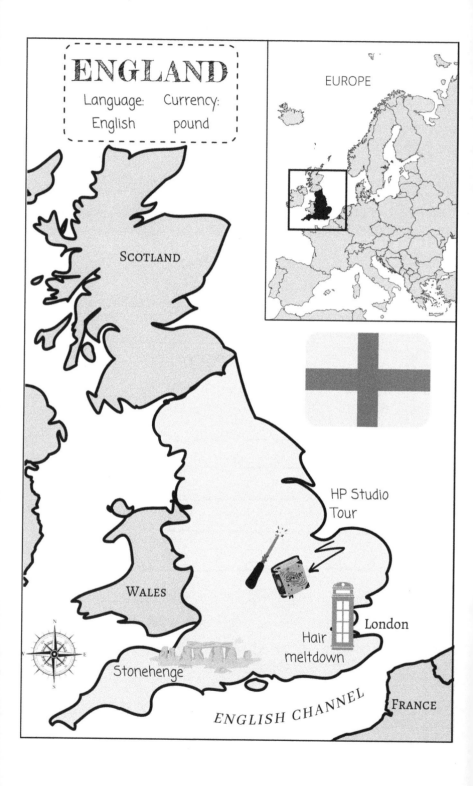

9.

Hunting for Harrys

October 19–24

The biggest difference between England and America is that England has history, while America has geography.

— Neil Gaiman, English author

Riley, 12

"That's our bedroom? And we have to share the bed?!"

Shoved against the right wall is a bed that's barely wide enough for one normal-sized adult or two very skinny kids. For once, I'm glad to be small for my age. The nightstand crammed between the left wall and bed is the only other piece of furniture in the room. We put our suitcases on the skinny strip of floor space and leapfrog over them to get to the bed.

"See, if we were home, you would have your room and bed all to yourself," Delaney says.

I don't know why I'm surprised. I've watched a gazillion episodes of *House Hunters International* with my dad, so I've seen tiny bedrooms before. It's usually when an American family is moving to a big city like London or Paris.

"This is typical for London, especially to be in a great location with Tube access. At least you have a bedroom. One of you can sleep on the pull-out sofa if you want," Mom says.

"No thanks. I'm good," Delaney says.

"No way, José, on the sofa-ay. Sofa beds are the worst." It looks like I'm sleeping with the bed hog.

We are staying in a West London *flat* in between the Hammersmith and Goldhawk *Tube* stations. Even though they speak English here, they have funny words for things.

My home-for-the-week in this West London neighborhood is totally different from my neighborhood. Instead of having separate houses, one long building runs as far as you can see. There are no yards (which they call *gardens*), only a wide sidewalk with massive trees growing out of some of the squares. The three-story tan brick building is divided into equal sections that are exactly the same: a white bay window, concrete steps, black handrails, fancy white columns, and a black door. I bet little kids go to the wrong door all the time. Once you go inside the main door, there is a separate apartment on each level. That's why they are called flats. Because each family's space is flat.

"Where do the dogs poop?" I ask. "Molly would never poop on a sidewalk."

"Well, some dogs do." Delaney points at a doggie pile on the sidewalk outside the window.

"Ew, gross. Mom, are we gonna be here for Halloween? This is the perfect trick-or-treating street."

"Unfortunately not."

"All of my friends are going to the Sloss haunted house this weekend. Just one more thing I'm missing out on," Delaney says.

"Aww, don't remind me." Halloween in our neighborhood is a blast. Parents take little kids trick-or-treating on golf carts. And bigger kids still dress up because we love getting candy we don't have to buy with our own money. Then we roast marshmallows and have basement dance parties. Now I'm a little homesick too.

LONDON, ENGLAND: Our home for the week in West London.

Delaney, 14

I LOVE ENGLAND! For starters, my three favorite Harrys are from here: Harry Potter, Harry Styles, and Prince Harry. That's my Harry trifecta. Just being in London makes my heart sing. I will admit it (but not out loud, of course). This is better than middle school. I love the architecture, the historical sights, the shops, and even the taxis.

"Y'all, listen to this." I'm flipping through the London tourist guide I found on the coffee table. "You know how an American taxi is just a boring yellow car with some random guy driving it? Well, the London taxis are unlike anywhere else in the world. Those black cabs that look like old-timey cars, with rounded roofs and shiny chrome grills, are called *hackney carriages*. And not just anyone can drive a hackney carriage. The drivers have to memorize twenty-five thousand streets in downtown London and pass a test called The Knowledge."

"Wow. They're London's human GPSs," Dad says.

Maybe it's the accent (it's so much better than ours), but everything and everyone just seems classier here. London is a mashup of the old and new. It's historic and modern, all rolled up into one perfect package.

Things to Do in London!
1. Ride the London Eye (the biggest ferris wheel in Europe)
2. Check the time on Big Ben (London's famous clock tower)
3. Watch the Changing of the Guard at Buckingham Palace.
4. Find my three favorite Harrys!!!

"Do we have to take the Tube?" Riley says as we walk to the Hammersmith station. "I hate public transportation."

"Why would you say that? It's the best way to get around London," Dad says.

"Because I always worry about bad guys getting on. At least with planes, people have to go through security. But anyone can get on a subway or train. How is that safe?"

"You're worrying about nothing. I wish we had the public transportation infrastructure that Europe has," Dad says.

"So what are we doing today?" I interject. Riley's gonna keep obsessing on this if I don't change the subject.

"Exploring London," Mom says.

"I hope we see Harry," I say.

"Which one?" Riley asks.

"I don't care. Any of them."

"I just want to go to Abbey Road," Dad says. "We need to recreate the picture from the album cover."

My dad swears the Beatles' 1969 *Abbey Road* album cover is one of the most famous ever. It's the one with the four band members in a crosswalk, and Paul McCartney is barefoot. Beatles fans love to come to Abbey Road and recreate the picture. This should work out perfectly since there are four of us. But who will take our picture?

This turns out not to be a problem. I thought that this famous crosswalk might be on a side street or a road that has been shut down because of its popularity. Nope. It's a regular street in the middle of London with near-constant traffic. We arrive to find lots of tourists on both sides of the road. The drizzle isn't deterring any of these die-hard fans.

"Quick! Will you take my picture?" A woman shoves her phone into my hand and runs into the middle of the street.

I take her picture. She runs back just as a car drives through the crosswalk. As soon as the traffic clears for a second, a couple on the other side runs into the crosswalk. They get in the frozen walking position.

"I got it!" a person yells from across the street.

This goes on for several minutes. People line up on both sides and try to keep up with whose turn it is to go next. As soon as there is a traffic break, a person, couple, or entire family runs into the street just long enough for a stranger to take their picture and then jump on the sidewalk before becoming roadkill. Even though it is a crosswalk and people should have the right-of-way, the locals must be sick of tourists slowing down traffic for this cliché photo-op. So they barrel down the road like the crosswalk isn't even there.

When it's finally our turn, Mom hands her phone to a woman next to us.

"Who's Paul? Someone's gotta take their shoes off," Dad says.

"I'll do it." Mom strips off her shoes and socks, dropping them on the sidewalk in the rain.

We run into the street, lining up in the correct order, just in time to see a delivery truck racing toward us.

"Quick! Take the pic!" Dad yells as the truck gets closer.

"Got it!" the stranger with Mom's phone yells back.

LONDON, ENGLAND: The McIntyres cross Abbey Road.

We make it to the sidewalk just in time for the truck to hit a puddle, drenching us.

I turn to my dad, expecting him to be annoyed about the soaking. But a smile stretches like Abbey Road across his face.

After our Beatles' re-enactment, we explore the major tourist sights of London. I also go inside every single red phone booth we pass and pretend to make a call. Even the phone booths are classy.

"For once, I'm glad Mom and Dad are cheap!" Riley says.

"Why's that?" I ask.

"So we don't have to go into Westminster Abbey. What family's gonna pay seventy dollars to go inside a boring cathedral?"

"I'm starving. Can we eat now?" I spot a pub across the street.

"Me too. I wanna sit for a minute," Riley says.

We cross the street and enter the pub. We sit at a tall, round table and scan the menu. Our waiter, Chap, takes our order.

"I'll have the fish-n-chips," Dad starts.

"Me too. Hold the mayo, please," Mom says.

"We'd like to share a plain hamburger and French fries, please. Nothing on the hamburger, just plain." I order for Riley and me.

"Okay, so two fish-n-chips and one plain hamburger and chips, right?" Chap repeats our order.

"No. We'd like fries instead of chips," I corrected.

"French fries *are* chips." Chap grins and winks at me. "You must be from across the pond."

"We are," Dad says.

"Are you on fall holiday?" Chap asks.

"No, we're traveling for a semester. This is our second country," Mom says.

"Wow. You girls are lucky." Chap looks at Riley and me. "Best education you will ever get."

"Yes, sir. It sure is." I flash a fake smile.

Why does every single adult say this when they hear about our trip?

AFTER LUNCH, my Harry dreams come true! I meet and take pictures with all three Harrys in one place. We waited in line for over an hour to get in, but it was so worth it.

"Look at all these celebrities, Ri!" I've never seen so many famous people in one place.

"Who do you want to meet first?" Riley scans the room.

People surround the celebrities, waiting for their photo-op. But these superstars are so patient. Even my parents are excited. My dad loves meeting Nicole Kidman, and he even puts his arm around Julia Roberts. Mom doesn't care because George Clooney has his arm around her. But the highlight is when Ri and I hang out on the bleachers with One Direction! Riley snags the seat by Harry Styles, and I squeeze next to Niall Horan. They just smile while my parents take a million pictures. After that, I get to hug Prince Harry and Harry Potter (Daniel Radcliffe).

Today is the Best. Day. Ever!

Okay, so maybe we are at Madame Tussauds Wax Museum, but you wouldn't believe how lifelike the figures are. From Einstein to Princess Diana, you can meet just about any famous person you want.

Wax Harrys are better than no Harrys at all.

"WHY IS ENGLAND THE WETTEST COUNTRY?" Dad asks.

"I don't know. Why?"

"Because the queen has reigned here for years."

Where does he come up with these? Today we are doing something very un-McIntyre. We're on a tour bus full of strangers headed to Stonehenge and Bath for the day. The bus might be fun if some teenagers were along, but it's a bunch of old people and us.

"Why are we on this tour?" I ask. My parents are very anti-tour groups.

"There's no easy way to visit both Stonehenge and Bath using public transportation. It would be a hassle to rent a car for a day. So this is the easiest way to see both places," Mom explains. "Plus, I found a Groupon."

Ah. That explains it. The good ol' Groupon, even in Europe. The good news is the bus is super comfortable. The bad news is the two old ladies behind me won't shut up about their heartburn and hemorrhoids. Talk about TMI. I'm actually glad when the tour guide starts talking.

> ### Stonehenge according to Simon-the-tour-guide!
>
> Stonehenge was built 5,000 years ago, around 3000 B.C. That was four to five hundred years before the Pyramids of Giza in Egypt were built. Scientists believe Stonehenge was built by the Druids as a temple for worship, but no one knows for sure. The end.

When Simon finishes his tour guide spiel, he starts telling jokes. He must be a dad, because he thinks his jokes are funny. They're not.

"Who knows what kind of music they play at Stonehenge?" he asks the bus. No one answers. "Hard rock!"

I tune them all out and open the dog-eared page of *The Redheaded Princess*. It's the story of Queen Elizabeth I. Two hours later, we pull into the parking lot.

The massive rocks greet us from a distance. Each stone stands taller than a two-story house. A worn path surrounds the most famous prehistoric stone circle in the world. But unless those rocks start singing and dancing, this historic sight is a historic waste of time. I don't understand my parents' fascination with the Wonders of the World.

"Here." Dad hands me a headset. "You can listen to the history while we walk around."

I push *play* and step onto the path. The narrator sounds like a ghost. I learn one thing before turning it off: *Trilithon* is the name of the dinosaur-sized prehistoric Pi symbols, made from two standing rocks with a third stone lying across the top.

Every time we stop to get a family picture in front of the famous trilithons, an obnoxious tourist with a selfie stick photobombs us. Selfie sticks should be banned.

"Y'all put your palms up flat, like you're holding Stonehenge," Mom says.

She loves getting cheesy tourist pictures. When my mom is finally satisfied with our photos and video (of Riley and her baton), it's time to go.

"That was lame," I whisper to Riley as we climb aboard the bus.

"For real. I bet the English kids hate coming here for field trips," Riley says.

At least when school field trips are boring, you have your friends to make it fun. But not at world school. So let me give you some advice: If you go to London and have the choice of going to Stonehenge or somewhere else, choose somewhere else. It doesn't matter where. It has to be more interesting than this big pile of rocks.

AMESBURY, ENGLAND: Stonehenge

Riley, 12

WHEN MY PARENTS told me we were going to Bath, I thought it was a play on words. I mean, who names a city "Bath?" Turns out, it's named after its ancient Roman Baths. Even if the name is strange, Bath is way more interesting than Stonehenge. And we've only been here fifteen minutes. I usually get super bored looking at cathedrals, but the one here is 10/10. Plus, it's free. So we don't have to stay long "to get our money's worth."

The town square is full of street performers and fun things to do. A guy painted in gold from head to toe—hair, skin, glasses, and clothes—pretends to be a statue. Somehow, he looks like he's sitting in a chair, but there's no chair. I can't figure out how he does it. My parents drop a few coins in his gold-painted money bag as we pass by.

"Hey, look! There's a TK Maxx." I point to the store across the street.

TJ Maxx is my favorite store—and this looks just like one— but it has a *K* instead of a *J*. I would love to go shopping. I'm sick of my clothes already. Plus, I need a fleece, but I can't tell my parents or they'll kill me. (And we haven't been gone long enough for my RRP growth spurt to kick in.) Right across the street is the Pound Shop. It looks like a Dollar Tree. Since they use pounds instead of dollars, it's the Pound Shop. It reminds me of the popular Thai saying—same same but different.

Our second social studies lesson for the day is visiting the ancient Roman Baths.

"Man, I'm glad we don't live in ancient times," Delaney says as we wander past a giant community bathtub.

"Ew. That would be so weird to bathe with our neighbors," I say.

"For real. We just did that in Iceland. I'm still not over it."

Like Stonehenge, we listen to an audio guide. But, shocker, this one is interesting. The best part of the exhibit is the see-through container filled with a rainbow collection of gemstones. Workers found the jewels in the pool drains before the bathhouses became a tourist attraction. Rich women used to wear their jewelry into the baths, so everyone would know they were wealthy even if they were naked. The minerals in the water dissolved the wax that held the stones in place. When the wax melted, the diamonds and rubies fell out.

"I bet those show-off society women freaked out when they realized their jewelry was missing," I say.

"No wonder the mineral water at the Blue Lagoon was a nightmare for our hair. If it can dissolve wax, we're lucky our hair didn't fall out," Delaney says.

"I wish your hair had fallen out. That would've been the perfect revenge," I say, reminding her I haven't forgotten her mean prank.

"So, GIRLS, have you decided on your topics for your Iceland blog posts?" Mom asks while we wait for the bus.

"I call the Blue Lagoon," I say, before Delaney can.

"You can have it. I'll do the locker room. It's my duty to society to warn travelers about it."

"Yay, there it is." Our comfy bus pulls in. It's sooo much better than public transportation.

I'm pooped from Stonehenge and Bath, and I'm ready to be back at our flat. I plop down in the aisle seat next to Delaney. I bend over and pull *London Eye Mystery* out of my backpack. It's a good time to catch up on my required reading.

"Hey D—," I turn to ask Delaney a question. Her cheek is smooshed against the window with a wad of gum about to fall out of her mouth. She's already asleep. Ugh! How does she do that?!

TODAY WE'RE GOING to a real castle: the Tower of London. This should be way more fun than a museum. The Tower of London is almost one thousand years old and isn't a regular ol' castle. It's been a prison, a zoo, and lots of people have been executed here. Most of them had their head chopped off. I hope it isn't haunted.

"Hello, young ladies." A tour guide in a fancy costume tips his cake-sized hat at us. "Welcome to the Tower of London. May I help you with anything?"

"Thank you," Dad says, then strikes up a thirty-minute conversation with the man.

It turns out that he's no tour guide. He's a palace guard called a *Beefeater*. And the fancy costume? It's actually a uniform that is sewn with gold thread and costs over $9,000!

Back in the olden days, they used to get paid in beef. Now, it's a big deal to get to be a Beefeater. To qualify, you must serve at least twenty-two years in the British military and have medals for Long Service and Good Conduct.

"Let's check out the torture devices in the Bloody Tower," Delaney says.

"Ew, no. That's scary. I wanna see the thirty-two billion dollars of jewels."

"Are you sure? I heard Anne Boleyn's headless ghost haunts the crown jewels."

LONDON, ENGLAND–OCTOBER 2013: Beefeater educates visitors at the Tower of London.

"No, it doesn't!" I say, hoping she's just trying to scare me.

We spend the entire morning exploring the Tower of London. When we leave the medieval castle, we just start walking. We have no plans for the afternoon. I glance at my watch. My friends are just waking up for middle school, and I've finished another day of world school. I was wrong about Europe. It's not boring at all.

LONDON, ENGLAND–OCTOBER 2013: Beefeaters pose with Delaney and Riley at the Tower of London.

"Riley, look!" Delaney points ahead.

"Oh my gosh! I can't believe it! Let's go!" We fast-walk-run all the way to the Millennium Bridge. I didn't know it was a real bridge. I thought it was just a movie set.

"What is it?" Mom asks when they catch up.

"It's the bridge the Death Eaters destroyed in the *Half-Blood Prince*," Delaney squeals.

Delaney, 14

RILEY AND I have been Harry Potter fangirls for as long as I can remember. We've read the books, watched the movies, had the birthday party, and taken the quizzes. I'm a Hufflepuff, and she's a Ravenclaw. Years ago, our library hosted a Harry Potter event. I dressed as Luna Lovegood, and Riley dressed as Hermione. We drank Butterbeer, made crafts, and competed in HP contests in the library-turned-Hogwarts.

Even though my parents don't like theme parks, we convinced them to take us to Universal Studios in Orlando when The Wizarding World of Harry Potter opened. I imagined I attended Hogwarts and that Diagon Alley and the rest of Wizarding World were real. It's the one place teenagers (and some adults!) can still play make-believe without shame. Riley wore her Hogwarts robe, scarf, and goggles the entire time. She swore she wasn't hot, even as sweat poured down her bright red face.

We spent one summer creating elaborate wands out of craft paper, caulk, and paint. Our collection rivaled the ones from the Universal Studios gift shop. While we were at camp, Mom transformed Riley's bedroom with Dumbledore wall quotes, candlesticks, and flickering-flame antique lamps.

To say that I'm excited about the Warner Bros. Studio Tour is the understatement of the century.

OUR DAY at the studio begins exactly where it should: King's Cross Station Platform 9 ¾. I run and push the trolley into the brick wall. Dad waves goodbye while Mom takes my picture. The trolley and I magically disappear through the wall, and I land in a train headed for Hogwarts.

Well, not exactly. In my imagination, it works that way. I do have pictures of me pushing the trolley through the wall at Platform 9 ¾. But after the photo-op, you have to get on a real train to make the journey.

My heart races when we reach the studio entrance. Not from anxiety for once, but from anticipation. I cannot believe I am actually here, seeing the sets, costumes, and props from my childhood fantasies. Goosebumps pop up on my arms and legs when I enter the Great Hall. How many hours of my life have I spent imagining myself seated in the Great Hall as one of the wizards-in-training? My "Muggle" (non-wizard) parents move quickly through the sets, but not me. This is the only place in the world that could convince me to miss eighth grade. I intend to savor every second.

"Aren't you glad I pitched a fit so we could come here?" I'm smiling so much it hurts.

"Yes! *Obliviate* Iceland locker room." Riley uses her arm as an imaginary wand to cast the memory-erasing spell.

"Nothing will erase that," I say.

LEAVESDEN, ENGLAND: Warner Bros. Studio Tour

I imagine eating dinner with the Weasleys at the plaid-table-cloth-covered table in The Burrow. And seeing Godric's Hollow, where Harry's parents were killed, makes me sad. The details of every little thing are mind-blowing. I know it's all make-believe. But there is one wizard who is real—J. K. Rowling. Only a wizard can write an 870-page book (*Order of the Phoenix*) that kids beg to read. That is magic.

As we're leaving, I see my solution to this ridiculous global field trip—the Flying Ford Anglia. The light blue flying car is invisible to Muggles.

"Quick, Riley! Get in!" We jump into the car. I cannot believe I'm actually sitting in *the* Flying Ford Anglia. If only its flying magic were real. Now that I've checked off my bucket-list dream, I would engage the invisibility device, ditch my family, and fly home.

This week in London has been even better than I imagined. But now I have over four months to go before I get to be a normal eighth grader. The daily countdown app on my iPad is still in the triple digits. How did I let them talk me into this???

LEAVESDEN, ENGLAND–OCTOBER 2013: Harry Potter fans take a seat in the Flying Ford Anglia.

Riley, 12

"I'M READY to leave London! I can't wait to get out of this flat!" I plug in the vacuum again. "Delaney's hair is everywhere, and it's grossing me out!"

Delaney has the hair of ten humans and sheds worse than Molly and Jingles combined. What's worse? She doesn't even care! Last April Fools' Day, Delaney cleaned out her hairbrush and left her hamster-sized hairball on my pillow. I'm still planning my revenge. There's nothing grosser than someone else's hair. Nothing. Her hair is on the floor, in the bathroom, and in the bed. I CAN'T GET AWAY FROM IT.

"You have *issues*," Delaney says.

"No, I don't. I have *an* issue. Singular. You!"

"Riley, you're getting your wish. We're leaving in the morning," Mom says.

"So what's the plan again?" Dad asks.

"I found a group charter flight to Italy that has a few empty seats. They were dirt cheap because they wanted to fill the plane. So we'll fly to Naples tomorrow and stay the night. We'll head to Sorrento the next day," Mom says.

"So what has everyone thought about London?" Dad asks. "Was it worth changing the entire plan to come here?"

"Yes!" We all agree on something for once.

"This is the most un-foreign foreign place we've ever been. Nothing was really different except for the accent. The hardest part about being here was remembering to order chips instead of fries," I say.

"True. This felt like a real vacation, not like most of our trips," Delaney says.

"How so?" Mom asks.

Delaney continues, "Well, most times when we travel, there's something hard about it. But that's the part that makes it memorable. Like the culture is different, or the language is difficult, or … the people are naked."

"So true. Remember the toilet disaster in Thailand?" Riley says. "I'll never forget that!"

***

PASSPORT LESSON #2:
While all travel transforms, the most life-changing transformation happens when you're farthest from your bubble.

ENGLAND High-Low Report Card	☺	☹
Delaney	HP studio tour	Stonehenge
Riley	HP studio tour	Delaney's hair in the flat
Mom	Visiting Bath	The food
Dad	Tower of London	Cost of living

10.

A Tragic Toilet Tale

Two years ago

Experience is not the best teacher. Other people's experience is the best teacher.

— Andy Andrews, American author

Riley, 12

Before we travel to a new country, my parents always make sure we know certain basic things. First, we have to learn the following words and phrases in the other country's language:

- Good morning/goodnight
- Hello/goodbye
- Please/thank you
- Where is the bathroom?
- How much is ...?

You'd be surprised at how nice and helpful people will be if you just try to speak their language. Even if you totally butcher it, which we usually do, that just makes them even nicer. Because they know you care enough to try.

The other things we have to know when arriving in a new country are the exchange rate and tipping rules. The exchange rate is how much of their money equals one dollar. When you arrive in a new country, the first thing you do is get their money. The easiest and cheapest way is from the ATM, just like you would at home. Except it spits out baht or kronas or pounds instead of U.S. dollars. If you don't know the exchange rate, then you don't know if you should get 300 baht or 3,000 baht from the ATM. Three hundred baht sounds like a lot, but it's really only ten dollars.

After you figure out the exchange rate, then you have to figure out tipping. Everyone knows that you're supposed to leave a fifteen-to-twenty percent tip when you eat in an American restaurant. But other countries have their own rules about tipping. Some cultures don't tip at all. Other cultures tip just about everyone. If you don't know the rules, then you'll end up either looking like a big cheapskate or a big sucker. Neither one is good.

So we have to learn those things for every single country we visit. But then my parents also make sure we know other stuff, so we don't make any dumb mistakes. Because some mistakes can land you in jail. Like you can't joke around about guns or bombs in an airport, or you may be arrested. These things are super important to know ahead of time.

So two years ago—while we waited in the immigration line to enter Thailand at the Bangkok airport—Mom gave us one of her quick lessons.

"Be sure you don't say anything negative about the Thai king or royal family to anyone," Mom warned. "It's illegal, and they can take you to jail."

"You can *go to jail* for saying something mean about the king in Thailand?" I asked.

"Yep. One guy was just sentenced to thirty-five years in prison for posting something rude about the royal family on Facebook," Mom said.

"Are you serious?! If that was the law in the United States, then half the population would always be in prison. Insulting the president is practically a sport in the U.S." Delaney chimed in.

"I know. Many countries don't have the same freedom of speech laws that Americans have."

"Dang. That's crazy," I said.

My parents are great at teaching us the things that can send us to prison, but they sometimes forget the stuff that would be way more helpful. Like how to use a toilet. The chance of me randomly making a rude comment about the Thai king and his family is .00000000001 percent. The odds of me needing to use the toilet? One hundred percent!

Too bad they didn't teach me that lesson.

On our second morning in Thailand, our driver, Somchai, picked us up to take us to the Damnoen Saduak floating market. On the way, he stopped at a 7-Eleven to fill up. While Somchai pumped gas, we ran inside to buy snacks and use the bathroom.

"I feel like I'm in preschool again," I said, staring at racks full of snacks I didn't recognize.

"Why is that?" Delaney asked.

"Because I can't read the writing. I have to study the wrappers to figure out what the snacks are." I bought a few mystery snacks before announcing, "I need to go to the bathroom."

"Me too," Mom said.

"Me three," Delaney added.

We found the restroom around the back. We filed into separate stalls and closed the doors. Unlike the Western-style toilet in our hotel, the gas station had authentic Thai toilets known as *squatters*. A squatter looks like a toilet that is built into the floor. The rim of the potty is floor level, with grooves on the sides.

THAILAND: Squatter potty in a gas station outside Bangkok.

"This toilet is so weird!" I laughed.

"For real! I hope I pee in the hole and not on my feet," Delaney said from the stall next to mine.

"What are you talking about?" Why would she pee on her feet? "Hey Mom, open my door and take a picture of me sitting here."

"Did you say 'sitting,' Ri—" Mom pushed open my door. "GET UP! GET UP! GET UP! You don't *sit* on the squatter. You squat! Your feet go on those ridges and you squat over the hole!" she yelled.

EWWWW! I jumped up, violently scrubbing gas-station-squatter-nastiness off the backs of my legs and buns. "HOW AM

I SUPPOSED TO KNOW THAT?!" I yelled back. Through the crack in the door, I saw Delaney. She stood folded in half, hands on her knees and her shoulders jiggling. "STOP LAUGHING, DELANEY. IT'S NOT FUNNY!"

"Maybe not to you, but it is to me." She half-snorted and half-laughed.

Ugh! Why can't that stuff ever happen to Delaney?!

Four VERY IMPORTANT
Things to Know before Visiting a New Country:

1. Basic words and phrases
2. Tipping rules
3. Exchange rate
4. HOW TO USE THE TOILET!!!

PASSPORT LESSON #3:
If you insist on doing things your way
in a different culture, things could get nasty.

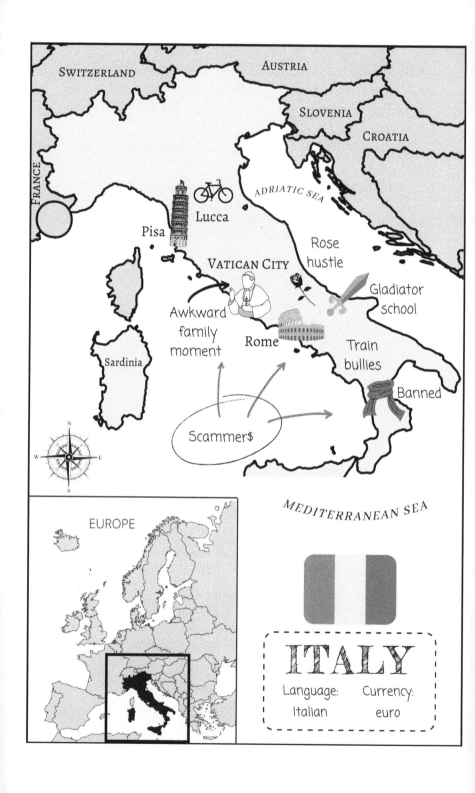

11.

A Series of Unfortunate Events

October 25–November 11

Never travel faster than your guardian angel can fly.

— MOTHER TERESA

Riley, 12

"Can we get pizza before we get on the plane?" I ask.

"Ew. I'm not eating pizza until we get to Italy and don't have other options," Delaney says.

"I can always eat pizza." Mom hands us some pounds. "I'll save our seats. Y'all get the food."

We scatter to different parts of the Gatwick London Airport food court and return with our last meal in London. We won't miss the food here, that's for sure. A friendly-looking man and his little boy walk up to our table.

"Are these taken?" The man points at the only empty seats in the food court.

"They're all yours," Dad says.

We strike up a conversation with Luigi and his son, Mario. No lie. Just like on Mario Kart. Luigi is from Italy and gives my parents tons of travel tips.

"You must be careful in Italy," Luigi warns. "There are a lot of scammers and pickpockets. Be especially careful on public transportation and in the main tourist areas. Are you going to the Colosseum?"

See! I knew public transportation was dangerous.

"Yes. We're starting in Sorrento then working our way north to Rome, Florence, and Venice," Mom says.

"I'm going to tell you the secret to visiting the Colosseum. Lots of scammers hang out front. They'll tell you they are 'official guides,' and you must hire them to skip the long lines. Just ignore them and keep walking. At the main entrance to the Colosseum, you will see three lines. The one on the left is for groups. The one in the middle is for people buying a tour inside the Colosseum. And the line on the right is for everyone who doesn't know the secret. Which is most tourists. Just use the middle line and go straight inside."

"Awesome. Thank you," Dad says.

"And I'm assuming you're going to visit the Leaning Tower, right?" Luigi asks.

"Definitely," Mom says.

"Be sure to visit Lucca the same day. You can ride bikes along the tops of the old city walls."

"Oooh, now that sounds fun," I say. Bike riding beats visiting ancient sights any day.

The grown-ups keep talking while Delaney and I look for ways to entertain ourselves. Travel days are so boring. We usually use our airport time to get caught up on homeschool stuff, but sometimes we just people watch.

"Fashion alert! Fashion alert!" I elbow Delaney.

Speed-walking down the terminal is a tiny man wearing maroon-and-navy plaid pants, an orange-and-black checkered shirt, a black felt hat with a red feather, and a yellow bow tie.

"Where?" Delaney asks.

"There," I say under my breath, using my head to point in the right direction.

"Oh. Wow. That's impressive. Looks like a mashup of a pirate, an elf, and Bill Nye the Science Guy."

"Someone call the fashion police. He should be arrested for mixing patterns like that," I say.

And that is how the Root Beer game began. At first, we called it the Atom Bomb game. We changed it because it's not smart to use the word "bomb" in airports, and airports are one of the most popular places to play it. Plus, root beer is funnier. Here's how our invented game works: When you spot an especially tragic fashion disaster, you say "root beer." Since you don't want to be rude and point, you use an imaginary clock to show where it is. A fashion catastrophe straight ahead would be "at noon." A person on your right would be "at three o'clock." So in real life, it sounds like this, "Hey Delaney, wanna get a root beer at three o'clock?"

Like all games, the Root Beer game has rules. You can't call root beer on:

1. Old people
2. Outdated clothes, like mom jeans
3. Poor people ('cause that's mean)
4. Religious/cultural clothing ('cause that's ignorant)

By the time we board our flight, we've had eight glasses of root beer.

Delaney, 14

NAPLES IS A NASTY, historic dump. Graffiti covers the statues. And not artistic graffiti, just straight up spray-paint vandalism. We've been here ten minutes, and I'm thrilled we're leaving in the morning. We're on a bus that's taking us from the airport to drop us near our bed-and-breakfast. The moonless sky makes it feel creepier than it (hopefully) is. Our B&B is only two blocks from the bus stop, but that may as well be two hundred miles. There's no way we'd walk two blocks after dark in the graffiti-vandalized area of our city. Why are we doing it here?

"We should've taken a taxi," Mom says, stepping off the bus into the darkness.

"Too late now," Dad says.

The fact that they both don't feel good about this makes me feel even worse. If I'm scared, Riley must be terrified. I grab her hand.

"This is sooo much scarier than Sloss," Riley whispers, squeezing my hand.

Mom digs a piece of paper out of her backpack. She squints under a broken street lamp to read it.

"I think we go that way." Mom points down the empty street.

Surrounded by our suitcases, I feel like a neon sign flashing ROB US. We walk a block with our heads on swivel. Our luggage bounces across the concrete, announcing our presence to whoever lurks in the shadows. Two guys turn out of an alley, coming toward us.

"Turn around," Dad orders.

We quickly drag our bags back to the bus stop. The men follow us for a bit, then turn down another alley. Mom and Dad stare at the paper again, trying to figure out the directions to the B&B.

"Can't you call?" I ask.

"Our phones don't work, and we don't have SIM cards," Mom says.

"We've gotta get moving," Dad says. "We're targets."

Behind us is the ocean, so it's not that way. We must choose between the two remaining directions: scary and terrifying.

"Let's try that way." Mom points toward scary.

"I don't think that's it." Dad shakes his head.

My parents are pretending to be calm, but I know they are freaking out. They aren't very good at faking it. In the distance, four shadows emerge from a corner headed our way.

"C'mon. Now!" Dad herds us toward terrifying, creating distance between us and the approaching danger.

The other four don't have suitcases and backpacks, so they are gaining on us quickly. The group is shouting. I don't know if it's at each other or at us. We don't want to get close enough to find out. We walk fast. They walk faster. When I stumble on the uneven cobblestone, the suitcase handle slips out of my hand and crashes next to me. Their voices—so close now—drown out my thudding heart. That's when I realize they aren't shouting. They are singing. And they sound very happy. We stop and let the shadows catch up.

One man and three women stroll toward us, swaying back and forth. Their arms are hooked at the elbows, forming a human chain. With every step, a wine glass gently bounces against each person's chest. Does everyone in Italy wear wine-glass necklaces?

"Ciao!" the man greets us like we're old friends.

"Ciao," my parents reply.

The Italian man says something else which we don't understand.

"Do you speak English?" Dad asks.

"I do." The shortest woman smiles.

"Thank goodness! We're lost. Can you tell us which direction our B&B is," Mom blurts out, handing the woman the sheet of paper.

"This is not a good place to be lost." The woman frowns. The group studies the paper. They talk to each other in Italian, then turn to us.

"We will take you," the tallest wine-glass-wearing woman says.

Hallelujah!

The Italian four-pack leads us a few blocks past run-down buildings and delivers us to the doorstep of our B&B. The man presses the worn call button by the building's front door and lets the owner know we've arrived.

"Grazie, grazie, grazie," my mom gushes, wrapping her arms around each of them. She gives them an air kiss near each cheek, like I've seen in the movies. After we all take turns exchanging air kisses, they lock arms again and walk away. We can hear them singing long after they disappear into the darkness.

"What if they hadn't shown up when they did?" My stomach is still somersaulting.

"Y'all, think about it. One man and three women appeared out of nowhere." Mom exhales slowly. "Those were our guardian angels."

Riley, 12

SORRENTO, FINALLY! I love it. Sooo much better than Naples. Sorrento is a forty-minute boat ride from Naples but forty million times better.

"Did y'all hear about that famous Italian chef who just died?" Dad asks.

"What happened?" I love watching cooking shows.

"He pasta way!"

"That was actually funny," Delaney says.

"Oooh, look at all the fun shops. Can we go shopping later?" I ask, our suitcase wheels clack-clacking on the cobblestone as we walk.

"Sure. Another day, though. We need to eat and then find our place," Mom says.

Five pieces of pizza later, I decide I'm going to move here when I grow up. After eating, we board a little bus that drives us to the village of Massa Lubrense. It's just two miles from Sorrento but less touristy.

"We get our own house here?" I ask. "Does this mean I don't have to share a bed?"

"Yep. You don't even have to share a room. The villa has three bedrooms," Mom says.

Delaney and I run inside and claim our bedrooms. I snag the one with the small desk. It will be perfect for homeschool. Outside is a huge patio overlooking vineyards. Lots of wine comes from Italy, and the grapes come from these vineyards. Wine drinking is such a big part of Italian culture that it's even normal to see teenagers drinking it with their parents!

"Hey Dad, can we shave your head here?" I ask. "You promised we could."

Delaney and I have been begging our dad to shave his head for months. He promised we could do it on the big trip. That way he could get used to being bald before seeing people he knows.

"I guess so. But I need to charge the clippers first."

A couple of hours later, we gather on the patio. Dad sits in a plastic chair with his back to the vineyard, and I spread a towel across his shoulders.

"I can't believe I'm letting you do this." He shakes his head.

I can tell he's nervous about shaving his head. I don't know why. He's bald on top with hair around the sides, so his head looks like a horseshoe. That's why we call him "horseshoe head." He doesn't think it's as funny as we do.

"There's no turning back," Mom says, as Delaney runs the clippers across Dad's head.

"You do that side, and I'll do the other side," I tell Delaney. "Then we'll both do the back."

Delaney and I giggle as we pass the clippers back and forth. We take turns mowing the lawn on Dad's head. We mow up-and-down and side-to-side. It takes lots of turns because it's not a razor blade. The hair doesn't just come off. We finish the sides, then focus on the back.

"The sides look good." Dad checks out our progress with a handheld mirror.

"It looks so much better already." Mom videos with her phone.

"You're gonna lov—" I drop the clippers as Delaney is handing them to me.

Crash! The clippers shatter into pieces. Delaney, Mom and I glance back and forth at each other. Then at Dad's head. Then at the broken clippers. We squeeze our lips to keep the giggles inside. We quickly turn away from each other to keep from exploding with laughter. The back of Dad's head looks like it's been cut with a weed eater. Flashback to my preschool botched haircut and laundry basket episode!

"Oh no. Please tell me you were finished." Dad angles the

mirror to see as much of his head as possible.

"Oh, it's fine," Mom jumps in. "They were basically finished with the back. It looks good," she says with a totally straight face.

"At least you no longer have a horseshoe head," Delaney says.

She's right. Now, he has a weed eater head. But that's our little secret.

"How long does it take to get to Pompeii?" I ask as we enter the Sorrento train station.

"Only twenty minutes," Mom says. "Did someone grab the book?"

"Got it," I say.

"Alrighty, you're the tour guide," Mom says as we take our seats on the train.

"Welcome aboard, folks," I say, using my best Italian-tour-guide accent. "I'm gonna tell you just what you need to know and leave out the boring stuff. Got it?

"Pompeii is an ancient city that was destroyed when Mount Vesuvius erupted in 79 AD. That's almost two thousand years ago, folks. The city was buried under fifteen to twenty feet of volcanic ash, so everything underneath was frozen in time."

"You sound just like Stephano-the-Italian-man." Delaney snorts. We love imitating Count Olaf from *A Series of Unfortunate Events*.

The train stops and a teenage girl—wearing skin-tight jeans, a crop top, and bedazzled high-tops—steps on. Thick black eyeliner circles her raccoon eyes. Hot pink fingernails unscrew the top to her hot pink lip gloss. She eyeballs the passengers while applying a coat, then slides the tube back in her pocket. She walks up to my mom and sticks her palm out. Mom pretends to read her book. The girl does the same thing to my dad. He just shakes his head. She walks through the train with her hand out, as if we are all riding *her* train. She shoves her hand in the face of everyone who doesn't look Italian. No one gives her a single euro. She gives a mean-girl glare to the entire train and gets off at the next stop.

"See! That would never happen on a plane. I bet that train bully spends the whole day riding back and forth," I say.

"I wonder how often people actually give her money," Delaney says.

A few stops later, we arrive in Pompeii. Yay. There are no lines. We're the first ones here. Then we find out why. The time changed last night, and we didn't know. An hour later, we buy tickets and explore the two-thousand-year-old city. Some houses still have paintings on the walls.

"See these trenches cut in the street?" Dad points to the gutters that we're walking beside. "That's where the sewage used to flow."

"Can you imagine walking down the street and a gigantic pile of poop floats by? I bet it was really smelly back then," I say.

"That's so nasty," Delaney says as we explore the ruins. "This is how life was in Bible times. That's pretty interesting to think about,"

We enter the ancient bathhouse. It's pretty fancy to be so old.

"Whoa. The ceiling is so high." I tilt my head up. "What a cool place to get a twirling video."

"It sure is," Mom says, pulling out her phone. "Hurry, there's a huge tour group about to come in here."

I whip out my baton and do a quick routine. I toss my baton toward the ancient ceiling dome, making my final catch as the tourists enter the room. Confusion washes across their faces when they see me twirling. We scoot out the other door and finish exploring.

The saddest-coolest part of Pompeii is the bodies. When

archaeologists found the skeletons, they were in the same position—crawling, praying, or kneeling with their face in their hands—as when they died. Using plaster, archaeologists have recreated the bodies of the victims at the moment they flash-fried from the intense heat. A plaster body lies in a glass coffin. His mouth is wide open, like he is screaming. It's the creepiest thing I've ever seen.

POMPEII, ITALY: (top) Victim of the Mt. Vesuvius eruption in 79 A.D. is preserved as a plaster cast. (bottom) Ancient Pompeii with Mt. Vesuvius in the background.

POMPEII, ITALY: Riley and Delaney explore the ruins of Pompeii.

"Do we have time to shop before our train?" I ask, fingers crossed.

"We have about an hour. Do you wanna look for scarves?" Mom replies.

"Yes!" Delaney and I say. "Jinx! One-two-three."

Scarves are *the* fashion accessory right now. Plus, they barely take up any room, so it's the perfect souvenir. We hop from shop to shop, looking for the perfect scarf. Most shops sell scarves for five euros each, or three-for-twelve euros. After visiting several shops, we finally go into one where we each find a scarf we love. But we don't see a 3 FOR €12 sign.

"Luigi said we should bargain in the shops," Mom whispers to Del and me.

She approaches the shopkeeper. "Buongiorno. Will you take twelve euros for three scarves?"

"No discount. You pay fifteen euros." He narrows his eyes and frowns.

"Grazie, anyway," Mom says to the man.

"So much for Luigi's great advice," Delaney whispers.

Mom heads to the entrance. "C'mon y'all. We'll find them in another shop. I remember seeing them around the corner."

We wander from shop to shop for thirty minutes and can't find the scarves anywhere. Ugh! I hate when this happens. When we were at the floating market in Thailand two years ago, I saw the cutest beaded sandals in the world. I spotted them right behind a man with a ginormous yellow python draped across his shoulders. That's one way to get people's attention! Mom promised me we'd see them at other markets and would buy them later. We never saw them again. I'm still mad about that.

"Can we just go back and buy them from the grumpy man?" I beg. At least he's not wearing a snake scarf.

Mom agrees. Yay!

When we get back to the shop, Mom hands me the money. "You go pay for them. He'll be nicer to you since you're a kid."

Delaney and I find the three scarves, smile, and hand the man fifteen euros.

"YOU ARE BANNED FROM STORE! GO SOMEWHERE ELSE!" The shopkeeper yanks the scarves out of our hands.

I leave Sorrento empty-scarf-handed and wear my disappointment to the train station instead. I don't want to live here after all.

Delaney, 14

I CAN'T BELIEVE that man kicked us out of his store! I've never been kicked out of anywhere. It's funny and humiliating all at the same time. We take our seats on the train. I like that it has rows facing each other, so we can talk and play cards. Riley and Mom sit in the aisle seats on the left with our luggage piled in the window seats next to them. Dad and I sit in the window seats on the right side of the aisle. The aisle seats next to us are empty.

We are heading to Rome, but we have to change trains in nasty Naples. I'm not looking forward to that. I dig in my backpack until I find my required reading for Italy, *The Smile*. It's about Mona Lisa, the woman with the most famous portrait in the world. I'm just getting to the good part when a scary dude jumps into the seat next to me. My book falls to the floor. He's all in my personal space. His leg presses against mine. My scalp tingles as stranger-danger bells go off. He leans across the aisle toward my mom and barks something in Italian. She grabs her handbag and gives him the I-have-no-idea-what-you're-saying look. Dad gives me the he's-bad-news look. The musclehead spins around in his seat and shoves his hand in my dad's face, demanding money. Dad gives him the over-my-dead-body look and shakes his head. I clutch my backpack to my chest. The MacBook Air is in it.

The nerve-wracking stare down begins: a fifty-ish dad with detached ACLs versus a guy half his age with twice the muscles. The odds are not in Dad's favor. This train goon leans toward my dad and sticks out his lower jaw. He narrows his eyes and makes boogeyman faces. When Dad doesn't cough up any euros, he gives my dad the finger. Dad's face turns red, and he clenches his fists. I've never seen him this angry.

I want to jump up and run to safety, but I'm frozen in place.

Why did we have to leave our bubble?! I guarantee none of my friends will be mugged today.

"Ignore him," Mom mouths to Dad.

Riley has a death grip on her backpack, too. Her eyes ping-pong between the dirtbag and our dad. The jerk growls like a rabid dog. He makes more evil faces and gives Dad the finger again. All eyes on the tensely-silent train stare at us. Using daughter-to-father telepathy, I tell Dad not to do anything crazy. I hope he gets the message. After several more minutes of growling and scary faces, the train scum stands up and struts down the aisle. He passes all the Italians, then plants himself next to an old couple. They're dressed like Americans. He strikes out again. When he gets off the train at the next stop, everyone in the train car exhales.

"What a jerk!" Dad spews, his red face fading to pink.

"See! *This* is why I hate public transportation!" Riley says, releasing the grip on her backpack.

AFTER GETTING YELLED at in the Naples train station for ordering a slice of pizza too slowly, and then getting scammed in the Rome train station, we are finally on the bus to our Rome neighborhood. Luigi warned us about pickpockets, so the four of us stand back-to-back like an outward facing X. After the train incident, we are on high-alert. Our backpacks hang across our chests. Our pockets are empty. One arm holds the backpack and the other grips the suitcase handle. There is zero personal space on this bus. Every time someone bumps against me, I'm sure they are slipping a hand in my pockets.

Twenty minutes later, the bus drops us in Trastevere. Our home for the next week is a two-bedroom apartment with grandma furniture. We don't normally stay an entire week in one location. But this isn't just anywhere. It is Rome, the capital of the Roman Empire. I hope things turn around here. We've been in Italy for five days. The only thing I like about it so far is the gelato.

WE HAVE A NEW GAME. It's called Genovia. As in the fictional country from *The Princess Diaries*. We're tired of people hassling us. So now *we're* messing with them. We figured out that when shopkeepers and "guides" (and all the other people trying to scam you) ask where you're from, it's not because they care. It's because they are trying to figure out how much to charge you. The United States equals the highest prices. So now, we tell everyone we're from Genovia. Everyone. And we use a fake accent too. The reactions are hilarious. Sometimes they ask where Genovia is, and we have to make up something fast. But usually they say, "Oh yes. We have many customers from there."

Riley, 12

"Mᴏᴍᴍᴍ, what are we doing today?" I call from my bed where I'm bingeing on Netflix. Our parents think we're doing home-school stuff, but I'm sick of online math lessons.

"I wish we could stay in bed all day and watch *Suite Life on Deck*," Delaney says from the other twin bed. "I would gladly miss eighth grade if that's how we were doing it."

"Y'all get dressed. We're going to Gladiator School," Mom yells from their bedroom.

"Sounds like Mom found another Groupon." I close my laptop and hop out of bed.

An hour later, we're walking down a dusty path on the outskirts of Rome.

"If you're an American when you go into the bathroom, and you're an American when you come out of the bathroom, what are you while you're in the bathroom?" Dad asks.

"European!" Delaney and I say together. "Everyone knows that one, Dad."

"How are your London blog posts coming?" Mom asks.

"I'm almost finished with my PSA about Stonehenge. Trav-elers need to know it's just a pile of rocks."

When we reach the "school" (it's more like a warehouse), a gladiator greets us.

"I'm Ougflak. I'm going to train you to become gladiators."

Ougflak's wearing a short red tunic that hits mid-thigh and gladiator boots. He would get dress-coded at our school for wearing something that short. Scratch that. No one's gonna dress-code this guy for anything. His tattooed arms are bigger than my dad's legs. And his legs are bigger than tree trunks. Even his muscles have muscles. I bet this guy never has prob-lems with train bullies.

"First, we learn. Next, we train. Then, we fight." Ougflak hands us four tunics. "Put these on."

Dressed like undernourished gladiators, we take turns holding real medieval weapons—like tridents, spears, and swords. Ougflak puts a helmet on my head. The metal digs into my shoulders, and my head falls forward under the helmet's weight. My gladiator lessons begin.

> Gladiators fought to the death in ancient Rome. It was their version of sports and entertainment, like going to a football game today. They fought in the Colosseum—a massive arena that held 50,000 to 80,000 people. Most gladiators were slaves, criminals, or Christian martyrs. But some were rich men seeking fame and fortune as professional gladiators.

After the classroom lesson we go outside and warm-up with an obstacle course. It is the ancient version of *American Ninja Warrior*. After we dodge swinging sacks of sand and attempt one-arm push-ups, Ougflak hands us our weapons: duct-tape-wrapped-pool-noodle swords and shields. Ougflak teaches us to hit and block. Now we get to fight!

Here's how gladiator scoring works: Arms and legs get one point per blow. Stomach and back earn three points. The head is off-limits. The first person to score five points wins.

"Who will fight first?" Ougflak yells at his gladiators-in-training.

Not us, not us. Another family with two boys is here. Please pick them.

"Delaney and Riley, you will start."

Ougflak scratches the fighting circle into the dirt, using a real sword. Delaney and I go to opposite sides of the ring. The boys are watching. This is sooo embarrassing.

"Fight!" he yells.

We run toward each other with raised noodle-swords.

Delaney whacks me on the arm. Dang it! She gets the first point. Round two starts and I whack her as hard as I can on her knee. That was fun. 1-1. In the next round, Del gets lucky again and taps me on the shoulder. Ugh! I can't let her win. At the beginning of the fourth round, I picture the train bully's face on Delaney's body and attack. Score! 2-2. Delaney laughs. She isn't taking this seriously. Next thing you know, she is ahead 4-2. How did that happen?! This is the final round. I have to hit her in the back or stomach to win.

ROME, ITALY–NOV 2013: Delaney and Riley fight at Gladiator School.

I picture her hairball on my pillow. "Aaagh!" I run at her like a medieval gladiator, and—*bam!*—I stab her in the chest.

"Five-to-four, Riley." Ougflak lifts my arm in the air.

But Delaney doesn't care. She's doubled over laughing. The British boys fight next. Then my mom and dad. Mom acts like this is real. Like she's a gladiator fighting for her life. She wants to beat my dad. But he wins, and she's annoyed. I may not be mom's younger clone, but I got her competitive genes. The British boys' parents don't wear gladiator tunics or fight. How lame.

I loved Gladiator School for two reasons: One, I didn't have to listen to a boring audio guide. And two, I had permission to fight Delaney.

"GROSS! DOES EVERYONE IN ITALY SMOKE?" I wave my hand in front of my face as we walk to the Colosseum.

"For real. Italy may look like a boot, but it smells like an ashtray." Delaney pinches her nose.

I don't know a single person in real life who smokes. My Papaw used to smoke, but that was like fifty years ago. He quit before I was born.

"Would you believe that when I was a kid people could smoke on airplanes?" Mom says.

"Are you serious? How dumb is that?" Delaney says.

When we get close to the Colosseum, a man approaches us, just like Luigi warned.

"Hello, are you going to the Colosseum?" he asks.

"We are," Mom answers, not slowing down.

"Where are you from? Do you have a guide?"

"We're from Genovia." I jump in, in case Mom forgets.

"And no, we don't have a guide," Mom says.

"Ah, you must have a guide. Tickets are sold out. I am the last guide of the day," he continues.

"No, thank you. We're good." Mom gives him the talk-to-the-hand sign, and he gives up.

The entrance to the Colosseum looks exactly the way Luigi described it. There is a line on the left for tour groups. Thirty to forty people wait in that line. The line on the right is for individuals. It snakes around the building and has at least two hundred people in it. There is no middle line at all. As we walk past those two hundred right-liners into the main entrance, I keep expecting one to throw a tomato (or cigarette) at us. Once inside, we march straight up to the ticket booth, buy our tickets, and sign up for a tour. No waiting at all. Grazie, Luigi!

Going to Gladiator School yesterday helps me understand what really happened at the Colosseum. I can picture the people cheering as the gladiators fought to the death. The real tour guide takes us to the tunnels beneath the Colosseum that the animals and gladiators used to enter the arena. After the tour, Delaney takes some cool baton video of me in the two-thousand-year-old stadium. Did they have majorettes back in the Roman Empire? Or am I the first to twirl in the Colosseum?

ROME, ITALY: The Colosseum

We spend the rest of the afternoon eating gelato, watching street performers, and avoiding scammers. The coolest street vendor is a woman who makes paintings of Rome with spray paint. She starts with a blank poster board and in less than five minutes, *voilà!*, she hands me a painting of the Colosseum. Delaney and I each buy one. Then, we walk to Trevi Fountain.

We stand with our backs to the most famous fountain in Italy. "Make a wish," Mom says, before throwing a coin over her left shoulder into the water. We all do the same.

"What'd you wish for?" Delaney asks.

"I'm not telling. That would jinx it."

I wish to not get mugged. I bet Delaney wishes to go home. Then, we walk to the Spanish Steps. With people packed on Rome's most famous steps, they look more like bleachers than a monument.

"Oooh, I have an idea. Let's all sit in different spots, and Mom, you take a picture. It'll be our very own *Where's Waldo* at the Spanish Steps," I say.

"Great idea, Ri," Mom says, before we scatter across the steps.

I'm standing by myself for two whole seconds, when a dark-haired man walks up and hands me a rose. "Hello, Beautiful. Where are you from?"

"Genovia." I clench my hands into fists.

"Here, for you." He shoves the rose in my face. "A beautiful girl deserves a beautiful flower."

"No, thank you." I squeeze my fists tighter. He's not gonna scam me. I know all about the *rose hustle*. These men trick girls into taking the rose and then demand money. Even if you don't want the dumb thing, they won't take it back.

"Genovians aren't dummies, ya know." I fling my ponytail and walk away.

Delaney, 14

Vatican City fun facts!

Vatican City is the Catholic capital of the world and the home of the Pope. It is also the smallest country in the world—smaller than my neighborhood! But this tiny country has three gigantic tourist attractions:

1. St. Peter's Basilica (so big that two football fields and the Statue of Liberty would fit inside). The Apostle Peter is believed to be buried here.
2. Vatican Museums (filled with Renaissance art).
3. Sistine Chapel (where Michelangelo painted the most famous ceiling in the world in the 1500s).

"Do we have to go in?" Riley points at the 200+ people ahead of us.

"Yes!" Dad, Mom, and I say.

"Ugh. This is gonna be so B-O-R-I-N-G. I wish Luigi had a skip-the-line tip for this place."

"Someone pull out the guidebook and share some fun facts," Dad says.

I skim the book.

"This is interesting," I say. "The Swiss Guard, not the Italian Army, protects Vatican City and the Pope."

"You mean those guys dressed like clowns wearing berets are Swiss Guards?" Riley asks.

She's right. They look like deck-of-card jokers in their blue-red-and-yellow-striped outfits.

"Yep. And get this: In order to be a guard you must be Swiss, Catholic, male, and five-foot-nine or taller. You've gotta have a great reputation and served at least two years in the Swiss military."

VATICAN CITY–NOV 2013: A member of the Swiss Guard stands at attention, protecting Vatican City and the Pope.

"So they're sorta like the Beefeaters of Vatican City," Riley says.

The line moves quickly, and soon we are inside. For two hours, I walk with my head swiveling up-and-down and side-to-side. The chapel is supposed to be amazing, but that's at the very end. I didn't know every inch of the Vatican Museum would be mind-blowing, too. I take picture after picture, but they're so lame on my phone. You have to see Renaissance art in person to appreciate it.

When we finally reach the door to the Sistine-cherry-on-top-Chapel, a guard says, "Cameras and phones away, please. No pictures and no talking."

He lets us in. The room is packed and silent. It's a weird combination. I'm glad they don't allow cameras in here. Those selfie-stick people would ruin the experience. We stand shoulder-to-shoulder with dozens of strangers. Every mouth hangs open as we stare at *The Creation of Adam* on the ceiling.

WE HAVEN'T BEEN out of the Sistine Chapel for ten seconds when Riley asks, "Can we get gelato now?" She sounds like a parrot. *Riley want a gelato. Riley want a gelato.*

"St. Peter's first. Then gelato," Mom says.

Good call. Riley is obsessed with Italy's version of ice cream. If we break now, there's no way she's getting up for a cathedral. Even if it's the most important Catholic church in the world. We step through the towering doors into St. Peter's Basilica, and my mouth falls open again. It's hu-mon-gous.

"We need to find the Pietà," Mom whispers. "It is one of Michelangelo's most famous sculptures."

It's easy to find. It is the only sculpture behind bulletproof glass. The Pietà is a statue of Mary holding Jesus's body after the crucifixion. Her face is so sad. I can barely make a stick man out of Play-Doh. How did Michelangelo carve this out of marble?

As we're exiting the basilica, a massive pack of worshippers parade toward us. A group of priests in flowing white robes leads hundreds of singing followers. The priest in the center carries a golden staff topped with a large cross. The priest behind him carries a Bible with a fancy metal cover. We stand against the wall beside the entrance as the parade enters St. Peter's.

"It's gelato time," Riley announces as the last worshipper passes us.

Out of nowhere, Dad says, "Let's join in," and disappears into the procession.

We see no other option but to follow. We're swallowed into the sea of singing, chanting Italian Catholics. And we can't escape. Wooden barriers line both sides of the procession, trapping us in this holy parade. The tourists are supposed to be outside the barriers—the Catholic worshippers inside the barriers. Dad clearly didn't think this through before jumping in. And he thinks teenagers are impulsive?!

I shouldn't be surprised. He's that dad, the guy in the audience who's always first to volunteer to go onstage and mortify his kids. He's the dad the school calls when they need someone to wear a dorky costume. Lucky me. It could be worse, though. My grandfather was Birmingham's Bozo the Clown when my father was a kid. Dad thought it was super cool that his father was a TV celebrity clown—until third grade. Then he became son-of-a-Bozo, which was tragically uncool.

But now, I'm dealing with my own father-created-crisis. Mom and Riley mumble fake Italian words, trying to sound like they belong. I smile awkwardly at the tourists snapping pictures of *me*.

This. Is. A. Nightmare.

The barriers are too tall to jump without looking like even bigger weirdos. So we keep walking and chanting, trying to blend in. With our fair skin and cameras in hand, we're not blending. At all.

"When you see an opening in the barriers, get out," Mom whisper-mumbles in my ear.

I nod. She and Riley stare at the ground to contain their giggles. If they make eye contact, it's all over. I shuffle alongside the worshippers, alternating glances at the picture-snapping tourists and the floor. Am I supposed to smile for their pictures? I don't know. Why can't the floor part like the Red Sea and let me join Peter down below?

Finally, the barriers end. We jump out and join the normal tourists. Some are laughing at us. Others scowl. The parade ends at the tomb of St. Peter. The worshippers continue singing and chanting around the tomb for twenty minutes. Then, they begin the procession out of the church. We move out of the way this time.

After they leave, we ask the guard to explain what we had taken part in. Thankfully, this wasn't some rare holy event that we crashed. It's a daily ritual for priests and devoted Catholics.

"Dad, don't ever do that again," I beg. "That was so embarrassing."

"Can we get gelato now?" Riley asks.

VATICAN CITY–NOV 2013: Roman Catholic worshippers parade into St. Peter's Basilica.

Riley, 12

 History fun fact!

Old towns across Europe are built around squares.
The most important buildings in a town, like the
government buildings and cathedrals, are found in
the main squares. Besides the important buildings,
there are also cafés, statues, and shops. In Italy,
these squares are called piazzas.

"I LIKE FLORENCE better than Rome already," I say, my suitcase bouncing across the cobblestone.

"Me too. Much better vibes," Delaney agrees.

We're walking from the train station to our apartment in a *piazza*.

I don't care if our piazza has important buildings. I just hope there's a gelato shop nearby. After walking for ten minutes, we find our square and building.

"Whoa." I point at the numbers *1294* scratched into the building. "This building is old."

We drag our suitcases three floors up the narrow staircase.

"Scusi," a hunched lady says as she passes me. I press against the wall, making room for the tiny woman who looks as ancient as the building.

We enter the musty, two-bedroom flat Mom booked online. But there's a problem.

"How can they call this a two-bedroom? Isn't false advertising illegal?!" I'm so mad. The second "bedroom" is really the living room with a pullout sofa. Sleeping with Delaney on a pullout sofa is double tragic. When we find the sheets in the stinky wardrobe, it becomes triple tragic.

"EW! These sheets smell like B.O.!" I gag.

"Stop being dramatic," Dad says.

Delaney takes a whiff and jerks her head back. "Nasty. They are gross. Smell them." She shoves the sheets toward Mom.

"I believe you," Mom says, backing away.

I bet if my parents' sheets smelled like this, we'd find somewhere else to stay. But their room has fresh sheets and a view of the piazza. So I've got three nights on a sofa with Delaney and gag-a-maggot sheets. For once, I hope she hogs the covers.

PISA, ITALY: The Leaning Tower

WE SPEND three days exploring Florence and Tuscany. The *Duomo* in Florence (that's Italian for cathedral) is the prettiest one

I've ever seen. It looks like a giant gingerbread church built out of white and green sugar cubes.

An hour train ride from Florence is the Leaning Tower of Pisa. It leans so far that you think it's going to topple right over. Mom gets the cheesy pictures of us pretending to hold up the tower. Then I pull out my baton and she gets some twirling video. The Leaning Tower makes a great backdrop. After climbing 294 steps to the top of the cattywampus tower, we catch another train to Lucca. That is the town that airport Luigi told us to visit and the best place in Italy!

It's a medieval town that still has the original walls circling the city. Lucca reminds me of a cereal bowl. The city walls are the rim of the bowl, and the city is the Lucca Charms. The "rim" is thick enough for trees and a bike path, and the entire loop around the city is less than three miles. That's smaller than my neighborhood.

We rent bikes and pedal up a ramp to the top of the wall. From there you can watch the entire city as you ride. When you see a "marshmallow" you want—like a gelato shop or play-ground—you coast down the nearest ramp into the bowl. We spend the afternoon riding up and down the city walls.

"I loved Lucca," I say, walking from the Florence train station back to our piazza. "Bikes and a playground. That's a perfect day." Too bad I'm heading straight for B.O. sheets.

"And not one person tried to scam us," Delaney says. "That's a shocker."

"Oh no!" An old lady is lying on the side of the street. People step inches from her head but don't even glance at her. "She's been hit. Hurry! No one's helping her!!"

We run to the woman. She's not moving. She must be dead, but no one cares! When we get closer, we realize why everyone else is ignoring her. She's lying between cars with a cup begging for money. She's trying to be sneaky, but she's texting on the phone hidden underneath her long, black coat.

"A woman warned me about this. Same thing. She was about to help a woman lying in the street, when a black BMW pulled up. A 'poor' woman jumped out and switched places with the 'hurt' woman. It's infuriating because you never know who really needs help and who doesn't," Mom says.

Ugh! We pass the woman like everyone else. Sadly, the only things stinkier here than the scams are my sheets.

PASSPORT LESSON #4:
Visitors will love or hate your school, your community, and your country based on the people they meet. Don't be a jerk.

ITALY
High-Low Report Card

	🙂	🙁
Delaney	Florence	Cigarettes everywhere
Riley	Kiwi-banana gelato	B.O. sofa bed in Florence
Mom	Florence	Scammers & smoking
Dad	Gladiator school	Jerk on the train

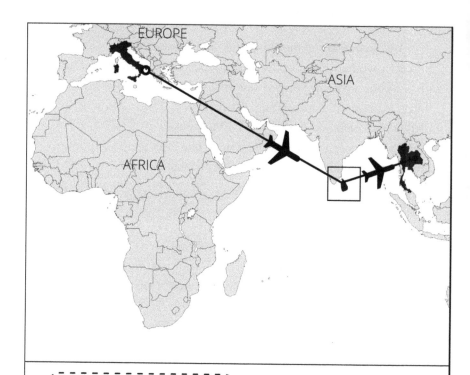

missing
backpack

Colombo

AWKWARD

INDIAN OCEAN

12.

Dress-Coded

November 12

The only real voyage of discovery ... consists not in seeking new landscapes but in having new eyes, in seeing the universe with the eyes of another.

— Marcel Proust, French novelist

Delaney, 14

"Dress comfortably. We've got a long travel day ahead of us." Mom zips her suitcase.

"What's the itinerary?" I ask, trying to figure out what she means by "long."

"We're training back to Rome, then flying to Sri Lanka, then catching another flight to Kuala Lumpur, and then *another* flight to Phuket. Then, it's a one-hour drive to Khao Lak."

That. Sounds. Miserable. But at least we'll end up at the beach. I'm over Italy. Several hours later, we board the first plane. It's an overnight flight to Sri Lanka (SREE lahn-ka), an island off the tip of India.

I take my seat and pull out *First They Killed My Father* while the other passengers board. Cambodia is Thailand's next-door neighbor. They suffered through a tragic genocide in the 1970s under their psycho-evil leader, Pol Pot. He was the Hitler of Cambodia and murdered millions of his own people. It's a depressing-but-important read. Ten hours later, we land at the Colombo airport looking and feeling nasty.

"Once again, I didn't sleep at all." Riley pulls her backpack from the overhead compartment. "And once again, you slept like a baby."

"If it makes you feel better, I still feel awful." I fish for gum in my backpack and hand her a stick. "Have some travelers' toothpaste."

We find our gate, plopping into four seats for the two-hour layover.

"So what are your Italy posts on?" Mom asks. "They're due in—"

"I call Gladiator School," Riley speed blurts.

"No fair! She always gets the good ones." I cross my arms and think for a second. "I'll do our humiliating experience at St. Peter's. All my posts are what *not* to do when traveling."

"Where's the backpack with the medicine bag?" Mom asks, her head swiveling in every direction. "Dale, you had it."

"I thought it was here." Dad looks around his feet.

"Everyone. Search," Mom orders.

"You two stay here with the stuff. We'll look for the bag," Dad says.

A few minutes later, they return with the backpack. Dad left it in a chair when he stopped to tie his shoe.

Mom holds the backpack in the air like it's an Academy Award Oscar statue. "*This* is our most important bag. Everything else can be replaced. Except this." She exhales and sits down.

A few minutes later, Riley's pointy elbow pokes me in the arm. "Everyone is so …"—her eyes dart around the room—"fancy."

One side of the first-aid kit.

I survey the gate. Most women are wearing beautiful *saris*, a single piece of fabric wrapped around the body. The rainbow-colored saris and headscarves sparkle with sequins and beads. The sari-wearing women each have a single dot decorating her forehead. A few women wear *burkas*, which are like giant capes covering everything from head to toe. These women peer through the skinny window framing their eyes. The men wear loose tunics and flowy pants. Some men wear turbans on their heads, the way I wrap my hair in a towel after I shower. Three men have handlebar mustaches.

On the other hand, we're wearing the official American travel outfit. Yoga pants. And we look like bums. The women remind me of Mrs. Hawk-Eye, the teacher who tries to catch girls violating the dress code. Are they staring at us because we are White? Or because of how we're dressed? Probably both. I feel naked without something covering my head—like I'm wearing a bikini in church.

It feels weird to be the ones who are different. The ones who are judged by our unusual clothes. Then it hits me.

"Riley! *We're* the root beer!"

"I knooow," Riley whispers. "They're acting like we have the Cheese Touch."

I make eye contact with a woman wearing a black burka. My eyes try to tell her that just because I'm dressed differently doesn't make me a bad person. I hope she understands. I smile at her. Her eyes squint through the tiny slit in her head covering. I think she smiled back.

After two hours that feel like ten, we board our next flight to Malaysia. The plane smells like curry, an Indian spice I don't like. I slink down in my seat, using a blanket to hide my outfit. The flight attendants look like goddesses in their saris. The gorgeous fabric is carefully wrapped to cover most of their bodies, except for the area Mom calls her muffin top. But it doesn't look bad—which is interesting because American flight attendants would never show their muffin tops. Ever.

When the safety video starts, we know we hadn't imagined the stares. The cartoon passengers look nothing like us. Their coloring and clothing match the people from the gate. It's so awkward to be the one who is different. The one not represented in ads or videos.

"I don't want to play Root Beer again," I say, settling in for another long flight.

"Me neither," Riley says.

I hate feeling judged because of my clothes and skin color. I think about a few kids at my school. Do they feel like this every day? Because it's a million times worse than wearing Fuggs.

please ensure
that your seat belts are fastened...

COLOMBO, SRI LANKA: Airline safety video on the flight from Sri Lanka to Thailand.

PASSPORT LESSON #5:

People are like presents. Some come in fancy wrappings and others in plain bags. Either way, the best part is what's inside.

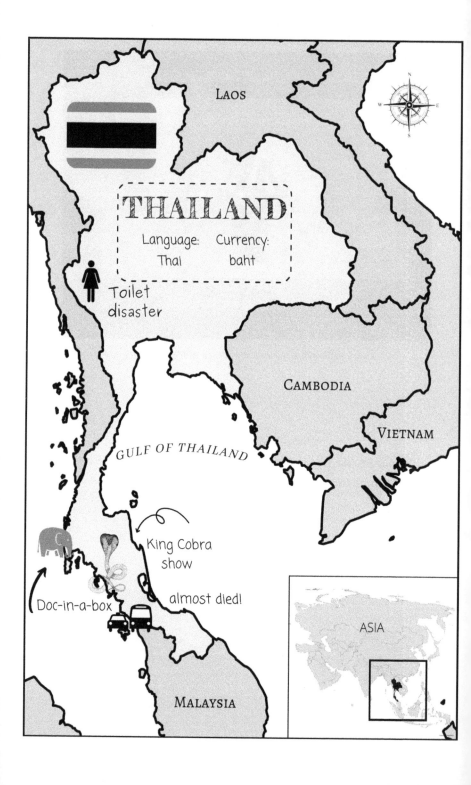

13.

Land of Smiles

November 13–28

Pull a thread here and you'll find it's attached to the rest of the world.

— NADEEM ASLAM, *THE WASTED VIGIL*

Delaney, 14

Thirty hours, four countries, three flights, two continents, and one throw up later, we make it to Thailand. I survived the curry flight by bingeing on beef sticks instead of eating real food. It seemed like a good idea at the time, but I barfed them up right after we landed. It was a hideous combination of starvation, exhaustion, and nothing looking good to eat. I'm ready for some chicken fried rice and a banana smoothie. That's my go-to Thai meal.

I'm ready for quality veg time in Khao Lak. This beach is an hour north of Phuket (POO-ket) but so much better. When we enter the Khao Lak Orchid Beach Resort, the staff greets us with a *wai*. We wai back. Just one of many reasons that I. Love. Thailand.

The wai is the Thai version of shaking hands and a sign of respect. To wai, put your palms together like you are praying and bow forward.

"Let's explore," I say to Riley while our parents are checking in.

We drop our bags and run to the pool. This is paradise. Massive palms surround the pool, providing the perfect place to read. I've never been here before, but it seems familiar. I don't know why.

"Oooh. Massages." Riley points to the thatch hut sandwiched between the pool and beach. "They're two hundred fifty baht for an hour. That's only eight dollars."

That's another thing we love about Thailand. Stuff we never do at home, we get to do here.

"C'mon y'all." Mom motions for us to join them.

We follow Chai Son to our room, a two-bedroom apartment minus the kitchen. The bedrooms and living room each have a flatscreen TV. Not that it matters since most of the shows are in Thai. This is the fanciest place we've stayed in yet. And it's on the beach.

"This is one of our splurges," Mom says. "We'll be here for five nights."

"Sweet." Riley kicks back on the sofa with her hands clasped behind her head.

"Heck yeah. Can we eat dinner now?" My stomach tells everyone I'm hungry.

It's been over thirty hours since we've had a proper meal. We head to the open-air restaurant by the ocean. Twenty minutes later, our server, Pakpao, sets a plate of steaming chicken fried rice in front of me.

"Kop khun ka," I say to Pakpao before shoveling the Thai dish into my mouth with a fork. I'm too hungry to even attempt the chopsticks.

"This is the best meal I've had since we left home," I say, not even bothering to swallow first. Thai food is so much better than Italian food, which is better than English food, which is definitely better than Icelandic food.

"Slow down," Dad says. "You act like you haven't eaten in a month."

"I basically haven't." I wash down the rice with my banana smoothie.

"I've got one for ya'," Dad says. "What did the head waiter say when a Vietnamese, a Laotian, and a Cambodian walked into a fancy restaurant?"

"What?" we all say.

"Sorry, no service without a Thai."

"Hey, your jokes are getting better," I say.

With my back to the water, I scan the resort. I can't get over the eerie déjà vu vibes. I'm taking a food-inhalation-break when it hits me.

"This is the resort from *The Impossible*! The movie about the tsunami. I watched it at Olivia's. It's the true story of a family that was here during the tsunami." I gulp my smoothie as this reality sets in.

"Why did you have to tell me that?" Riley's head swivels between the ocean and the resort.

"That's so unnerving." Mom wipes her mouth and leans forward. "I remember seeing a ten-year-old British girl interviewed. She saved her family and a lot of others at her resort in Phuket. Just two weeks before their trip, she'd watched a movie in science class about tsunamis. The girl was playing in the ocean when the water started bubbling. She had learned that was a warning sign. She told her parents, they told the lifeguard, and everyone ran inland and up the mountain. Just think if she'd missed school the day they showed the video. She was the only one who recognized the signs."

The 2004 Indian Ocean tsunami hit on December 26. This resort, and all of Thailand, was packed with tourists on winter break. With no warning, a massive underwater earthquake caused mountain-sized waves that wiped away towns and villages in Thailand, Sri Lanka, and Indonesia. Over 225,000 people died in fourteen different countries from the tsunami that day. It was the most destructive in history. Khao Lak was one of the hardest-hit communities.

Scenes from *The Impossible* swirl around my head. People like me were sitting right here, drinking smoothies, and swimming. Then they were dead. How do we know another tsunami won't wipe us away this week?

I was in Kindergarten the year it happened. I don't remember the tsunami, but I do remember that our school raised money to send the victims. We had a contest to see which homeroom could raise the most money. My class won, and we had a popsicle party.

Now I'm sitting in the very place that we raised money to help. They were nameless strangers at the time. Now I know their names. And they are not strangers. It's like the world is a giant dot-to-dot. Eventually, it all connects.

KHAO LAK, THAILAND: *The movie about the 2004 tsunami, The Impossible, was filmed at the rebuilt Orchid Beach Resort.*

"YOUR CAREER PREDICTION is finally coming true, Dad." I wrap a giant leaf around a slice of a banana tree trunk. It looks like a plate-sized disc of foam.

"You're right. Let's see how I do," Dad says.

In the ninth grade, my dad took a career test. It said he should be a florist, which is bucketloads better than a clown. But he was so embarrassed, he didn't tell anyone his results. He made up something much cooler instead. Since today is *Loi Krathong*, we're gonna find out if that career test was accurate.

Malee, our favorite hotel employee, explains, "The Thai believe the krathongs take away your bad luck when you float them down the river. Some people include strands of hair or nail clippings as another way of sending off their negative energy."

> Loi Krathong falls on the full moon of the twelfth Thai month, which is usually in November. The first step in celebrating is making a krathong, which is a floating basket of flowers.

Exotic blooms, banana leaves, incense sticks, and pins cover the table in front of us. We pick our favorite flowers and carefully arrange them on our slices of banana trunk. But our family-friendly holiday activity quickly turns into *Krathong Boss*.

"Quit taking all the good flowers, Dad." I snatch a bloom out of his hand.

"Hey, stop!"

"You know what would be good luck for me?" Riley asks.

"What?"

"If you'd put half your hair in yours. Think about all that bad energy you'd send away," Riley says.

"Well, maybe you should send away your cringey dance moves."

Riley and her floating krathong.

We may never celebrate Loi Krathong again, so we go all out making our krathongs. The final step is placing a candle in the center. Time's up. We step away from the table. It's time to find a judge.

"Malee, will you please pick your favorite?" With huge eyes and a round face, Malee looks like a baby doll. She inspects them carefully.

"They are all equally beautiful," she says.

"You have to pick one," Mom says.

"This one," Malee whispers, pointing to my dad's krathong.

Malee jumps when we bust out laughing. It's official. Dad should've been a florist. We return to our room to get ready for dinner. Mom, Ri and I put on the only dress we each packed. After a special Loi Krathong dinner, the hotel guests parade to the river carrying their krathongs. We light our incense and candle. Pravat plays the guitar while a small group sings the Loi Krathong song.

Delaney lights her krathong before placing it in the river.

When it's my turn, the moonlight guides my feet down the wooden steps. On the opposite side of the world from everyone I know and love (besides my parents and sis), I am strangely at peace. Thailand has that effect. I kneel on the small dock and place my flower raft in the river. My flickering krathong joins dozens of others in the floating flower flotilla. A smile sneaks across my face as I send my negative energy away. Maybe I can't control *where* I am, but I can control *how* I am. And I'm turning over a new banana leaf.

OUR FIVE-DAY SPLURGE has turned into eight. We were supposed to leave days ago, but my mom is sick. Really sick. The first clue that she was sick was during our day trip to the Similan Islands. Dad, Ri, and I spent the day snorkeling with rainbow fish, swinging on rope swings, and hiking to the famous boulder teetering at the top of Koh Similan. Meanwhile, Mom spent the day shivering under her beach towel in the tropical sun.

THAILAND: Koh Similan

That was three days ago. She is still in bed with a fever of 103°F. In my fourteen years of life, I cannot think of a single day my mom has spent sick in bed. Much less three. She has taken two different antibiotics and isn't getting better.

"I need to take your mom to a doctor," Dad says. "The clinic is only open from five-to-eight in the evening. The hotel is arranging a ride. It'll be here any minute."

"I wanna come," I say.

"Me too," says Riley.

Twenty minutes later, we arrive at the Thai-doc-in-a-box. Its neon-green sign, sliding glass doors, and plastic chairs look more like a 7-Eleven than a medical clinic. Outside the front door, a pile of shoes greets us. We kick ours off and go inside. Isn't that ironic? At home, you wouldn't be allowed *in* the doctor's office barefoot. Here, it's the exact opposite.

It is 5:23 p.m., and there is already a long line. The woman behind the desk smiles and bows when we enter. The clinic has three waiting areas: a few chairs across from the check-in desk, a separate waiting room, and outside. The few seats near the counter are the only ones with air-conditioning. Too bad those are taken. Mom completes the paperwork, and we are sent to the second waiting room.

The three patient rooms in the clinic are spitting distance from our seats. A sign hanging on door one reads EXAM. The sign on door two, TREATMENT. No sign hangs on the third door. The first room is where the doctor is. He sits behind a small desk without a sink or any sort of medical supplies besides the stethoscope hanging from his neck. The only other furniture in the tiny room are two chairs.

Most of the people coming and going from Room Two have wounds, most likely from moped accidents. A twenty-ish girl with bandages on her knees and hands sits next to a guy with a bandage wrapped around his head. Blood oozes through his gauze. A nurse comes in and out of Room Two several times carrying a metal tray with scary instruments. She is wearing gloves. She touches everything with those gloves. Does she only wear them for her protection? Or does she change them for the patients' sake too? I hope Mom doesn't have to go into Room Two. If she does, I'm gonna make sure the nurse changes her gloves.

Mom sits next to me, blankly staring out the window. She mumbles, "Am I hallucinating, or did a baby elephant walk by?"

I turn around just in time to see an elephant mosey by as casually as a stray dog.

"Don't worry. You're not hallucinating." I squeeze her hand.

A nervousness washes over me. I don't like this feeling. At all. Mom takes care of us, the travel plans, everything. We're all alone here. Just the four of us. But she's the team captain. What if she doesn't get better. Then what?

They finally call Mom's name. She gets to go to Room One. Yay. We all cram in. My parents sit in the chairs. Riley and I stand behind them. The doctor puts the stethoscope on Mom's chest and back. He mashes on her face and ears. She tells him her symptoms and hands him a piece of paper. The two medications she's taken are scrawled on it. When he reads the paper, his eyes widen like he just opened the Willy Wonka Golden Ticket.

"You *have* these medicines?" he asks.

"Yes, in our medical kit."

"These are very important medicines. We do not have them here." He continues, "You are sick."

"I know," Mom says. "Could it be the flu? Since the antibiotics aren't making me better."

"Yes, it could be." He nods. "Or maybe not."

"Can she get a flu test?" Dad suggests.

"Ah yes. Flu test would be good." The doctor nods again.

Finally, we're getting somewhere. "Okay. Let's do it!" I jump in.

"Oh, no. Sorry. We do not have flu test."

"No flu test?" Mom asks, her eyebrows squished together.

"No flu test. We are a very poor country. For flu test, you must go to hospital. One hour away."

"Kop kuhn krup." Dad thanks the doctor and bows in a wai. Using both hands—because it is rude to exchange money with one hand in Thailand—he pays the receptionist 500 baht (about $15) and we leave.

Even though we returned to the hotel with no answers, I did learn one thing. Mom was right. Our first-aid kit is irreplaceable.

Riley, 12

YAY! MOM IS FINALLY BETTER. At least she got sick while we were staying at an awesome hotel without B.O. sheets. After a ten-day stay, we say *sawasdee ka* to our friends at the Orchid Beach Resort. We had plane tickets to Laos next, but we missed our flight when Mom got sick. Now we're going to Krabi, Thailand instead.

Sunan, our driver, loads our bags into the van. Del and I climb to the back row. Mom and Dad take the middle. While the bookworms pull out books, Dad and I pull out earbuds. I listen to my tunes and watch the tropical scenery whiz by. And I mean *whiz*. Sunan drives fast. Really fast. When he goes around a curve, our bodies lean one way, then back up. Like a Weeble. Mom looks up from her book, frowning. She whispers something to my dad.

"Sunan, could you please drive a little slower? Kop kuhn krup," Dad says.

Sunan looks at my dad in the rearview and smiles. He slows down.

Mom turns around. "This is why I'd rather take a train than a taxi. You never know what kind of driver you're getting," Mom whispers.

My mom hates being a passenger. Hates. She always drives at home, not my dad. Something terrible happened when she was a teenager, and she can't stand to let other people drive. While Delaney and I are dividing up blog post topics—like we divvy up chores at home—Sunan speeds up.

"Shhh! No talking," my mom hisses at us in a panicky-angry voice this time.

"Sunan, *please* slow down," Mom says.

He glances into the rearview, smiles, and the van slows. Mom releases her death grip on the headrest in front of her. Del goes back to her book. Dad and I gaze out the windows. But Mom fixates on the speedometer, like she can slow it down if she stares hard enough. A few minutes later, the van is racing again. Mom glares at the numbers on the dash. The red arrow moves higher and higher. The roads are curvy. You can't see what is coming in the other lane. We're flying now. Sunan crosses the double yellow lines to pass the car in front of us. And then—*bam!*— there's a tractor-trailer barreling toward us. I grab Delaney's sweaty hand. Dad yanks his earbuds out. Sunan swerves the van in front of the car we passed. Brakes squeal. Horns honk. The semi barely misses us.

"SLOW DOWN!!!!!!" Mom's bottled-up fear explodes, filling the van.

Even though Sunan deserved it, Mom just did the worst thing a person can do in Thailand. She made Sunan *lose face*.

> "Saving face" is super important in Asian culture. Especially Thailand. You should never show anger toward another person. Ever. Yelling at someone is like slapping him across the face. Anyone that embarrasses someone else is guilty of this colossal cultural no-no.

But saving face doesn't just apply to anger. If someone's zipper is down, you wouldn't point it out. Not even privately. Because that would be embarrassing. They'd rather walk around all day with their fly down than for one person to tell them in private. I don't know about you, but if I have a booger hanging out my nose, I want my friend to give me the nose-wipe sign. That's way better than people laughing behind your back all day.

The rest of our drive is super awkward. No more smiles from Sunan—just the evil eye and silent treatment. The only good thing is he drives slower now. Even though my mom did this bad cultural thing, what else was she supposed to do? They asked him politely to slow down. Twice. Then we almost died. You know what Americans say? Rude-and-alive is better than polite-and-dead.

Sunan drops us off at our guesthouse and squeals away without wai-ing.

He hates us.

"I wish we were back at the Orchid." I unpack in our new room.

"Me too," Delaney says. "I'm not feelin' this place."

Bright yellow paint covers the walls like a mask. But the room still feels like a dungeon. Our guesthouse is a block off Ao Nang beach, behind a spa/massage parlor. Our parents' room is just up the steps from ours. I sorta wish we were all in the same room. A clicking-hissing sound comes from the wall. Every five minutes, a plug-in air freshener squirts out fake tropical smells. It's gross.

"Too bad Delaney and Dad are missing this," I yell, while clinging to the limestone cliff.

I hope the guy holding the rope knows what he's doing. If he doesn't, I'm a goner. Railay Beach near Krabi is one of the coolest rock-climbing places in the world! Mom and I take turns climbing the massive rocks until we are pooped.

"Are you ready for some beach time?" Mom asks.

"Yessss!" I step out of my harness.

We find the path to Phra Nang Beach and speed-walk past the monkeys. I'm no longer a fan. The creepy kleptomaniacs will snatch your stuff if you're not careful. I turn around. Mom is hobbling.

"Why are you walking so slow? I wanna get past the monkeys."

"My feet are killing me. My sandals rubbed blisters from the sand and water."

"You shoulda listened to me. I told you to get Chacos."

A few minutes later, we reach the beach. WOWZA! A row of colorful *longtails* bobs along the shore. And a giant limestone mountain juts out of the ocean behind them. Longtails are the authentic boats featured in pictures of Thailand. They remind me of the dugout canoes in Panama, except they are bigger. These longtails aren't here for the photo ops, though. They are food boats. Yippee! I order mango sticky rice and a mango smoothie from the burka-wearing woman on the longtail. How is she not suffocating in this heat? Mango meal in hand, I plop down next to Mom on our sarong towels.

"I hate Delaney is sick," Mom says. "What a great day they're missing."

"I'd pick feeling bad on a real tropical beach over a fake tropical dungeon any day."

Delaney says she's sick, but I know she's faking. She's either bingeing on Netflix or has her nose stuck in a book in the air-conditioning.

The beach begins filling up. Couples mainly, and a few families with babies. Since it's November, there aren't many families with older kids traveling. At the far end of the beach, I spy a purple unicorn. Just kidding. Even better, I see a girl my age!

"You should go introduce yourself," Mom says.

She's right. I can't be shy. I haven't hung out with anyone besides my fam for six weeks. I neeeed to play with her. I'm doing it. I stand up, wipe off the sand, and walk up to the girl.

"Hi, I'm Riley. Do you speak English?"

"A little. I'm Hanna. I'm from Norway."

"Wanna swim?"

"Okay."

Well, that was easy. Hanna and I spend the afternoon playing in the ocean. When we get hungry, we visit a longtail for snacks.

We're sharing a plate of fresh pineapple when we spot people coming out of the cave at the end of the beach.

"Let's check it out," I say. We jump up and run down the beach to explore the cave. As soon as we get inside, our hands fly up, covering our mouths. And then our eyes. We spin around and run right back out. We fall into the sand, laughing in the same language. *Phra Nang* means Princess Cave. But there's nothing princess-y about it. I've got to bring Del here to see this!

"PACK YOUR STUFF. We're moving somewhere else," Delaney announces when I open the dungeon door.

"Yay! Why?"

"Mom and Dad think it's creepy too."

"Coolio. BTW, you missed the best day ever." I cram packing cubes into my overstuffed suitcase.

"How's that?"

"Well, first, the rock climbing was awesome. Second, the beach was a-maz-ing. And third, I met a girl from Norway. We hung out all day."

"Did she speak English?"

"Enough. Hanna takes it as her foreign language. I was good practice for her. You know what's crazy? She's only six days older than I am. Anyway, we found a ... uh ... *special* cave. You've got to see it."

Fifteen minutes later, our *songthaew* picks us up. A songthaew is a pickup truck that has benches in the bed. It's a Thai group taxi. The nice ones have a roof. We pile in and wave *sawasdee ka* to the dungeon. I'll barf if I smell tropical air freshener ever again.

Our new place isn't close to the beach, but it's sooo much better than the last one. It's in a compound with a dozen matching houses and a swimming pool. But the best part of all?

The owner's two Pomeranians who like sleepovers with the guests! I can't wait 'til bedtime. I hope these dogs snuggle like Molly. I miss her so much. What if she doesn't even remember me when I get home? Or worse, what if she remembers me but won't forgive me for abandoning her?

Del and I unpack our bags and run to the pool. Thirty minutes later, loud chants interrupt our swimming.

"What's that?" I swivel my head, looking for the source of the noise.

"It's coming from loudspeakers over there." Delaney points toward the hills.

We don't understand what they are saying. The chanting lasts about five minutes, then it stops. A few minutes later, the owner walks by.

"I see you found the pool. Do you need anything?" Lars says. He's the one who said the dogs can sleepover.

"No, thank you," Delaney says. "But I do have a question. What was just playing from the loudspeakers?"

"Oh, that was the Muslim Call to Prayer. There's a mosque nearby. Muslims pray five times a day. You'll hear the call to prayer at those times."

"But I thought Thailand was mainly Buddhist," Delaney says.

"It is. Let me explain. Imagine that Thailand is shaped like the letter P. The northern round part is almost entirely Buddhist. As you travel south down the straight part, there are more Muslims. Krabi is toward the bottom of the straight part. If you keep going beyond Thailand, you'll be in Malaysia. And if you keep going, you'll end up in Indonesia. Those countries are mainly Muslim. Make sense?" Lars says.

"Sure does."

I wondered why so many of the women in Krabi cover their heads, compared to the rest of Thailand. Social studies lesson for the day: check.

KRABI, THAILAND: Riley and Ronald McDonald greet customers with a wai. Used with permission from McDonald's Corporation.

Delaney, 14

"WHOSE BRIGHT IDEA WAS THIS?" Dad shakes his head.

"Mom's," Ri and I say at the same time. "Jinx! One-two-three."

"C'mon, y'all. You can't go to Thailand and not see a king cobra show."

"I could," I say. Dad and Ri agree.

We enter the cobra show arena. On the floor is a ring that looks like a giant baby pool. The edge stands about a foot high. Four rows of wooden bleachers curve around the snake stage. We climb to the third row. We are the only people here, so we could sit in the front row. But what moron would sit four feet away from a fifteen-foot-long snake?

The king cobra is the longest venomous snake in the world. They can grow up to eighteen feet long. One bite and you're dead within thirty minutes. Even an elephant can die within three hours. And here we are, sitting less than ten feet from the circle-of-stupidity.

"Welcome to the Krabi King Cobra Show!" a man yells into his microphone—like there's an audience of four hundred instead of four. "Introducing the bravest cobra charmer in Thailand ... Paithoon."

Paithoon enters the ring, where a couple of large boxes already sit. He opens box-number-one. Using a long hook, he pulls a cobra out. Then another. And another. Three six-foot cobras slither around him. Paithoon gets down on his knees and elbows. He clasps his hands in front of his face like he is praying. Which is exactly what I'd be doing if I were in his flip-flops. The three cobras form a semicircle around him. They're in cobra pose with their necks standing tall and hoods flared. The hairs prickle on the back of my neck and my arms breakout in goosebumps, even though it's ninety degrees out.

Paithoon grabs one. He holds the serpent in one hand with

his arm outstretched. The cobra stiffens into a six-foot rod. I want to die. After showing us a few more cobra tricks, Paithoon puts the snakes back into their box. Hallelujah. It's over.

"Let's G-O." I stand, rubbing the goosebumps off my arms.

"It's not over." Mom nods toward the ring.

Paithoon opens box-number-two and pulls out a monster-sized king cobra. This snake—that's longer than an SUV—slithers around the ring. Ri and I move up to the fourth row. We sit glued together like Siamese twins.

I picture the snake turning into a king-cobra-rocket and launching at us. The cobra is longer than the distance between the ring and the fourth row.

I. Hate. This.

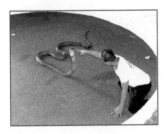

KRABI, THAILAND: King Cobra charmer teases snake at cobra show.

My heart races. Paithoon teases the cobra like he wants it to strike him. He kneels and stares in its eyes. The cobra flares its hood, bobbing his head back and forth like a boxer. Paithoon moves closer and blows in his face. The snake strikes! Paithoon ducks to the right just in time. Paithoon continues to harass the snake by tapping on its head or pointing his finger right in its face. And just as the cobra strikes, Paithoon moves out of the way.

I'm frozen in the tropics when Paithoon puckers his lips and moves in for a kiss. He is going to die! And then we're all gonna die! Will my school yearbook include a page dedicated to my tragic death-by-king-cobra on a stupid family trip? All the kids in my school will be so glad they have normal families.

The announcer yells into his microphone, "SAVE YOUR LIPS, MAN. SAVE YOUR FACE!" over and over.

Paithoon slowly goes in for the smooch. Somehow, he plants

a kiss on the cobra's head without getting a fang in the face. The torture is over.

"Y'all need to give him a good tip. He deserves it," I tell my parents.

"No doubt," they agree.

Dad two-hands Paithoon a wad of baht, and we leave. Alive. No yearbook dedication page necessary.

KRABI, THAILAND: Riley and Delaney huddle together at the King Cobra show.

Random fun fact!

The first "Siamese twins" (a.k.a. conjoined twins) were Chang and Eng Bunker (1811-1874). They were from Thailand, formerly known as Siam.

Riley, 12

"HAPPY THANKSGIVING." I nibble my corn-on-the-cob-on-the-stick.

We buy our Thanksgiving feast one item at a time from the longtails. Of course, it's not Thanksgiving in Thailand. It's just another Thursday in November. But for us, it's Thanksgiving. And we are spending it at the best place near Krabi—Railay. I lie back on my sand recliner, catching some rays.

"So, what's everybody thankful for this Thanksgiving?" Mom asks like we're sitting at our dining room table.

"I'll start," Dad says. "I'm thankful to be on this crazy adventure with all of my favorite girls."

"I'm thankful that as Americans we have the freedom to travel to most countries in the world. Not everybody is that lucky," Mom says.

"I'm thankful that we speak English since so many people learn it as a second language. We're lucky that lots of people can talk in our language, even if we can't talk in theirs. But that sorta feels like cheating. I'm gonna learn another language in high school," I say.

"Besides English, do you know the next most common language?" Mom asks.

"Spanish," I say.

"Nope, but good guess," Mom says. "Mandarin Chinese."

"Back to Thanksgiving. My turn," Delaney says. "I'm thankful for clean clothes. When you travel long term, you really appreciate fresh laundry."

No joke. On the smell-o-meter, our clothes usually fall somewhere between stale and stinky. In countries like Thailand, it's normal to send your clothes out to be washed. But you never know where they are washed. Even though they never smell as fresh as laundry at home, they're usually an improvement. One time, though, they came back way stinkier than when they were dirty.

"When are you gonna show me the special cave?" Delaney shovels her last bite of mango sticky rice into her mouth.

"Now! Follow me." I jump up and run for the cave.

When we get to the entrance, I stand behind Delaney. I cover her eyes with my hands.

Using my official-tour-guide voice, I say, "This is the most interesting cave in the world. You will be surprised by its … uh … uniqueness." We shuffle-walk into the cave. "Welcome to Weenie Wonderland!" I announce, unmasking Delaney's eyes.

"O. M. G. What. Is. This?"

Delaney bug-eyes the dozens of ding-dongs standing like trees. Some of the gigantic wooden weiners tower over us. Others are painted red, gold, or black. Scarves and ribbons dangle from some of the strange statues. It totally looks like a prank middle-school boys would pull on a dare. And then get suspended.

A sign hangs near a pile of privates stacked like firewood. It explains that this isn't a middle-school prank but a shrine to the goddess Phra Nang. Women who want to have a baby come to the Princess Cave. So do fishermen wishing for good luck and a safe journey. They are supposed to leave special gifts for the goddess, then hopefully their luck will turn around.

I don't know much, but I know one thing: Phra Nang Cave is a field trip for world-schoolers only. There's no way this weenie wonderland is in any of my textbooks.

KRABI, THAILAND: Food boats at Phra Nang Cave Beach.

PASSPORT LESSON #6:

Life's most memorable lessons don't come from textbooks.

THAILAND
High-Low Report Card

	☺	☹
Delaney	TIE: Thai food and Orchid Beach Resort	Guesthouse with gross air freshener
Riley	Similan Islands	Rice with every meal
Mom	Rock climbing on Railay	Getting sick
Dad	The Thai people	Mom being sick in the Similans

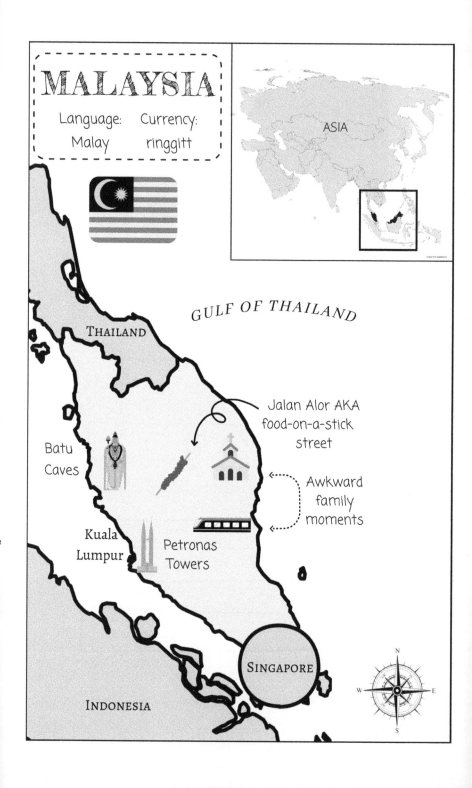

14.

Finding Our People

November 29–December 2

We may have different religions, different languages, different colored skin, but we all belong to one human race.

— Kofi Annan, Nobel Peace Prize recipient, seventh
Secretary-General of the United Nations

Delaney, 14

"What are you gonna do while we go Chaco hunting?" I ask Dad.

"I'm going barber hunting. I need someone to fix the hack job you did on my head in Italy."

"Whoops. Sorry 'bout that," I say.

"I hope we both find what we're looking for. I've gotta find something better than these dollar flip-flops." Mom holds up her Thai night-market bargain.

If Mom can't find Chacos here, she won't find them anywhere in this part of the world. Imagine the largest mall you've ever seen. Now multiply that by four. That's about the size of *a* mall in Kuala Lumpur (KL). Pretty big, right? You might even think a mall that size would be the main attraction in a city.

Wrong. KL has more than twenty mega malls. And our guest-house in Bukit Bintang is walking distance to at least five of them.

"Good luck finding a barber," I say as we walk out the door.

Riley bounces down the front steps. She's secretly thrilled that Mom's feet have blisters, because now we have to go shopping. We rummage through the pile of shoes to find ours. We are used to leaving our shoes outside. But when I don't spot mine right away, I always flashback to when my mom's favorite flip-flops were stolen off the boardwalk in Gulf Shores, Alabama. No one's ever stolen our shoes in Asia.

We stroll a few blocks to the first mall: Berjaya Times Square. This A/C paradise is a welcome relief from Malaysia's heat. A click-click-click noise roars above. An amusement-park-sized roller coaster winds through the mall filling it with screams of thrill and terror. Super fun mall, but no Chacos.

Our next stop is The Pavilion.

"Awww, it's decorated for Christmas!" I squeal the second we step inside the fancy mall.

We did not expect to see this in a Muslim-majority nation. A massive Christmas tree fills the atrium, along with garland, lights, polar bears, and poinsettias. Santa sits in an SUV-sized sleigh where children wait to sit on his lap. It makes me so happy—and so homesick—at the same time. I had finally settled into this crazy adventure. And now, this beautiful Christmas scene has slapped me in the face. It is a rude reminder of all that I miss. It is so hard to be away from my friends, my grandparents, my life. Will they even remember me when I return?

Unfortunately for Mom, the bougie Pavilion is more Kardashian than McIntyre, more Golden Goose than Chaco. Although we didn't find shoes, we did find the fanciest movie theater in KL. And they show Hollywood movies in English!

Riley, 12

"You look good bald!" I say, when I see Dad's shiny pale head. "Goodbye, weed eater. Hello, cue ball."

"Can I rub it for good luck?" Delaney reaches for his head.

"Sure thing," Dad says. "I'm shocked, but I like it too."

"I love it." Mom pulls out her phone. "How much was it? I need to put it in the Trail Wallet." She tracks every krona, euro, and baht we spend in this app.

"A whopping ten ringgits. Three dollars."

"Gotta love that," Mom says.

"Did you find some shoes?" Dad asks, as we walk down the guesthouse steps.

"Nope. No luck. A luxury designer on every corner, but no Chacos," Mom says.

We've been gone for over two months, and I've hit the mega-mall jackpot here. But my body hasn't added a single inch, ounce, or curve. So I haven't outgrown anything. Meanwhile, I bet my friends are sprouting new curves daily. I don't know which is more depressing—not getting new clothes, or curves.

"So, what are we doing for dinner?" I pull my flip-flops out of the pile.

"We're going to Jalan Alor. It's the most famous place for street food in KL. It's just a block away." Mom ties her shoelaces.

A few minutes later we reach the famous street. It is insane.

Jalan Alor is a street-long Asian smorgasbord. Even though it's a normal city street, you can't drive on it because plastic tables and chairs cover the pavement. Neon food carts line the road as far as we can see.

This street should be called Everything-on-a-Stick Street. Because that is what it is. Chicken-on-a-stick, frog-on-a-stick, fish-on-a-stick, broccoli-on-a-stick, unidentified-object-on-a-stick. You get the picture. The only thing not on a stick is soup. I peer through the glass of the hawker carts, trying to find something I'm brave enough to eat.

I chicken out and get chicken. It's hard to mess that up.

"Where do koalas go on vacation?" Dad asks, taking a bite of something weird.

"Koala Lumpur!" Del and I say at the same time as we walk along the street.

"That was too easy," Dad says. "The next country will be harder."

"Hey, check it out." Mom points at a building in the distance.

Dotting the end of the street like the letter *i* is Kuala Lumpur Baptist Church. That's weird. Like the Christmas decorations at the mall, I didn't expect to see a Christian church in a mostly Muslim country. But there it is. Service times scroll along the electronic sign hanging above the door.

"They have an English service on Sundays," Delaney says. "We should go."

We've been *in* a lot of cathedrals and Buddhist temples over the past seven weeks. But we haven't been *to* church. Big difference.

"I hope they don't sing as many songs as Papaw and Nanaw's church," I say.

My grandparents go to a Baptist church, and they sing way too many songs. Papaw and Delaney keep count. There should be a law. Five songs max. Three is perfect. One Sunday, they sang *twelve* songs. Luckily, I got a terrible earache. So Mom and I snuck out.

"Good idea, Del. Sunday morning church it is," Mom says as we walk back to our guesthouse.

Delaney, 14

"Do we have to go inside?" Riley whines as we stand outside the Islamic Arts Museum. "It sounds sooo boring."

"You can't visit Malaysia and not learn something about Islam," Mom says.

After an hour in the not-so-boring museum, we head to KL's most Insta-famous building, the Petronas Towers. After taking selfies in front of the twin skyscrapers, we grab some lunch.

"You know what I'd kill for right now?" I ask while finishing my millionth dish of chicken fried rice.

"What?" Riley says as we walk to the KL Sentral train station.

"Chick-n-Minis," I say.

"Me too," Mom and Riley say as we enter the train terminal.

"A Chick-fil-A sandwich would be so good right now," Dad says.

"If I lived here, I'd open a Chick-fil-A. I'd be rich," Riley says.

People smush together in the terminal with the same goal: to snag a spot in a crowded train car. We join the mob and wait for our train to the Batu Caves. About ten minutes later, we hear the train roaring toward us. People shove their way to the front of the platform. Getting onto crowded trains is always dicey. What if one of us doesn't make it on? And we get separated?

"Look down there." Riley points down the platform to a handful of people calmly entering a nearly vacant train car. "Let's go to that one."

We race down the platform, jumping into the train car as the door closes behind my dad. Score! There are plenty of empty seats. We take four together. People stare at us, but we're used to it.

"Good eye, Ri," Mom says.

"What is wrong with those people? How did they miss this empty car?" Dad says.

"For real. We're tourists, and we figured it out," Mom says.

While they're high-fiving each other, I notice the sign. The pink sign. The very important pink sign that stretches across most of the train car: COACH FOR LADIES ONLY. Holy moly! What have we done? This is bad. Very bad. Muslims have very strict segregation policies for men and women. My dad sitting in a female-only train car in Malaysia is worse than bad. It's disastrous.

I elbow my mom.

"Ow!" She doesn't look up from the pamphlet she's reading.

I elbow her harder.

"What?!" she says, turning toward me.

I flick my eyes toward the sign.

"Oh my gosh!" She jerks her head toward Dad. "You're not supposed to be here!"

KUALA LUMPUR, MALAYSIA: Train car for women only

Once again, all eyes are on us. But this time, we don't have to guess why the women are staring. We jump up, gushing apologies in English. Our brains freeze. We can't think of "sorry" or any other words in Malay. We hope they understand. The train is moving, but we have to get out of this car. Now. We pull apart the doors like I've seen in the movies. The ground races below. We open the doors to the next compartment and force our way in. Everyone stares at the White man who just entered from the female-only car. I hold my breath. But no one says a word. And no one takes him away in handcuffs or with a pillowcase over his head.

KUALA LUMPUR, MALAYSIA: The Petronas Towers are the tallest twin towers in the world.

Riley, 12

WELL, THAT WAS AWKWARD! Thirty minutes later, we exit the train station in search of the Batu Caves. It's easy to spot. A shiny gold statue, the size of the Statue of Liberty (minus her pedestal), guards the entrance.

Delaney looks up from the guidebook. "That's the Hindu god Murugan. This is the largest Hindu statue in Malaysia and one of the most important Hindu shrines outside of India."

SELANGOR, MALAYSIA: Hindu deity Lord Murugan stands at the foot of the Batu Caves temple.

Even though it's drizzling, this is the perfect place to get a twirling video. Standing in front of Lord Murugan and the cave entrance, I start my routine. I haven't twirled in a while, and I'm a little rusty. I begin with easy tosses and catches. After some twirls, it's time for my grand finale. I fling my baton as hard as I can. Whoops! The wet baton slips, flying toward a baby in a stroller.

"WATCH OUT!" I scream at the family.

I don't think they speak English, but a screaming girl gets your attention in any language. The shiny baton lands inches from the stroller. I run to them.

"I'm sorry. I'm sorry." I pick up my baton lying next to the stroller's front wheel.

They can tell I feel awful and are super nice, considering I almost clobbered their baby. This isn't our day. I put my baton away, and we climb the steps to the cave's entrance.

"Good grief." Mom stops midway. "How many steps are there?"

"Two hundred and seventy-two according to the guidebook," Delaney says.

"You know what would be awesome?" I say. "A chair lift. Like at the ski slopes."

We finally make it to the top and enter the Batu Caves. Whoa. No ding-dong statues here. This Hindu temple-cave has brass railings, an altar, and fancy wooden doors. Colorful Hindu gods watch visitors from a ledge above. A shirtless Hindu priest wears a white sheet tied around his waist. For a donation, we can receive a blessing. Sign me up! After the day we've had, we could use one. With incense and candles burning, the priest chants some Hindu stuff. Using his thumb, he smears a white dash and a red dot on my forehead.

I hope it works.

Delaney, 14

THE LATEST *HUNGER GAMES* movie has just been released, and Ri and I are dying to see it. Even Mom has read the books, so she's pumped too. Plus, we all need something familiar—like going to the movies. That's the secret to surviving long-term cultural travel, getting little doses of home when you don't expect it.

We walk a few blocks from our guesthouse to The Pavilion. Once again, we enter the Christmas wonderland. It's Saturday night, and holiday shoppers pack the mall. The line for Santa now snakes past the carousel.

We find the ticket office. Buying movie tickets here is like buying plane tickets. They have three classes of seats, similar to first class, business class, and economy. We pay for the mid-level seats, a.k.a. the couple's chair.

Dad goes to the bathroom, and we look for our theater. We see a door with *Catching Fire* scrolling above it. We push through the door into a fancy lounge with a private concession stand. Chandeliers hang from the ceiling, and sleek modern furniture fills the room. Wow. We go through another door into the actual theater. Score! Inside sit ten pairs of leather recliners with coffee tables, service buttons, and blankets. This. Is. Awesome! We search for our couple's chairs and can't find them. Sadly, it's because we found the gold class (first class) theater, not the class we paid for. Bummer.

Disappointed, we leave and find Dad in the hallway. Then, we find our not-so-fancy theater. The couple's chairs are plush loveseats, not luxury leather. They fill the upper center of the theater. The cheapest (economy) seats are just regular ol' movie seats that fill the sides and bottom of the same room. Dad loves the couple's chair. And we would've too, if we hadn't just seen the gold class theater. It's the same feeling you get after walking through first class on a plane to get to your cramped seat in the back. It's just wrong.

After the movie, we stroll through the Pavilion's winter wonderland. A local band plays Christmas music. We stop and listen, soaking in the unexpected Christmas spirit. When we leave the mall, fake snow falls on us in the tropical night. What a magical ending to our day.

"AUBURN WON THE IRON BOWL!" I yell, waking the family.

It's Sunday morning in Malaysia, but it's still Saturday night in Alabama. For football fans, Alabama's annual Iron Bowl is the biggest event of the year.

"Be quiet!" Riley buries her head under the covers. "I threw up all night."

"What and what?" Dad looks at me, then Ri.

"Hang on, Del. We'll get to that in a second." Mom turns to Dad. "Riley had an awful stomachache all night. She threw up a few times. I went to the front desk in the middle of the night, and they gave her some charcoal tablets."

"Charcoal?" Dad asks.

"Yep, but they seemed to work," Mom says, then pivots toward me. "How do you know about the Iron Bowl?"

"I've been texting with Joey for the past hour. He's giving me the play-by-play. The game was tied with one second left. Bama missed a field goal, and Auburn caught it and ran a hundred yards and scored." I dig through my suitcase hunting for my dress. "They're calling it the Kick Six."

"Sounds like the Kick Sick to me. I'm glad I missed that one," Dad says, disappointed for his alma mater.

"Ri, you feel like going to church? We need to leave at nine-fifteen." Mom zips her dress.

"I think so." Riley moans a little and sits up.

Visiting a new church can be super awkward. Will we be

totally ignored? Will it last three hours? Will they do something weird, like handle snakes?

As we walk to the church, Riley says, "What if they make all the visitors stand up? That would be sooo embarrassing."

So, we come up with a church-visitation-survival-plan. It involves sitting in the back row and secret hand signals that mean *let's get out of here!* We all agree to the plan. When we arrive at the church, we're greeted by smiley Robert. He enthusiastically shakes our hands and directs us upstairs to the sanctuary. So far, so good. Being ignored won't be a problem.

At the top of the stairs, a tiny Malaysian woman welcomes us like we're celebrities. We make church-visitor-small-talk for a few minutes, then turn to make our way to the back row.

"I'll show you where to sit." The friendly church-drill-sergeant marches us straight down to the second row.

Oh boy. We obediently take our guest-of-honor seats. I hope there aren't snakes. There's no sneaking out, no matter what. Within seconds, we're surrounded by eager church members on a mission to make us feel welcome.

A few minutes later, the service starts with praise music. Some songs we know, others we don't. After the music ends, Riley's tragic prediction comes true. The pastor asks all visitors to stand, so we can be properly welcomed. This is so awkward. Church members swarm us again. This time, they point out the other visitors: a Black couple from Louisiana and a White family with two daughters from Sweden. Finally. Some people like us. I can't wait for church to end so we can meet them.

Besides the accents, everything about the service feels strangely familiar—the prayer requests, the mission teams, even the corny preacher jokes (which are basically a different version of dad jokes). The only difference is how they collect the offering. Instead of passing a brass plate or plastic bucket, they pass a purple velvet bag hanging from silver bars.

When the service ends, Mom says, "Let's go talk to our people."

"Yes! I want to meet them too," I say.

We make a beeline for Maurice and Aliyah, the couple from Louisiana (even though they're probably LSU fans). For the first time in seven weeks, we hang out with people from our part of the world. People who know what the Iron Bowl is and say "y'all." We eat lunch together in the church cafe where we bond over the Southeastern Conference (SEC) college football, craving Milo's sweet tea, and all things Southern. It's a family reunion with two people we just met. It's the most at-home I've felt in two months. It's a good day. We just found a little piece of the Southeast United States in the middle of Southeast Asia.

PASSPORT LESSON #7:

Our country, culture, and interests
bond us as humans—not our skin color.

MALAYSIA
High-Low Report Card

	☺	☹
Delaney	The Christmas spirit	'Bama losing the Iron Bowl
Riley	Fancy movie theater	Being sick/ taking charcoal
Mom	Visiting church & meeting couple from LA	Not finding Chacos
Dad	Finding a barber	Female-only train car

15.

The Girl in the Photo

December 3–21

We cannot change history. With love, we can heal the future.

— Kim Phúc, Napalm Girl

Riley, 12

"The first thing you must learn in Vietnam is how to cross the street," Phuong tells us.

"No joke. This is insane," I yell, so Phuong and Duc can hear me over all the honking.

Today is gonna be super fun because our guides are college students! Standing on the sidewalk in Hanoi, we watch millions of motorbikes zoom by. They fill the street like runners during a marathon. The drivers smush as many motorbikes into the lanes as possible. The only cars are taxis.

"Wow. That's impressive." Delaney points at a motorbike carrying a family of five.

"Check that out." Dad points to one with a passenger balancing a gigantic flat-screen TV across his lap.

HANOI, VIETNAM: It's astonishing what the Vietnamese can carry on a motorbike.

Mom gasps. A woman holding a baby in one arm steers her motorcycle with the other. Another bike zooms by carrying a tower of moving boxes bungee corded together. Behind it is a motorbike with a door wedged between the driver and passenger. The guy in the back holds it straight while they zip through traffic. Vietnam's moto-motto should be: No SUV? No problem!

Crossing the street in Vietnam is the exact opposite of how we do it at home. And it is terrifying! Here's what you do:

1. Look at the oncoming traffic, which means both directions.
2. Make eye contact with the drivers heading straight at you.
3. STEP INTO THE TRAFFIC, KEEP WALKING, and DON'T STOP.

"Follow me, and you'll be fine," Duc says as we step off the sidewalk into moto-madness.

"Whatever you do, don't stop walking. If you stop, they will hit you," Phuong warns.

This is the most dangerous thing we've done yet! We leave space between us and walk at a steady pace. The drivers weave around us, missing us by a hair. Miraculously, we make it across alive.

"Today, we'll visit Hanoi's most famous sights," Phuong says. "The Ho Chi Minh Mausoleum, Ho Chi Minh's home, One Pillar Pagoda, and the Temple of Literature."

"Then, we'll go to our favorite place for lunch," Duc adds.

Mom whispers to Del and me, "Phuong and Duc are majoring in tourism, so they give free tours to English-speaking visitors so they can practice their English. We aren't even allowed to tip them. We can only buy them lunch."

Our first stop is to see a dead man. Outside of the massive square building, crowds are waiting on the skinny red carpet that leads to the front door. You might think people are lined up to see a movie star or celebrity. Not the body of Communist leader Ho Chi Minh. He died the same year my mom was born, so he's been dead a long time. What's he gonna look like?!

My mom pulls out her camera to snap a picture of the building. A guard dressed in all-white yells at her to put it away.

"When we get inside, you must be completely silent and walk single-file with your hands at your side. Don't put your hands in your pockets or cross your arms," Phuong says as the line creeps down the red carpet.

Duc explains how scientists keep Ho Chi Minh's body in tip-top shape. He goes to Russia each fall for a couple of months of R&R (restore and refurbish).

We enter the mausoleum and robot-walk into the room with Uncle Ho (that was his nickname). Ho Chi Minh is lying in a glass case, like a bizarre version of Sleeping Beauty. We're lucky. He just returned from his anti-aging treatment at the Lenin Lab. Those Russian scientists really know what they're doing. Besides looking a little plastic-y like a Ken doll, you would never know Uncle Ho's been dead almost fifty years!

After we visit the other places on the list, it's lunchtime. We follow Phuong and Duc into their favorite restaurant. My stomach growls when I inhale the smell of Asian food. It's a hole-in-the-wall restaurant we never would've found on our own. Phuong and Duc lead us up a narrow, creaky staircase to a private room. Two coffee tables sit in the middle of the jail-cell-sized room. We plop down on straw mats and lean against the old brick walls.

Phuong and Duc order since we can't read the menu or speak Vietnamese. The servers cover our table with dishes of Vietnamese yumminess. We don't ask for forks or spoons. After weeks in Asia, we are chopstick champs. After sampling all the dishes, the noodle soup is the winner.

"This is my new BFF. Best food forever," I say, slurping the last of my *pho* (rhymes with duh) from the bowl like a local.

HANOI, VIETNAM: Dinner at New Day

Delaney, 14

"CHÀO BUỔI SÁNG," Mary greets us from behind the front desk.

"CHOW boy saan," we repeat back with our Alabama accent.

"That was much better." Mary smiles.

Mary is our favorite employee at the Charming II hotel. Every morning she gives us a quick Vietnamese lesson. When we return in the afternoon, she quizzes us to see if we still remember what she taught us. Vietnamese is a tricky language, and we usually fail the afternoon quiz. But Mary just laughs and tries again the next day. She's a patient teacher.

When we finish breakfast, Mary asks, "What are you doing today?"

"We're going to the Hanoi Hilton," Mom says. "What should we do after that?"

"You should visit the Vietnamese Women's Museum," Mary says. "Visitors say good things about it."

"That sounds sooo boring," Riley whispers when we reach Charming's front door.

"Why are we going to visit another hotel?" I ask, stepping out of our quiet hotel into honking Hanoi.

"Huh? What do you mean?" Mom says.

"You said we're going to the Hanoi Hilton. Why?"

"Oh, right. I guess that is confusing. The Hanoi Hilton isn't actually a hotel. It's the prison where American prisoners-of-war were held and tortured during the Vietnam War. That's what our POWs sarcastically named it," Mom explains. "But now it's a museum."

It's a good thing Phuong and Duc taught us how to cross the street yesterday, because today we're on our own. We explore the Old Quarter, taking in the local life. Along the sidewalks, people sit on plastic stools and eat. The tiny red and blue seats remind me of preschool. The men sit with their knees bent chest-high, like giants sitting on dollhouse furniture. Those who aren't sitting on stools just squat. Most smile and wave their chopsticks as we walk by. Women wearing cone-shaped rice farmer's hats wander through the streets selling fruit. Long bamboo poles see-saw over their shoulders with large baskets of fruit hanging from each end. Other women have baskets filled with mangos, star fruit, and rambutan creatively attached to their old-fashioned bicycles. Every woman we pass wants us to buy some. But my dad is wearing a backpack full of bananas provided by our hotel.

"Không, cám ơn," we politely decline and keep walking.

Fifteen minutes later, we arrive at the Hoa Lo Prison a.k.a. the Hanoi Hilton. A thick concrete wall surrounds the prison. Jagged glass juts from the top like shark teeth. Questions flood my brain faster than the motorbikes whizzing by. Did any Americans ever escape over that wall? Why would Vietnam make a museum out of place that tortured American POWs? It didn't make sense at first, but now I understand.

HANOI, VIETNAM: A cell door inside the infamous "Hanoi Hilton."

The French built the prison back in the late 1800s when they occupied Vietnam. Ninety-eight percent of the museum is dedicated to educating visitors on the brutal treatment of the Vietnamese people by the French. Only a tiny portion of the museum covers its role as a prison for American soldiers during the *American* War. Senator John McCain is the most famous American who was imprisoned here.[1] I've seen him on TV. I know he can't raise his arms over his head because of the torture he suffered for nearly six years. But the photographs hanging on the walls show American POWs playing basketball and decorating a Christmas tree, as if the Hanoi Hilton offered its "guests" fun activities to pass the time.

I call BS.

"That was hard to see," Dad says after we leave. "The propaganda was disgusting."

"They made it seem like a country club for the POWs." Mom shakes her head.

"Every country gets to tell their version of history, don't they?" I ask.

We walk in silence to the Vietnamese Women's Museum. Even Riley doesn't complain. It's weird to think America was part of a terrible war here less than fifty years ago, when my parents were kids. And now we're visiting a place where many Americans died. In thirty years, will I take my kids to visit the countries that are war zones right now? Will the dangerous destinations we wouldn't dream of visiting today be tomorrow's vacation hot spots?

HANOI, VIETNAM: Local woman sells fruit from bike.

We spend a couple of hours in the Women's Museum. A documentary explains what the fruit sellers must do every day to survive. Their day starts at three in the morning and goes downhill from there. I'm ashamed at how easy my life is compared to theirs. I'll never complain about my measly chores again. When we leave, we buy fruit from everyone.

Riley, 12

"MARY AND TUON would make a cute couple," I say as we pedal along the Thu Bon River in Hoi An.

"Aww, they would," Delaney agrees. "But they should definitely live here. Hoi An's so charming."

Tuon is the host of our guesthouse. He is so cute and friendly, just like Mary from Hanoi. He organizes group dinners for guests twice a week. I sure hope some other kids are staying there.

We explore the ancient town on bikes. Bright-colored lanterns fill the shops and hang across the streets like banners. We ride across the bridge that crosses the river. Two tiny women with giant smiles greet us. They carry baskets of fruit swinging from the poles see-sawing across their shoulders. We stop and buy a couple of bananas.

"Can we take a picture with you?" I ask, making the camera-clicking sign with my hand. They nod and smile, and Mom snaps our picture.

HOI AN, VIETNAM–DEC 2013: Riley and Delaney with local women selling fruit.

"You know what I love about Vietnam?" I steer my bike with one hand while eating the banana with the other.

"What's that?"

"I'm tall here."

In elementary school, I was always assigned the same spot on class picture days—the end of the front row. That's where the shortest kids always sit. But here, I tower over adult women. It's so weird to go from being the "little seventh grader" to the "tall American girl" with nothing changing except geography.

"I'd gladly go to middle school here," I continue.

"Why's that?" Delaney cocks her head.

"Because no one is tall or curvy. I'd fit in perfectly!"

The girls in my school are divided into two groups: curvy and not-curvy. The boys are obsessed with the curvy girls. It's so annoying.

We meet up with a guide for the afternoon who takes us to Kim Bong Island. We ride bikes around the island, meeting the locals, and learning about their jobs as boat makers, noodle makers, and mat weavers. One of the mat weavers is a girl my age. I sit on the dirt floor next to Binh while she teaches me what to do. She spends every morning weaving mats with her mother and grandmother and every afternoon in school. And you know what's really crazy? I earn more money babysitting for a day than they make in a month. And their jobs are hard!

"Y'all follow me," Dad says, after our official bike tour is over.

He leads us on his DIY tour of Hoi An. We pedal to the South China Sea and lie on the beach for an hour. We bike past rice fields and water buffalo on the way back to the town, ending up at the Hoi An Cloth Market. Yay! This is the place that makes custom clothes for cheap. I'm sick of my clothes. I've been wearing the same four outfits for nearly two months. Just as we are locking our bikes, two women swarm my mom and attack both sides of her face. Their weapon? Thread.

"Ow! Stop!" Mom jerks her head away as a puff of peach fuzz floats off her face.

The women want to thread Mom's entire face, but she's not a fan of pain or forced facials by strangers armed with string.

"That felt like bee stings." Mom rubs her face as we walk into the cloth market.

The cloth market is a beehive. Unfortunately, the bees inside are even more aggressive than the ones outside. Stacks of fabric fill the stalls of the famous market. We want to browse, but random women keep shoving different materials in our faces.

"Do you like this? What do you want? Do you want jeans? How about a dress?" They fire questions faster than we can answer them.

"Come." One woman orders us to her booth. "Sit." She pulls out three red plastic chairs.

"She's scary," I whisper to Del.

I don't know why, but we obey her. And now we're stuck at Mrs. Scary's booth. She hands us clothing catalogs the size of textbooks and tells us to pick something out. While I flip through the book, dreaming of a new outfit or two, Delaney's eyes glaze over.

She leans over and whispers, "I can't handle this. I'm finding Dad and going back."

"You're not gonna get new clothes?" How can she turn this down?

"It's not worth it." Delaney buzzes out of the beehive before Mrs. Scary can stop her.

She's crazy. It is overwhelming, but I'll suffer to get new clothes. Plus, I get to pick the pattern, the style, and it's custom made just for me. No more dorky clothes from the children's department. I choose material for a dress, two shirts, and jeans. Mom picks out material for a dress, tank, and jeans. Mrs. Scary measures every part of our bodies and tells us to come back tomorrow. Woo-hoo for a new RRP wardrobe!

KIM BONG ISLAND, VIETNAM–DEC 2013: A local girl teaches Riley how to weave mats (top); a local man teaches Delaney how to make rice flour noodles.

Delaney, 14

"WE'RE DOING WHAT?" I nearly choke on my scrambled eggs.

"Spending the day at an international school. You'll get to be around kids your age. It'll be fun."

Seriously? How does Mom come up with this stuff?

"Yay! What are you gonna wear?" Riley asks as if tomorrow's the first day of real school and we have a closet full of cute outfits, instead of a suitcase full of crumpled clothes.

I should be hyped. This is my first chance to escape my parents' presence in two months. But I'm not. I've never been the new kid. Today, that's gonna change. As we ride bikes to Green Shoots International School, Mom fills us in.

"There are only sixteen students. Most are Australian or French, and they moved to Hoi An because of their parents' jobs. The kids go to this school because it's English speaking."

"This. Sounds. Awful. I don't want to do this." My sweaty palms slip on my bike handles.

"Well, we can't leave Riley all alone," Dad says. "It'll be fine."

Ugh. I want to go back to our guesthouse with them. That's how much I'm dreading this. But no amount of begging helps. We roll up to the campus—a white-and-green building with a few classrooms and a grass field surrounded by palm trees—and leave our bikes at the front gate. The principal introduces himself, and my parents hug us goodbye. How can they do this to me? Aren't they going to be bored without us? We kick our shoes onto the pile at the front door, and Mr. Stan takes us to meet our new classmates. I want to throw up.

An Australian boy runs up. "G'Day! I'm Max. Wanna meet my mates?"

"Sure!" Riley says.

His accent is so cool. Max leads us to the outdoor lunchroom. We sit on two empty stools at a bamboo table surrounded by palm trees. The students swarm us like kids to an ice cream truck. They range in age from seven to fourteen, and they are equally intrigued by the two American newbies.

"Come play our favorite game." Eleven-year-old Evie tugs my shirt and runs to the field.

Max explains the rules, but they make no sense. We just fake it and join the fun. Equal parts of sweat and dirt cover us when the game ends. Blood runs down the legs of two boys. No one whines or asks to see the nurse. There probably isn't one.

After the game, we follow the kids into a classroom. Three tables form a U-shape with ten chairs around it. Fans spin on the walls cooling down the tiny room with open doors and windows. Mr. Stan assigns us buddies. I'm paired with Max, the only other eighth-grader, to work on math. Riley works with a seventh-grader named Sean.

It soon becomes clear that we aren't going to get much work done. Max, Evie, and I are too busy discussing the differences between our school and theirs.

"There are five hundred students in three grades?" Max's jaw drops.

They laugh every time we say *y'all*. We can't get enough of their Aussie phrases like *mates*, *barbie*, and my personal favorite, *good on ya'*.

"I love your accent," I say.

"We don't have an accent. *You* have the accent," Evie jokes.

Mr. Stan finally gives up on teaching, and we play cultural comparison instead.

At the end of the day, my parents are waiting for us. They and the other parents line up on bikes and motos outside the gate. There are no SUVs or minivans in this carpool line. They seem absurd now, the giant vehicles Americans drive to haul purchases from Target and Costco.

"How was it?" my parents ask.

"It was the best day of my life! Can we enroll?"

HOI AN, VIETNAM–DEC 2013: Delaney is all smiles after a day at school (top). Barefoot students relax in the outdoor lunchroom at Green Shoots International School.

Riley, 12

"I can't wait to see my new clothes. Especially the dress." Mom and I pedal back to the cloth market.

We lock our bikes and find Mrs. Scary's booth. Our clothes are ready. Yay! New wardrobe coming up! My shirts and jeans turned out great. But my dress looks like something a mom would wear to work. Not a twelve-year-old girl. I hate it. Mrs. Scary mixed up the fabrics on Mom's order, so she's disappointed too. We ride our bikes back to the guesthouse.

Delaney is lying in bed under the mosquito net reading *Escape from Saigon: How a Vietnam War Orphan became an American Boy.*

"How are your clothes?" she asks without looking up.

"I hate the dress, and she messed up Mom's order."

"Told ya."

Ugh! I hate when Delaney's right.

"Well, I did get two cute tops and jeans. And they fit perfectly." I pull them out of the bag.

"Wanna hear some good news?" Delaney dog-ears a page and looks up.

"What?" I change into my new peach blouse and jeans.

"It's group dinner night, and two families from Australia and New Zealand just checked in. There are six kids, and four of them are in middle school!"

Delaney, 14

"THAT WAS SO MUCH FUN LAST NIGHT." I kick sand along the beach. "It's just our luck that kids would show up on our last night."

"I know. Riding bikes with them around Hoi An would've been a blast," Riley says.

The Salgados, from Sydney, Australia, have four kids: Zofia, Lucia, Zarah, and Salvador. Lucia and Zarah are in middle school. The Martins live in Christchurch, New Zealand. Their kids, Erin and Henry, are middle schoolers too. Last night, Ri and I hung out with people other than our parents for the first time in two months (except for our day at the international school). It was an epic boost to my non-existent social life.

"I definitely could've stayed there longer," Dad says.

"Me too," Mom agrees.

We just arrived in Nha Trang—a resort town on the South China Sea—where palm trees and sunbeds line the beach. Beach loungers rent for 30,000 dong a day. That sounds super expensive, but it's only $1.50. A park runs along the beach behind the sunbeds. Filled with bright blue exercise equipment, it's more like a playground for adults. We spend the next half hour twisting, crunching, riding, spinning, and pulling at the outdoor gym.

"I wish our beaches had fun stuff like this," Riley says, stuck in an awkward scissor-split position.

"For real. And the geometric trees are straight out of a Dr. Seuss book."

The weirdest thing keeps happening here. Every time someone greets us, like in a store or hotel, they speak to us in Russian. Store signs and menus are written in Vietnamese and also Russian.

When I was five, a seven-year-old girl from Belarus lived with us for the summer. My parents took Russian lessons before Svetlana arrived because she didn't speak English.

Mom made welcome T-shirts in Russian for us to wear when we met Svetlana at the airport. I don't remember many words, but I know Russian when I hear it. Everyone assumes that since we have pale skin, we must be Russian. This hasn't happened anywhere else in the world. Who knew that Nha Trang was a Russian-vacation-hot-spot?

Countries really aren't that different from middle schoolers. Every country has its squad. Vietnam and Russia are definitely in the same squad. The United States belongs to another squad. Usually, the different squads get along. But sometimes they don't. No matter what, you always stick up for your squad. That's how middle school works. And that's how the world works, too.

What if my squad doesn't have my back when I return? What if I have no friends at all? Being in middle school without a squad is one of the scariest places in the world.

ATLANTA, GEORGIA: Five-year-old Delaney wears a T-shirt at the Atlanta airport that reads "Welcome, Svetlana! My name is Delaney," in Russian.

Riley, 12

"IF THIS CABLE SNAPS, we're goners," Delaney says.

"Don't say that!" I stare at the whitecaps below.

"How long is it?" Mom asks, her knees bouncing.

"You don't want to know," Delaney says.

Mom hates heights, so I change the subject. "Today's gonna be sooo fun. I hope they have good roller coasters."

"I bet they do," Dad says. "It's Vietnam's best amusement park."

We survive the two-mile-overwater-cable-car ride to the private island and buy our tickets. A fake castle stands at the park entrance. In front of the castle is a fair-skinned, dark-haired princess surrounded by dwarves. Do the head honchos in Orlando know about this place??? Not that I care, because this theme park is a blast. We spend the day riding coasters and carousels, then cooling off on water slides and in wave pools.

"This amusement park reminds me of my Fuggs. It's the knock-off version of Disney," Delaney says.

"Without the Disney prices or crowds," Mom says.

We're heading to catch the cable car back to Nha Trang when I spot a new ride—a super tall tower with a ring of seats circling it. Each section of the ring has four seats. The ring moves up the tower until it reaches the top. Then it flips upside down and spins around. It looks so fun!

"Oooh! Can we ride that?" I squeal.

"I'm not getting on that," Mom says.

"No thanks," Dad says.

"Looks totally sketch," Delaney adds.

"You're a bunch of chickens. I'm riding it." I head toward entrance.

Yay. I don't spot a lame yardstick tool to check my height. Those are such a drag for short kids. There's no line, so I march straight up to the attendant.

She puts me in the end seat and lowers the black safety bar over my shoulders. My head doesn't even reach the part of the bar that goes over the shoulders. A tall Russian woman sits next to me. Her head sticks above the top of the safety bar.

The ride starts. The seat ring goes up, up, up the tower. This is so fun. My fam is a bunch of wimps. When we reach the top, I can see across the island to the South China Sea. What a view.

Bam! The compartment flips upside down. Oh my gosh! I'M GONNA DIE!!! This ride was not designed for short, skinny kids! Why did they let me on?! There's *no way* they would let a kid my size on a ride like this at Disney World. There's too much room between my body and the harness. I clutch the bar across my waist to keep from falling out of the shoulder harness. The upside-down circle at the top of the tower starts spinning. My death grip gets tighter. This was the worst decision of my life! And now I'm going to splat to my death. I try to spot my parents, but we're spinning too fast. Will they see me drop out?

When the upside-down spinning torture ends, the compartment flips upright, and the ring crawls down the tower.

I spot Delaney first. She's bent over laughing. My parents stand next to her with their eyes and mouths wide open. They aren't smiling at all.

"Told ya it was sketchy," Delaney says when I rejoin them.

Ugh. I hate being small, and I really hate when she's right!

NHA TRANG, VIETNAM–DEC 2013: Riley and a Russian woman survive the ride.

Delaney, 14

WHEN WE WERE IN HANOI, we asked Mary, "If you could visit anywhere in Vietnam, where would you go?"

Her answer? Da Lat.

She wants to visit the park for lovebirds, Valley of Love, and the Buddhist monastery. But there's no way those are better than The Crazy House.

"BOO!" Riley and I jump out from either side of the door, scaring the couple peering into our room.

"Agh!" they scream and scurry away.

A few minutes later, we hear more voices.

"Hide! Quick." We take our places by the door and hold our breath.

When two boys lean over the wooden gate to peek into our room, we leap out. "BOO!"

The brothers scream, bouncing backward. We crack up. When the boys see us, they do too.

We just checked into the Hang Nga guesthouse, a.k.a. The Crazy House. It's a tourist attraction by day and a hotel at night. If you put Dr. Seuss, Hansel and Gretel, Hogwarts, and Hobbiton into a blender, you would end up with The Crazy House. Secret tunnels, tree branch bridges, and hidden ladders connect the rooms throughout this magical treehouse-hotel maze. A spiderweb window sits next to a tree-hole balcony. It's the trippiest hotel ever.

Most visitors come for the day to explore the ten rooms and property, but we're spending the night! Since we just checked in, people keep poking their heads into our room. A locked gate keeps them from coming inside. Each room—designed like the inside of a tree trunk—has an animal theme (bear, kangaroo, termite, etc.).

We're staying in the Eagle room. A fire roars in the eagle egg fireplace. A pterodactyl-sized eagle with outstretched wings stands on top of the egg. Our round bed sits inside a cave on one side of the room. My parents' bed is on the other side of the monster eagle. The table and stools look like mushrooms. I've landed in a fairytale.

"This bed is so cool. I don't even care if we have to share." Riley stretches out across the circular bed. "Scaring people is hard work."

"For real. It's hilarious watching the tourists freak out," I say.

DA LAT, VIETNAM: The Crazy House is a kids' fantasy attraction by day and a hotel at night.

When the last day visitors leave Hang Nha, we begin an epic family game of hide-and-go-seek in our private theme park.

"Ready or not, here I come." I uncover my eyes. With endless nooks and secret passages on the ground and in the sky, our game lasts until it's too dark to play.

This is way cooler than middle school.

*DA LAT, VIETNAM: Riley and Delaney enjoy the balcony
view at The Crazy House hotel.*

Ri and I crawl into the circle bed and pull up the covers. We're waiting for Netflix to load when I hear Mom gasp.

"What's wrong?"

"Uncle Charles died," her voice cracks.

"Which one?" Mom has an Uncle Charles on both sides of her family. She adores them both.

"The musical one. From St. Louis," she says.

"What are we gonna do?" I ask. Will we go home? If we do, we'll be home in time for Christmas. I feel guilty even thinking that.

"We'll continue our journey. It breaks my heart to miss his funeral, but we'll be there in spirit." She continues, "This is definitely the hardest part of long-term travel. I worried something like this would happen. But if you spend your life worrying about the what-ifs, instead of chasing your dreams, you will always regret it."

Riley 12

"WHY ARE THERE SWASTIKAS HERE? Isn't that, like, majorly un-Buddhist?" I ask as we wander around the Truc Lam Monastery campus. We're looking for the visitors' meditation pagoda.

"That makes no sense. That's completely against Buddhist teachings," Mom agrees.

Zen is one of those words that you hear a lot. But I never really understood what it meant. Now I do. This place oozes zen. The shrubs and flowers have fresh haircuts. Not one leaf is out of place. Even though we're outdoors, everything looks freshly vacuumed. (Which I haven't had to do since my hair freak-out in London. Yay!) We see other visitors, but everyone's super chill. No screaming babies or whiney little kids. A large yellow pagoda—topped with two tile roofs—stands in the middle of the campus. We peek inside. Worshippers kneel facing the Buddha statue. They rest their hands in a prayer position against their forehead. This isn't the one for tourists. Outside the main pagoda stand smaller pagodas and perfect gardens.

A smiley monk walks by. His orange robe and pants hang loosely from his body.

"Excuse me," Dad says. "We're looking for the visitor meditation place."

"That is very good. I will take you. Follow me." He smiles like my teachers do when kids act interested in their lesson. While we walk, Mr. Monk teaches us all about Buddhism.

DA LAT, VIETNAM: Buddhist monk at Truc Lam Monastery

Buddhism according to Mr. Monk

Buddhism is more like a way of life than a religion. But it's still considered the fourth most popular religion in the world. A Hindu named Siddhartha Gautama was born in Nepal around 563 BCE (over 500 years before Jesus). He tried Hinduism and other belief systems, but none worked for him. So he started his own: Buddhism. It means "the enlightened one." Pretty much anyone can be a Buddhist, but Siddhartha is the head honcho, or Buddha.

Fifty monks and fifty nuns live at the Truc Lam monastery. Since meditation is a big part of becoming *enlightened,* the monks and nuns meditate six hours a day. The meditation times are: 3:30-5:30 a.m., 2:30-4:30 p.m., and 7:30-9:30 p.m. That makes going to church once a week pretty lame!

"It looks like we have the same barber," Dad jokes, rubbing his head. The monk laughs and rubs his own.

"All monks must shave their heads with a razor. It's called *tonsure.* It's a way of publicly renouncing worldly things, like vanity. Even the nuns must shave theirs."

"No way." Delaney pets her long, fat braid.

"Sooo, what's with all the swastikas?" I ask.

"Ah, yes. That confuses a lot of Western visitors. The swastika is an ancient Asian symbol. It has been around for thousands of years. It means good luck."

"So Hitler and the Nazis took a symbol that means something good and turned it into something evil?" I ask.

"That is correct." He nods his head with his hands clasped together.

We follow Mr. Monk into the tourist meditation room. It is empty except for the Buddha statue. He hands us a square foam mat and a round pillow, then gives the following instructions:

How to Meditate

1. Put the pillow on top of the square. Sit in a full or half-lotus position with your booty on the cushion and your knees touching the mat. If that's uncomfortable, you can sit criss-cross-applesauce.
2. Keep your eyes slightly open and stare at the floor three feet in front of you.
3. Here's the hard part: Erase any thoughts from your brain. If you feel an idea trying to pop up, imagine erasing it with tissue on a whiteboard. Stay still and deepen into relaxation.

We sit on the pillows in our official meditation poses. When we go silent, the meditation master sneaks out. Two minutes into our meditation session, Dad stretches his legs. He's done. I'm trying to focus, but dumb thoughts keep jumping into my head. I can't wipe them away fast enough. Dumb thought. Wipe. Dumb thought. Wipe. Dumb thought. Dumb thought. A minute later, I'm out. But Mom and Delaney keep on meditating, for a whole six minutes.

"That was hard!" Dad rubs his knees.

"I'm impressed they do that six hours a day. We barely made it six minutes," Mom says.

"I don't know about y'all, but I received enlightenment," I say, using my official voice.

"Oh really? How's that?" Delaney gives me the side-eye.

"I received a clear message that you must become a Buddhist nun. It's the *only* path for you," I say to Delaney. "And the first thing we must do … is shave your head."

After our failed meditation experiment, we get lunch. "If you're sick of Asian food, raise your hand." I put my chopsticks in my empty bowl. Everyone but Delaney raises a hand. After six weeks of rice and noodles, I neeeed a hamburger.

"Hang in there for three more days. We're heading to Ho Chi Minh City tomorrow and then to Australia," Mom says. "Maybe Santa will bring you a hamburger for Christmas."

DA LAT, VIETNAM: Truc Lam Buddhist Monastery

Delaney, 14

"Do y'all remember how to do this?" Mom yells, motorbikes flying past us.

The honking and fumes drown my senses. "Ho Chi Minh City is even crazier than Hanoi! See you on the other side." Boldly defying school-crossing-guards across America, I take a deep breath and walk straight into traffic. The carpool moms at home would wet their workout clothes if they saw me now.

We survive the crossing from the hotel to the restaurant across the street and grab a table on the covered patio.

"That was close," Riley says, as raindrops splatter on the road.

"This should be interesting." Dad nods toward the street.

We order dinner and watch the creative ways people deal with rain on motorbikes. Many wear ponchos, some wear umbrella hats or hold an umbrella, but most get drenched. How miserable. It's not like motorbikes are their fun vehicles for sunny days. It's the only vehicle—rain or shine.

Two couples sit at the table next to ours. They are watching the torrential street show, too. Always eager to talk to non-family members, we strike up a conversation.

"Where are y'all from?" Dad asks.

"Germany. How about you?" Inge asks.

"The United States," I say.

"Are you here on Christmas break?" Inge's boyfriend asks.

"No, we're traveling for several months," Dad says.

"Really? That's awesome. I wish my parents had done that," Kurt says.

"How can you do that? What about school?" Kurt's girl-friend, Anika, asks.

"We're homeschooling. The girls will go back to regular school when we return," Mom says.

The Germans tilt their heads and scrunch their faces. "You

can do that in America?" Kurt asks.

"Homeschool? Sure. Anyone can. Lots of people do it," Mom explains.

"It's a good thing you don't live in Germany, or you'd be thrown in jail," Anika says to my parents, then turns to us. "And you'd fail your grade. Homeschooling is illegal."

"Which is crazy," Kurt continues, "because you're learning so much more traveling than you ever would in the classroom. But that's the law."

Wow. If we lived in Germany, this world-school adventure never would've happened.

"Whoa. I'm glad we're not German," Riley says.

Six months ago, I would've given anything to be German. Now, I'm not so sure.

HO CHI MINH CITY, VIETNAM: Crossing the street is not for chickens.

Riley, 12

Social studies lesson

Cao Dai is a new religion that began in Vietnam in 1925. It combines the major world religions, believing that all religions come from the same God. They have worship services four times a day: 6:00 a.m., noon, 6:00 p.m., and midnight. Most visitors attend the noon service.

FINALLY!! A temple that isn't boring! The Cao Dai (cow die) temple in Tay Ninh looks like a stop on Candyland. We're watching the worship service below from a bright blue balcony hanging from sunny yellow walls. Fluffy clouds cover the ceiling. Green dragons with red-and-white-striped horns twist around twenty-eight massive pink columns. Gum-drop-colored swirly designs cover the dragon poles. The all-seeing Divine Eye stained-glass windows watch everyone. The Cao-Dai-eye symbol reminds me of the tattoo on Count Olaf's ankle in *A Series of Unfortunate Events*.

The worshippers wear solid white robes from neck to ankles. They file in—forming perfect rows—before sitting criss-cross-applesauce on the floor. Women sit on the left side of the temple, men on the right. The leaders wear bright yellow, red, or blue robes. Each color represents a major world religion. Some of them wear special hats that look like tall, square chef hats with the Cao-Dai-eye monogrammed on them. While the orchestra plays, worshippers sing and chant. Visitors cram into the narrow balconies to observe this unique service.

Staring at the hundreds of worshippers and visitors, I whisper to Delaney, "I hope we can find our shoes when this is over."

An hour later, we dig our shoes from the pile and head for the van.

"I wonder how the worshippers feel about their service being a tourist attraction," Dad says.

"They didn't seem to mind," I say.

"I guess it's the best way for people to learn about their religion," Delaney says.

"Good point. None of us had ever heard of Cao Dai before this week," Mom says.

"Awww." A man with a twisted body sits lop-sided in an old wheelchair on the sidewalk ahead. People parade past him like he's invisible. "Nobody's helping him. Can we give him something?"

Dad gives me 100,000 dong, which sounds like a ton, but it's only five dollars. Then again, five dollars here is a lot more than back home. I stick it in his cup. His sweet face beams.

We climb into the van, but I can't stop thinking about the man. We all watch him in silence as our van drives away.

"That was so sad seeing everyone walk past him," I say.

"I know. He's not like those fakers in Italy," Delaney says.

Mom and Dad read each other's minds.

"Turn around," Dad tells the driver. "Go back."

Mom fishes into her bag. She keeps the big bucks. She hands me a thick wad of dong that won't make a difference in our world. But it will make a difference in his. When I jump out of the van, the man's face lights up. His contorted body shifts slightly as he tries to lift his head. I help him find a safe hiding place and tuck the money away, so no one will steal it. He can't really talk, but he squeaks with joy. His little body shakes as he smiles with his mouth wide open. My hands are empty—but my heart is full—when I hop back in the van. We wave to each other as the driver pulls away. The ear-to-ear grin never leaves his face.

Or mine.

TAY NINH, VIETNAM: Tourists observe noon mass at the Cao Dai church.
This new religion includes spiritual leaders from the East and West, including
Buddha, Jesus, and Mohammed, as well as others.

Delaney, 14

The Vietnam War in a nutshell

North Vietnam and South Vietnam were fighting each other over communism. North Vietnam (capital Hanoi) was pro-communist, and South Vietnam (capital Saigon) was anti-communist. China and Russia joined the North Vietnam squad. The United States, Australia, and other anti-communist countries joined the South Vietnam squad. In the end, North Vietnam won. Saigon was renamed Ho Chi Minh City, and all of Vietnam became a communist country.

"TODAY IS A GOOD DAY to be small." Riley creeps ahead of me through the underground dirt tunnel.

"A lot of Americans are too big to fit. But this part of the tunnel has been enlarged for tourists," our guide, Minh, yells back, his voice echoing in the dark.

"This is torture on my knees," Dad says.

We are crawling through the famous Cu Chi tunnels outside of Ho Chi Minh City (Saigon) on our field trip to learn more about the Vietnam War.

After crawling through a section of the tunnels, Minh leads us to a secret door in the ground. He lifts the square cover, revealing a hole. It's much skinnier than the American-sized tunnel I just crawled through. I hop in. Balancing the leaf-covered concrete square on my head, I slip underground, sliding the camouflage cover in place.

HO CHI MINH CITY, VIETNAM: Cu Chi Tunnels

The Viet Cong soldiers hid and lived in these tunnels during the war—literally under American and South Vietnamese soldiers' feet. The tunnels stored weapons and supplies. They also provided living quarters, and even a hospital, for the Viet Cong fighters.

"The Viet Cong soldiers were South Vietnamese who joined the communist movement under Ho Chi Minh. The Viet Cong fought with the North Vietnamese against the South Vietnamese and Americans," Minh explains.

"After Saigon fell to the North Vietnamese, lots of South Vietnamese fled to the United States. They would rather go to a new country with nothing but the clothes on their backs than live in a communist country," Dad says.

"That's right. One of my high-school friends escaped on a boat in the middle of the night. She was six-years-old. Some of her siblings didn't make it out," Mom says. "Can you imagine that?"

As annoying as Riley can be sometimes, I cannot imagine us being ripped apart. My stomach swirls just thinking about it.

"Come see the booby traps," Minh says.

The poor soldiers who stepped on the camouflaged jungle doors fell into a deep hole with metal spikes in the bottom. The Viet Cong covered the spikes with poop. If the metal daggers didn't kill the enemy, infection would. Although I'm impressed with their cleverness, all I can think about are the horrible deaths that their victims suffered.

War. Is. Awful.

ON THE WAY to our last stop of the Vietnam War tour, Dad and Minh get into an intense conversation about communism. Minh is in his twenties, so he's spent his entire life under communist rule. Our driver, Mr. Quan, jumps into the conversation.

"I didn't even know he spoke English," I whisper to Riley. Mr. Quan is around Papaw's age. He hasn't uttered a single word—Vietnamese or English—all day.

"Communism" was Mr. Quan's chatterbox on-switch. It turns out our silent driver was an English interpreter for the South Vietnamese army! He begins telling stories about the war. My parents scooch to the edge of their bench seat. Minh has been sharing information he memorized from a tourism script. But Mr. Quan's stories come from his heart. And they are fascinating.

The funniest are the stories about the American soldiers who returned to Vietnam forty years after the war to reunite with their Vietnamese girlfriends. The looks on the war-time love-birds' faces when they reunite are *always* the same. Disappointment.

"The sixty-year-old version looks nothing like the twenty-year-old that's been living in their heads," Mr. Quan jokes.

But the stories about his two years in a "re-education camp" after the fall of Saigon aren't funny at all. They sound nothing like camp to me.

"Most South Vietnamese who are my age are very pro-American." Mr. Quan glances at Minh, then meets our eyes in the rearview mirror. "And no matter what it says on a map, our city is still Saigon."

After an awkward silence, Minh asks, "Would you like to drive through Kim Phúc's village on the way back?"

"Absolutely!" Mom says.

"Who's that?" I ask.

"She's the girl in the most famous photo from the Vietnam War. The one with the naked girl running down the street screaming. The napalm girl." Mom continues, "Everyone my age or older knows who she is, even if they don't know her name."

Instead of passing through, we stop at Kim Phúc's (rhymes with book) family's restaurant. We are the only people here. The gut-wrenching photo hangs next to a small TV. The picture shows terrified children running in the street. One girl, front-and-center, is completely naked. Whatever she is running from is a million times worse than being seen in her birthday suit. We take our seats in the metal chairs, and Ms. Phúc's sister-in-law starts the video. In this little family restaurant in Trang Bang, Vietnam, I learn the story of the girl in the photo.

June 8, 1972

The villagers of Trang Bang are gathered in the safety of the Cao Dai temple when they learn it is about to be bombed. The South Vietnamese think the villagers have evacuated and the Viet Cong are hiding in the temple.

While nine-year-old Kim Phúc and her older brother are running for their lives, a South Vietnamese plane drops *napalm.* This weapon of war instantly covers the village in fire, including Kim Phúc's clothes. She rips them off, yelling, "Too hot! Too hot!" At that moment, war photographer Nick Ut takes the picture that will change the world's view of war.

With third-degree burns covering much of Kim's body, the doctors said she would die within days. They were wrong. Fourteen months and seventeen surgeries later, Kim Phúc left the hospital.

Years later, Ms. Phúc married, and they honeymooned in Russia. On the way home, their plane stopped in Canada to refuel. The couple seized this chance at freedom from a communist government. With only the clothes on their backs, they got off the plane and requested political *asylum.* The Canadian government granted their request.

Ms. Phúc has forgiven the men responsible for her pain and suffering. Today, she lives in Canada and is an ambassador for peace and forgiveness.

Silence fills the room when the video stops. Mom speaks first. "Wow. All these years I assumed she was taking a bath when she had to flee. I've always wanted to know her story."

"That's so powerful that she forgave the men who dropped the napalm. What an important lesson for us all," Dad says.

Learning the story of the girl in the photo opened my eyes to the reality of war. It tears countries and families apart. It's hard to know which side is the good side because both sides tell their version of events. They share the evil acts of the enemy while hiding their own.

It's hard to wrap my head around being trapped in a war zone, much less catching on fire. And then forgiving the men responsible. Ms. Phúc is the world's poster child for forgiving the past to make way for a better future.

PASSPORT LESSON #8:
There are two sides to every story. Especially war. Most people only know the version their country tells. But there are two weapons more powerful than hate—love and forgiveness.

	VIETNAM High-Low Report Card 🙂	☹️
Delaney	Green Shoots School	Hanoi Hilton
Riley	Crazy House	Near-death at amusement park
Mom	Hoi An	Difficult working conditions for women
Dad	Hoi An	Hanoi Hilton

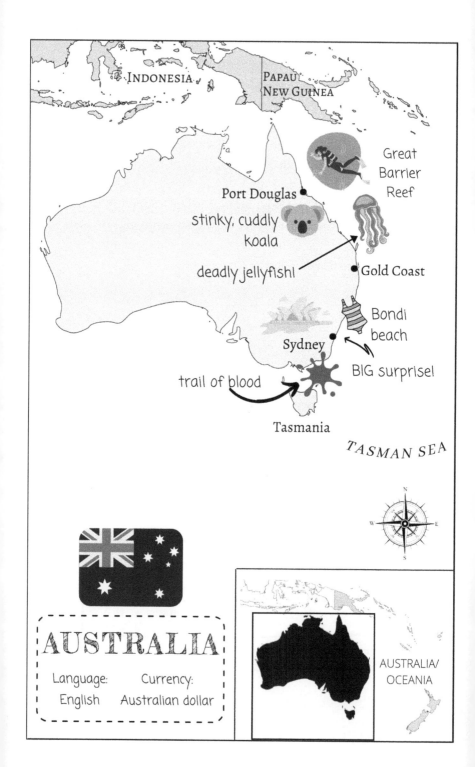

16.

At Home in the Land Down Under

December 22—January 3

Home isn't a place. It's a feeling.

— CECELIA AHERN, *LOVE,*
ROSIE

Riley, 12

After another miserable overnight flight, we land *Down Under* (Australia's nickname and an '80s song my parents keep singing). While Dad waits on our bags, we run to the restroom.

"A sign like this would've been super helpful in preventing my squatter tragedy in Thailand," I say from my stall. The cartoon picture hanging on the door shows how to use a Western toilet. A lot of potty-squatters must come here. Do the toilets confuse them as much as the squatter confused me? Do people try to stand on the rim of the toilet? Scary, Mary! That's almost as bad as me sitting on a squatter.

"And in other exciting potty news, we can flush the paper here," Delaney says from her stall.

GOLD COAST, AUSTRALIA: *Instructions posted in the airport restroom explain how to use the toilet.*

"Only three days 'til Christmas," I say, drying my hands. "I'm sooo excited."

"Me too. But Christmas in the middle of summer is so weird," Delaney says.

We find Dad and roll our bags outside. A man who reminds me of Papaw picks us up and drives us to his hotel by the Gold Coast beach. Red-and-white-striped hammock chairs sit in front of the seafoam green building. It's so cute. The owner leads us into our room, but he keeps his shoes on. Ew. We leave ours outside and go in. Bummer. We're all sharing one room with the World's Smallest Bathroom.

"This is tiny. Can't we get two rooms? Like in Asia?" I ask when the owner leaves.

"Nope. Australia is much more expensive than Asia. Besides, we're only here one night," Dad says.

"Who wants to find a hamburger?" Mom asks.

"MEEEE!!!" I squeal. Everyone else does too.

"I bet we'll find a place down the beach," Delaney says.

Del and I race to the sugar-white sand and kick off our flip-flops.

"This looks exactly like Gulf Shores," Mom says, "with the sand dunes and sea oats."

"There's a place." I point to a funky beach restaurant.

"Looks good to me," Dad says.

We grab a table—the first one with both chairs and forks in weeks—and scan the menu.

Dad's jaw drops. "Thirteen dollars for a burger? That's crazy. Our dinner last night was less than eight for all of us."

I don't care how much it costs. We all order burgers anyway. And when the server brings our juicy hunks of beef on buns, Del and I clap and squeal like kids getting their first phone.

"The prices may be higher than Southeast Asia, but at least we can drink the tap water. Cheers to a new continent." Mom raises her water, and we clink glasses.

Yay! We can finally drink the water and brush our teeth without getting travelers' tummy. This tragic problem goes by different names, depending on where you are:

- Bali belly (Southeast Asia)
- Montezuma's revenge (Mexico)
- Nile runs (Middle East)
- Delhi belly (India)

It doesn't matter what you call it. They all mean the same thing. Horror-movie amounts of puking and/or diarrhea. Luckily, we made it through Asia without any major stomach explosions.

"Who's up for a Christmas concert on the beach tonight?" Mom asks.

"I am," everyone says.

Delaney, 14

I HAVE A COUNTRY-CRUSH ON AUSTRALIA. Seriously. The people are chill, the accent is cool, and they speak English. But it's so much better than our version. They have cute names for everything, like:

- mosquitos = mozzies
- breakfast = brekkie
- sunglasses = sunnies
- swimsuits = swimmers

We catch the bus from the Gold Coast to Surfers Paradise, then follow the crowds across the street and under an archway with SURFERS PARADISE lit across the top. An Aboriginal man, wearing only a loincloth and red headband, sits on the sidewalk by the beach. Painted-on white stripes-and-dashes decorate his dark skin. He plays the *didgeridoo*, a wooden, flute-type instrument the length of a fishing pole. Aboriginal Australians are the original Aussies. Similar to the Native Americans, they were the first people on the continent until the White guys moved in.

The highrise condos in both directions remind me of Orange Beach, Alabama. A sea of people crowded on beach towels wait for their Christmas concert to begin. By distance, Australia is the farthest place in the world from Alabama. But right now, I feel more at home than I have in over two months. The four of us keep walking in circles on the beach, doing the same thing: smiling.

"Hey, look." I point toward the ocean. A speedboat barrels toward the shore. As it gets closer, we spot someone familiar waving frantically at the crowd. We wave back.

"SANTA! I KNOW HIM!!" Ri and I scream together.

Santa zips to shore. He hugs and high-fives his way through the crowd, paying special attention to the little kids. We sing Christmas carols, surrounded by strangers but soaking in the familiarity of this new continent. When the show is over, we join the crowd making their way back to their cars. When we reach the busy road —the one with the bus stop, traffic lights, and crosswalks—we do what has become normal. We walk straight into traffic. The blaring horns and creative hand gestures are the first hints we've messed up. I turn around. The holiday mob waits on the sidewalk, mouths hanging open, staring at us like we're barbarians.

"Whoops," I say. It's crazy how something so scary and foreign three weeks ago is now normal.

"Different culture. Different rules," Mom says. "Time to dig out the old playbook."

"I feel like we're in a cultural pinball machine. We're bouncing from one continent to another, and the rules change with each one. It's a lot to remember. The normal things in one place are bad in another. Like, do you wait at crosswalks or not? Do you wear your shoes inside or not? Do you shake hands or bow? Is it okay to show your knees and shoulders? Or is that offensive? Do you give someone money with one hand or two?" I say.

"Do you sit or squat?" Riley chimes in. "Who's the head honcho of rule-making, anyway? And why do all the rules have to be different?"

———

"THIS SHOULD BE INTERESTING," I whisper to Riley as we're getting into our rental car at the Cairns airport. My parents haven't driven in over two months. Now they have to drive on the opposite side of the road, with the steering wheel on the opposite side of the car. Even though Mom always drives at home, she's the co-pilot when we travel.

"You're too close on my side." Mom stares out her window at the road.

"No, I'm not. If I move over any more, I'll be over the yellow lines," Dad says.

"Are you sure? It feels like we're about to run off the road."

"Would you just close your eyes and take a nap."

I don't know why he would suggest that. Mom's the one who gives directions. Besides, she'll never close her eyes with someone else driving. I put my earbuds in. They'll figure it out. An hour later, we arrive in Port Douglas. When I open the car door, the heat and humidity smack me in the face.

"This is worse than Alabama in the summer," Mom says.

"I hope we have a pool." Riley's face is already turning red in the heat.

Our apartment, By the Sea, is awesome. We have two bedrooms, separate beds, a swimming pool with tons of toys, a Christmas tree in the lobby, and over five hundred videos we can check-out. Four Mile Beach is on the left, and Port Douglas town is on the right.

We change into our *swimmers* and walk to the beach. It's too hot to run. Even though it's four miles long, all the beach-goers cram into the same area. Yellow MARINE STINGER signs posted along the shore warn that today's stinger risk is moderate. For it to be the middle of summer, the beach is practically empty. It's nothing like the crowds last night at Surfers Paradise. Then again, the distance from Port Douglas to Surfers Paradise is the same as New York to Florida. Even though they are both on the east coast, they are very far apart.

A lifeguard leans against a sideways-propped surfboard near the water.

"Let's get in." Riley drops her towel. "I'm burning up."

"Hold up a sec," Dad says. "Let's ask the lifeguard about the signs."

A few minutes later, I'm learning all the reasons why I'm

NOT getting in the water. From November 'til May is *stinger season* for the top half of Australia's east coast. And this isn't like at home, where if you get stung by a jellyfish, it stings for a bit, and then it's over. Here, if you get stung by a jellyfish, YOU DIE. No wonder the beach is a ghost town. Mr. Cute Lifeguard explains all about the two deadliest kinds: Japanese Irukandji and Box jellyfish.

"The Box jelly is the most poisonous creature in the sea. One sting, and you're a goner. And it's basically invisible in the water. The Irukandji is as tiny as your fingernail. Its venom is so painful that even if you don't die, you'll wish you did," he says.

"Then why are those people in the water?" I point at the handful of idiots swimming.

"That area is enclosed by nets, so the Box jellies can't get in. But nothing can keep the Irukandji out. They're too small." He pulls his *sunnies* off, uncovering his baby-blues. "It's easy to know who the tourists are. They're the only ones in the water. You can't pay a local to go in during stinger season."

We pick up our towels and head to the hotel's pool. The water is so warm, it's more like a giant bathtub. After learning that Australia has more deadly animals than anywhere else on Earth, my country-crush is fading. Why did we come here? For the same reason everyone else does—to explore the Great Barrier Reef. Shark attacks have moved down on my list of ocean anxieties. I've *got* to talk my parents out of this.

Riley, 12

"I'M GOING TO THE GROCERY. Who wants to come with me?" Mom asks.

"I do." I love shopping, even for food. And we finally have a kitchen.

"You know what I'm craving?" I ask, while we walk to the store. "Bacon, eggs, and biscuits. Like a real Cracker Barrel breakfast."

"That sounds so good." We enter the grocery, grab a cart, and head for the cooler section.

"Oooh, look." Only three gingerbread house kits remain on the shelf. "Can we get them?" Delaney and I make gingerbread houses every year. Mom saves them, and now we have an entire village.

"It wouldn't be Christmas without gingerbread houses." Mom puts two kits in the cart.

We get the bacon and eggs, but we can't find biscuits anywhere.

"Ask her." An employee stacks cans on a nearby shelf.

"Excuse me," Mom says, "can you please tell me where the biscuits are?"

"Aisle three."

"I just went down aisle three. I didn't see any."

"All the biscuits are on aisle three," the grocery worker repeats.

"Aisle three just has crackers and stuff. We're looking for biscuits, like in the refrigerated or frozen section maybe ..."

"*All* of the biscuits are on. aisle. three," the stacker says, using the voice teachers use when a kid asks the same dumb question over and over.

"Oh my gosh. I totally forgot." Mom turns to me. "Biscuits are cookies here."

"No biscuits?" My visions of buttermilk-doughy-goodness fade away.

"No biscuits."

"If I lived here, I'd open a Cracker Barrel. And everyone would love me for introducing them to buttermilk biscuits and sweet tea."

"THIS IS THE GREATEST CHRISTMAS EVE EVER," I say, as we feed wallabies and kangaroos at the Wildlife Habitat. The cute little guys nibble pellets right out of our hands, and no one gets kicked in the face.

"Aww, the joey is poking his head out of the pouch." Delaney points to a cute mama 'roo nearby.

"That reminds me. What do you call a lazy baby kangaroo?" Dad feeds a wallaby.

"What?"

"A pouch potato."

"Take a picture," Mom says, squatting eye-level with a wallaby. They are staring at each other and holding hands. She's grinning, and the wallaby is smiling back. It's sooo cute! I could stay here forever. Then, my wallaby kisses my forehead.

"It's almost time," Dad says.

At two o'clock, we get to hold a Koala bear! We take our seats at the Koala exhibit and learn all about these furry balls of cuteness.

Did you know that Koalas only live in Australia? And they sleep eighteen hours a day? They only eat eucalyptus leaves—which are poisonous to most humans and other animals. And they aren't actually bears; they are marsupials. They have pouches for their babies like kangaroos.

Now comes the fun part.

PORT DOUGLAS,
AUSTRALIA: Riley holds a Koala
at the Wildlife Habitat.

"Put your hands together and form a cradle," the zookeeper instructs, "and be very still." When he places the Koala in my arms, my muscles tense under his weight. The Koala puts his little arms around me, squeezing with his claws. He nuzzles his furry head under my neck. I don't care how heavy he is. I could hold him forever.

"Koalas get stressed easily," the zookeeper continues, "so you must not move." Everyone takes a quick turn holding him.

"You know what I learned about Koalas that you could never learn from a book?" Del asks as we leave Wildlife Habitat.

"What?"

"Crikey, they stink!"

"No doubt." Mom turns to Del and changes the subject. "We can go shopping after Christmas to get you some new clothes."

"Sounds good. I need some jeans that aren't painful."

Ugh. It's not fair. Delaney has outgrown her clothes, and now she gets to go shopping. Meanwhile, my battery died on the Riley Reinvention Project. If it doesn't start charging soon, I'm still gonna be on version Riley 1.5—instead of Riley 2.0—when we go home!

Delaney, 14

THE ONLY DISAPPOINTING THING about Christmas in Port Douglas is that we couldn't find a Christmas Eve church service. It's especially disappointing because we figured we'd have a better chance of having a traditional Christmas with church and everything in Australia than Asia. I bet the church we visited in Malaysia had a wonderful Christmas Eve service. Celebrating Christmas without the church part feels like skipping the meal and going straight for the dessert.

"Merry Christmas!" my parents yell from behind the camera when Ri and I bust into the hotel lobby. They've hijacked the hotel Christmas tree as our own.

"Oooh, look. Gifts and everything," Ri says.

My expectations are low. The only store open when Mom went shopping was the pharmacy. It doesn't matter. It's not like we have room in our suitcases for anything anyway. But Mom always wraps our gifts, no matter how dinky, like fine jewelry. We take turns unwrapping a jar of Nutella, a twelve-pack of cream soda, Tim Tams (my fave Aussie cookie), lip balm, candy, and hair twisties. The final gift is an envelope.

"Y'all open this one together," Mom says, reminding me of the Christmas we got the blue laptop.

I keep my expectations low as we open an envelope with the hotel's name stamped in the corner. We unfold the stationery. It's a homemade gift certificate to snorkel or dive on the Great Barrier Reef. Redeemable tomorrow.

"Yay! I've always wanted to scuba dive!" Riley busts into a cringey dance move.

"Hello??? Stinger season anyone???" Am I the only person with good judgment in this family?! The blue laptop was lame, but this gift could kill us!

My mind races with the possibilities. What if I die? Even

worse, what if they all die, and I don't? I'd be trapped all alone on a continent on the other side of the world. Then what?

"We'll wear special stinger suits that will cover our entire bodies. It'll be fine," Mom says.

"Fine" does not sound fine to me. I've got twenty-four hours to talk them out of this.

My life depends on it.

Riley, 12

"WE LOOK LIKE A FAMILY OF TELETUBBIES." Del zips up her head-to-toe stinger suit. The only part of her body I can see is her face. "I will *not* be posting a picture of this."

GREAT BARRIER REEF, AUSTRALIA: *The McIntyres wear stinger suits to protect them from the deadly jellies.*

"Better to be dorky than dead," I say. Her face crumples up in a way that reminds me of the time we swam with sharks in Belize. We were six and eight years old. Delaney stayed on the boat and cried while the rest of us snorkeled with the nurse sharks. Once she realized they wouldn't eat us for lunch, she jumped in. But it was time to go.

On the way to the reef, Scuba Ben fills us in. We can either snorkel or dive. I'm definitely diving. Even though I'm not certified, like my parents, I can do an intro dive. No way am I gonna miss out on scuba diving at the Great Barrier Reef. But I'm not gonna lie, I'm pretty nervous about real sharks. Delaney's not excited about any of this, but she's gonna snorkel. At least she's not gonna sit on the boat and cry.

"The Great Barrier Reef is the largest reef in the world." Ben begins his talk. "It's even larger than Italy."

"At least the fish won't try to give us a rose," I whisper to Del.

Ben continues, "It's so big, astronauts can see it from the moon."

A few minutes later, Ben teaches me everything I need to know about breathing underwater. There are lots of ways to die if you mess up. When we get to our first dive site, I sit on the edge of the platform. As the boat bobs up and down, I squeeze my feet into the flippers. When Ben hangs the thirty-pound air tank on my back, I almost flip over. Thirty pounds is almost half my body weight!

"You won't feel the weight once you're in the water," Ben says.

GREAT BARRIER REEF, AUSTRALIA: Riley's getting ready for her first scuba dive.

Splash! I follow the dive master into the ocean. I grab the algae-covered rope and hold on. I slide down the line, going just a foot underwater. Ben tests the breathing skills he taught me during the boat ride. I put the regulator in my mouth. I practice breathing in and blowing out bubbles. Next, I practice expelling water from my regulator, in case some gets in my mouth accidentally. I have to get this part right, or I can't dive. When I master all the skills, we begin the fun part.

We shuffle our hands down the rope, deeper and deeper into the ocean. When we let go, I'm swimming in a tropical aquarium. The coral sparkles in shades of aqua, purple, orange, and blue. It's so bright it looks fake. Rainbows of fish wearing stripes and spots circle us. Some are tiny as insects; others are longer than skateboards. My favorite one wears bright red lipstick. Ben points to the different fish and writes their names on his underwater notebook. He swims over and picks up a sea cucumber with noodle-ish things poking out of it. After Ben releases it, the creature curls up and floats away.

All my years watching *SpongeBob* and *Shark Week* didn't prepare me for how a-maz-ing the Great Barrier Reef would be! Twenty-eight minutes later, Ben motions that we have to surface. We swim-climb up the slimy line and back into the boat. We spend the day snorkeling and diving at three different spots. At the last stop, I go down twenty-five feet and stay under for thirty-six minutes.

"What'd you think?" Dad asks after our last dive of the day.

"I loved it! It's so peaceful and beautiful down there. I wanna get certified." I peel off the stinger suit and wrap a towel around me.

"How was the snorkeling, Del?"

"Actually, great. I stopped thinking about the sharks and jellies once I saw all the fish."

"Did you see the Nemos? There were hundreds," I say.

We spend the entire ride back swapping fish tales. Mom dove with me and snorkeled with Del. She swears the snorkeling was just as good.

"Well, you're both ruined. You started at the pinnacle. After the Great Barrier Reef, anywhere else is gonna be lame. My first scuba dive was in a cold, muddy rock quarry with no visibility. Anything seemed good after that. But this ... this was magical."

Delaney, 14

THIS IS WHAT MOM'S BEEN HYPED about for nine months? She's been totally *puffing the goods*, which is what Dad says when a real estate agent makes a house sound way better than it is.

We just arrived in Sydney and checked into the Sydney Harbour YHA hostel. Mom busted into dance moves worse than Riley's when she snagged our reservation last spring. Based on her hype, I was expecting something fancier than two metal bunk beds and a micro-bath.

"I can't believe we're here," Mom sing-songs. She's bouncing on her top bunk like a summer camper.

I'd be that excited if we had free Wi-Fi. But Ri and I have to use our own money if we want to be connected. Ugh.

"Del, I'm picking up the network across the street," Riley says from the bunk above me. "Move to the corner."

I press my back against the wall and scooch into the corner. Score! There it is. Free Wi-Fi compliments of the library—as long as I don't move.

"You can sit there worrying about Wi-Fi, but I'm headed to the rooftop." Dad stands from the bunk across from me.

Did someone say rooftop? I drop my device. "Race ya', Ri!"

Riley and I sprint up the stairs to the terrace. We push open the doors, revealing the view.

"Whoa!" Two world-famous icons flank the Sydney Harbour —the Sydney Opera House and the Sydney Harbour Bridge.

"What a great spot for my twirling video," Riley says. "This is gonna be epic."

"Wow." Dad's mouth hangs open as he turns 360 degrees.

"See those hotels." Mom points at the high-rises that tower behind us. "Those rooms start around one thousand dollars a night, and you have to stay for five-to-ten nights. Our room is less than two hundred a night. Scoring a room here for New Year's Eve is winning the travel lottery. This is the only budget hotel that offers a front-row view of the biggest party in the Southern Hemisphere."

"If Mom hadn't gotten lucky, we wouldn't be in Sydney right now," Dad says.

"Dang. Go, Mom." I give her a high-five.

"Check out the bridge. Do you notice anything?" Dad asks.

"Other than it being huge? No," I say.

"Look very closely," Mom says.

"People are climbing across the very top! I see them next to the flags. They look like ants from here," Riley says. We zoom the camera lens to get a better view.

"Oh my gosh. That's crazy." The people-ants march up and over the top arch of the metal giant.

"Guess who's gonna be the ants in a few days?" Dad asks.

"Yay!!!" Riley squeals.

Oh, yay. Here we go again.

"O. M. G. That's insane," I say.

A sea of umbrellas stands between us and the most famous building in Australia: the Sydney Opera House. The iconic white landmark was designed with massive boat-like sails. We want to explore it, but we have to figure out how to navigate through umbrella-land first. Aussies and tourists have claimed every inch of concrete around the Sydney Harbour as their own. They huddle together under their umbrellas, seeking shelter from the mid-summer sun. It's New Year's Eve, and this is ground zero for the biggest party south of the equator.

A security guard lets us through a barrier.

"I wonder how long they've been here?" We tiptoe our way through the crowd. "It's not even noon."

"What do they do when they have to pee?" Riley asks.

"There's no way I could sit on concrete under this sun for

fifteen hours," Dad says. "That's why your mom is the best travel planner in the world."

"You can say that again," Mom says. "This. Is. Un-believable."

Who cares about free Wi-Fi. We hit the New Year's Eve jackpot.

SYDNEY, AUSTRALIA–DEC 31, 2013: Only fifteen more hours until midnight.

Riley, 12

"Don't forget your lanyard," Mom says, as Del and I run out of our room.

"We've got 'em," I yell back, as we race to the rooftop party.

"What do you wanna do first?" Delaney asks. There's lots of fun stuff—like a photo booth, lemonade stand, and fortune-teller.

"Oooh, the fortune-teller! I've always wanted to do that. Do you think she's real?"

We get lemonades and join the line. Thirty minutes later, it's my turn to sit across the table from the fortune teller. She wears a long, dark dress. A sparkly medallion necklace dangles from her neck, and a matching band circles her head. She looks legit, but it's hard to tell. She shuffles her cards and places them next to an old book like you'd see in Harry Potter.

"When is your birthday?" she asks.

"April seventeenth."

She flips to the April section. "You like to travel."

Well, duh. I have an accent and I'm staying at a hostel, so she knows I'm not from around here. I nod. She carefully spreads the cards across the table.

"You are organized and ambitious. When you set a goal, you go for it. Where others see brick walls, you see ideas. That is a good thing. It will make you very successful." The fortune teller peers through her pointy glasses.

That's creepy! She really knows her stuff. She tells me lots of other things that make me think she's been spying on me. I ask her questions about my future, carefully remembering the answers. Then the perfect question pops into my head to test if she's real or fake.

"When am I going home?"

"Hmmm." She peers into her ball, then studies the cards

spread across the table. "The sky is cloudy and the signs are unclear. It won't be soon, but it won't be long."

My turn is over. "She's a total fake," I whisper to Delaney. "No one knows when we're going home. Not even Mom and Dad."

After Delaney gets her fortune read, we meet a brother and sister our ages. We spend the night guzzling giant Pixy Stix and playing made-up games.

At nine-fifteen sharp, a blast fires from the harbor below. A burst explodes over the Sydney Opera House, and the sky rains white lights. Another blast turns the sky red, and the white opera sails glow against the crimson backdrop. Lights blaze from the Sydney Harbour Bridge. *Bam!* Fireworks explode on top of fireworks on top of fireworks. Back-to-back explosives launch from the opera house, the harbor, and the bridge. This is sooo intense! A parade of boats outlined in color-changing lights glides through the water below. I've never seen anything like this! And that was only round one. The kiddie round. Now the parents tell the little kids it's over and put them to bed. It's genius. The real New Year's Eve fireworks go off at midnight. You would have to see them yourself to believe it.

SYDNEY, AUSTRALIA: The rooftop view of the biggest NYE party south of the equator does not disappoint.

Delaney, 14

> ### Social studies lesson
> The Rocks is the historic part of Sydney, where
> England sent its prisoners to live in 1788.
> Today, tourists and locals hang out in the pubs
> and wander the old alleyways right
> by the Sydney Harbour Bridge.

"You can never go wrong with pancakes for dinner," I say, using my fork to swirl syrup designs on my plate. I just finished my last bite of Nutella pancakes at Pancakes on the Rocks, Australia's version of Cracker Barrel. Without the biscuits, of course.

"They may not have biscuits, but they have way better pancake options." Riley lifts her plate and licks the last bit of chocolate syrup from her Devil's Delight pancakes. With the plate hiding her face from my parents, Riley turns to me and mouths, "Bungee jumping."

I take a deep breath and try to sound sophisticated. "Riley and I have been researching things to do in New Zealand," I start. "And we've found something we really want to do."

"Awesome. I love when you help with the planning," Mom says. "What'd you find?"

"Bungee jumping," Riley and I say, our eyes darting from Mom's face to each other's.

"No way," Mom says. "Are you crazy?"

"C'mon, Mom. Bungee jumping started in New Zealand. We could jump off *the* bridge of the first bungee jump in the world. Wouldn't that be awesome?"

"No. It would not." She adds, "Climbing the Sydney bridge is our only bridge adventure."

"I'd do it," Dad chimes in. Cha-ching. Now he's on our side. It's three-against-one.

"Seriously? Mr. Bad Knees?" Mom crosses her arms and glares at him, then turns to me and says, "And who are you? And what have you done with my risk-averse daughter?"

Good question. The farther I get from my comfort zone, the braver I become. And the less I worry about what I'm missing at home, the more I enjoy this adventure. Bubbles are safe, but they are paralyzing too.

"Mommm, you always say we need to do authentic things when we travel. There's nothing more authentic than bungee jumping in New Zealand. Plllleeeease. Don't you wanna be Cool Mom?" Riley takes the point. She can usually talk them into anything.

"No one's bungee jumping. End of story," Mom says in her don't-bring-it-up-again voice. She changes the conversation. "So where should we go after New Zealand?"

"We're going to be there a month. Do we have to decide now?" Dad asks.

"Actually, we do. I just learned that we can't board our flight to New Zealand if we don't have proof that we're leaving New Zealand."

"Seriously? Why?" I ask.

"They want to make sure we won't overstay our visit. Each country makes its own rules about who can enter and how long they can stay. And the rules are different depending on which country you're from. It's our responsibility to know the rules and follow them. But, if we don't have the proper paperwork and the airline lets us on, then they have to fly us out at their expense. So the airlines are very strict about making sure we have what we're supposed to have. So, where do you want to go?"

"To a beach with warm water and no stingers," I say. Dad and Riley agree.

"I'll see what I can find. Y'all ready?" Mom stands, gathering her stuff.

"Can we go to that playground we passed?" Riley asks. She's still obsessed with playgrounds.

"I wanna go back." I yawn as I push open the front doors.

"Me too," Mom says.

"I'll take Ri to the playground. We'll meet you in the room later," Dad says. That's a good plan. Knowing Riley, she'll wear him out on the bungee jumping. Then maybe he can talk Mom into it. We leave Pancakes on the Rocks heading in opposite directions.

"Isn't it funny how the old buildings in Australia are the same age as the new buildings in London?" I say as we stroll back to our hostel.

"You're right. Like how buildings from the 1800s are old in the U.S., but that's considered new in other parts of the world."

"It's interesting how similar our country's history of colonization is to Australia's. But it's awful how the Aboriginal Australians were treated terribly, just like the Native Americans."

When we reach our turn—a corner with a pub on one side and a long row of old apartments on the other—a scream pierces the air, followed by a deep grunt. We freeze. A three-on-three street fight has broken out. Between five guys and one girl, a dozen fists and feet fly. Screams and cuss words break the silence of the bystanders. An older woman from the pub tries to break up the fight. But the girl punches her in the face.

"Oh my gosh!" Mom grabs my hand. I don't know if it's for her benefit or mine.

A shirtless guy wearing baggy jeans picks up a trash can and smashes it against another. Bottles shatter in the street. It feels like we're in the middle of a Hollywood movie, but they aren't actors. Minutes later, sirens interrupt the screams and thuds. Three of the bad guys take off when a pack of siren-blaring police cars arrive. The older woman staggers in the street, holding her head.

The police interview witnesses from the pub who saw the whole drama. They arrest the barefoot younger woman for attacking the older woman who was only trying to help. The officers put the scruffy girl in the police van. Her eyes dart like a madwoman while she pounds on the glass from inside. Meanwhile, the old lady lies in the back of the police car, cradling her noggin.

While the arrested woman's friend cusses at the cops, another scroungy neighbor yells at the cussing guy to shut up before they all get arrested. Given their scuzzy appearances, I don't think they were arguing over the last box of Tim Tams.

"We're definitely not in Liberty Park anymore," I whisper to Mom. When everything is under control, we skirt past the police cars down the sidewalk that leads to our hostel. I eavesdrop on the police as we pass by. They are trying to figure out where the bad guys went. Cops, radioing back and forth, swarm through The Rocks.

When we reach the concrete steps leading to our hostel, I spot a fresh drop of blood. And then another. Fresh red splatters lead up the steps, and blood smears cover the handrail. The hairs prickle on the back of my neck.

"I FOUND A TRAIL OF BLOOD," I scream to the police huddling around one of the squad cars.

As officers race toward us, one calls into his radio, "We found a trail of blood!"

We? Yeah, right. All those hours of watching *Criminal Minds* have finally paid off. Too bad none of the cops running past us is Derek Morgan. I follow the wet crimson trail. And Mom follows me, right into an alley. When I reach the dead end, the trail of blood stops. We're trapped at the back wall when a guy runs into the corridor. Yikes!

My survival instincts kick in. I bolt out of the bloody alley, thankful for every minute of cross-country practice over the past two years. I sprint all the way back to the hostel, doubling over when I reach the door. I'm still gasping when I realize what I left behind.

Mom!

Whoops.

"Thanks ... a ... lot," she says between huffs and puffs when she finally catches up.

"Sorry 'bout that. But at least we had an authentic experience." We sit on the back step, catching our breath.

"What are you talking about?" she asks.

"Think about it. We just witnessed a hard-core street fight and arrest. And then we assisted in a bloody police investigation. All in The Rocks—where the very first convicts who arrived from England were sentenced to live."

"Authentic experiences are overrated."

Riley, 12

"Wear your swimmers under your clothes. We're going on an adventure," Mom says. Yay! We're obviously going swimming. She continues, "We're going to do Sydney's famous beach walk from Bondi Beach to Bronte Beach. It's supposed to be spectacular."

"Ew. I hate hiking. How long is it?" I ask.

"It's only two miles. Besides, Bondi Beach is one of the most famous beaches in the world." Dad smears sunscreen on his head. "I think we're gonna like it."

"And we have a surprise for you when we get to Bronte Beach." Mom and Dad do the invisible conversation thing.

"You know I hate surprises. Just tell me what it is," Delaney says.

"Nope. You'll have to wait and see," Dad says.

We take the public bus from Sydney Harbour to Bondi Beach. At one stop, a backpacker—wearing a pack taller than her head—climbs on. A smaller bag hangs across her chest.

"Whoa." It's the biggest pack I've ever seen. I elbow Del. "She looks like a turtle carrying around a shell that's way too big."

The bus is packed, so the turtle-girl stands in the aisle. Every time the bus slows down or speeds up, she wobbles.

"There's only one word for the look on her face," Delaney says. "Regret."

When our bus turns a corner, the turtle-girl almost knocks a baby off her mom's lap.

"There's no way I'd lug that much junk around the world." I flashback to when I begged for a bigger suitcase. "What an amateur."

We hop off the bus and walk a block to Bondi Beach, a.k.a. people-watching paradise. Unlike the beach at Port Douglas, this one is a quilt of umbrellas, beach towels, and bronzed Aussies wearing colorful swimmers. Even though it's January, it's the middle of summer here.

SYDNEY, AUSTRALIA: *Bondi Beach*

"I've never seen such a vibrant beach in the middle of a big city," Mom says.

"Man, I'd love to live here." Dad scans the houses on the rocky cliffs.

We spot an empty patch of sand next to a couple of surfer dudes. We plop down on our towels.

"Aren't they worried about stingers?" I ask, watching bodies bob in the surf.

"That's only in the north," Del reminds me.

After a few minutes of ray catching, I ask, "So where's the surprise?"

"That's at Bronte Beach," Mom says.

"Then c'mon. Let's go." I jump up and shake my towel. "There's the trail." I point to the boardwalk along the cliffs.

We wave goodbye to Bondi from the boardwalk that connects separate beaches along the rocky coast. We stop for ice cream at Tamarama Beach. Only one more beach to go. I can't wait. I love surprises.

"I don't know why you're so excited." Delaney licks her ice cream. "You know it's probably one of mom's lame jokes."

Aw, man. She's probably right. We finish our ice cream and continue on the boardwalk. Ten minutes later, we reach Bronte Beach.

"So, where's the big surprise?" I ask, my arms folded across my swimmer.

"Right there." Mom grins and nods toward three kids playing on the beach.

"Delaney! Riley!" the curly-haired siblings squeal, running toward us. We hug, jumping up and down. It's Lucia, Zarah, and Salvador—three of the kids we met on our last night in Hoi An, Vietnam.

"Where's Zofia?" Delaney drops her beach towel in the sand.

"She's at our house helping my mom. You're coming to our house for dinner," twelve-year-old Lucia says. "Let's get in!"

When we get tired of swimming at Bronte, we walk to their house. It sits on a cliff with an insane view of the Pacific Ocean. We spend the afternoon and evening playing with our Aussie friends—the only people we know on the entire continent. After dinner, I meet my new BFF. It's no longer pho. Now, it's *pavlova*, a meringue-and-fruit cloud of Australian yumminess. Thank you, Ms. Emilia!

"That was a great surprise, Mom," I say, climbing into my bunk later that night.

"I thought so too. It was nice to hang out with another family at their house. It felt like home," Mom says in the darkness.

"It's so random. Three weeks ago, we met in Asia. And tonight, we had dinner together in Australia," Delaney says. "Have you ever noticed that the more you travel, the smaller the world gets?"

"And isn't it weird that it only takes one friend on an entire continent to make you feel at home?" I smile to myself as I snuggle under the covers on my last night in Australia.

SYDNEY, AUSTRALIA: Zarah and Riley at Bronte Beach.

PASSPORT LESSON #9:

In a sea of strangers, it only takes one friend to feel at home.
Be that friend.

AUSTRALIA
High-Low Report Card

	🙂	🙁
Delaney	New Year's Eve in Sydney	Heat in Port Douglas
Riley	Scuba diving on the Great Barrier Reef	Stinger season
Mom	New Year's Eve in Sydney	Stinger season
Dad	New Year's Eve in Sydney	Heat in Port Douglas

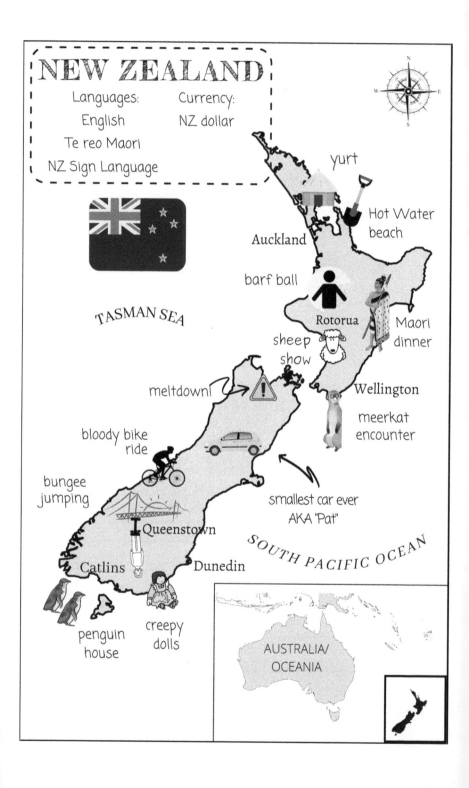

17.
Adventure Capital of the World

January 4–February 3

Life can be wonderful if you choose adventure rather than fear.

— CHIP GAINES, *CAPITAL GAINES*

Delaney, 14

"I think I'm gonna like it here," I say as we unload our bags at our new home on New Zealand's North Island.

"Do you mean 'here' as in the *yurt*? Or New Zealand?" Dad asks.

"Both." I step inside the gigantic, circular, heavy-duty tent with real furniture.

"Whoa, this is sooo cool. It's a convertible house. You can roll up the sides if the weather is good, or put them down if it's cold or rainy," Riley says.

Inside the yurt sit two queen beds, a sofa, and a kitchen. Stacks of books and record albums tower over a turntable. The bathroom is outside. Since the room is round, the furniture sits at weird angles. A note tops the fruit pile on the kitchen table.

ENJOY THE FRUIT IN THE ORCHARD.
WELCOME TO THE COROMANDEL PENINSULA.

I grab a plum and take a bite.

"I've got some good news and bad news about New Zealand. Which do you want first?" Mom flips through the guest manual.

"The good," Ri and I say. "Jinx! One-two-three."

"You won't be doing much homeschool over the next month. Because the bad news is that free Wi-Fi is basically non-existent in New Zealand."

"No Wi-Fi?!" How am I supposed to binge on Netflix when they think I'm doing homeschool?

"We don't need the Internet. New Zealand is the adventure capital of the world," Dad says.

"True. There are more ways to hurt yourself here than anywhere else. And don't even bring up bungee jumping again. There are plenty of other stupid things to do," Mom says.

"Like Zorbing!" Riley jumps into a hula-hoop move.

"Exactly. That's in Rotorua. We'll be there in a few days. The plan for the month is to drive from the top of the North Island to the bottom of the South Island. That's like driving from New York to California with super fun stuff to do at every stop. Today we're starting with Hot Water Beach."

"You know what that means?" Riley whispers as we walk to the tiny hatchback. "Dad's gonna want to stop at every brown sign he sees."

"Brown signs" is our code for stopping at every view, monument, and hike that we pass. Almost three thousand miles of boring brown signs and bad-dad jokes.

Kill. Me. Now.

Riley, 12

WHOA! WHAT A BIZARRE BEACH. Long shovels, not beach umbrellas, stick out of the sand. Women in bikinis and shirtless men dig furiously along the beach. With churned-up piles of gritty brown sand, this beach looks like a construction zone. Not a place to chill.

"What's the deal with this place? It looks like a scene from *Holes*. Except the diggers aren't juvenile delinquents," I say.

"It does. But unlike the characters in *Holes*, these diggers know what they're looking for. Hot water." Mom points to groups of people sitting in big sand holes. "See those people. They've found it, now they're relaxing in their personal hot tubs."

"So we've got to make our own," Dad says.

"Oooh, look! There's one!" I point to an empty, water-filled hole the size of a baby pool.

"Perfect," Delaney says. "Let's get it."

I dash across the sand and jump into my private hot tub. Bummer! The water is cold. No wonder it's empty.

"They need a map showing where to dig," I say, noticing the abandoned pools across the hot tub zone.

We spot a friendly-looking man taking a shoveling break.

"So, how does this work?" Dad asks.

"There are two geothermal fissures below the sand. You want to dig until you find a hot spring leak. Once you find your hot water faucet, then dig out your hot tub and let it fill with water. But be careful, it's scalding. Use a bucket to add ocean water so you don't get burned." He points to the plastic buckets scattered around.

This is gonna be so fun. I grab a nearby shovel and start digging. I plunge my shovel into the wet sand and toss it aside. I do it again. And again. And again. Ten minutes pass. The hole isn't even big enough for me, and I haven't found any hot water.

I'm out of breath. My back and arms are killing me. I take a break and stab my shovel into the sand. Resting against my shovel, I scan the hot tub zone to see if my family has had better luck. Wouldn't you know it? There's De-Lazy—chillin' with another family in their spa. Ugh! How does she do that?!

Mom waves me over. "Delaney made friends. They invited us to join them."

I squeeze between the Argentinian sisters. I lie back in their homemade hot tub, propping my feet on a bucket to protect them from a hot spot. Mooching off someone else is much easier than digging your own. My dad sits next to theirs. His name is Mateo, and he's in real estate, too.

"The six of us are traveling around New Zealand for six weeks in an RV," Mateo explains.

"Oh man. I'd love to do that," Dad says in his best Spanglish.

"It's a terrible idea," the oldest daughter whispers to Del and me, shaking her head slowly.

No way, José, would I spend six weeks in a hair-mobile with Del.

COROMANDEL, NEW ZEALAND–JAN 2014: Relaxing at Hot Water Beach

When spa time is over, we grab our stuff and walk to the car. "Can we get ice cream now?" I remember passing a cute ice cream shop in Hahei.

"First, we're going on a hike that Mateo recommended. It's only ten minutes from here. We'll get ice cream after that," Dad promises.

I whisper to Del, "Here we go. It's brown-sign time."

We drive to the trailhead of the mile-and-a-half *tramp* (that's what they call hiking in New Zealand). The paved trail starts near a bright green field overlooking the ocean. The ocean and sky, wearing the same shade of brilliant blue, blend together. Puffy white clouds fill the top half of the blue backdrop. We hike up steep trails into a forest, where tree-sized ferns form a tropical tunnel.

"I'm having Panama flashbacks," Delaney says. "But I'm not freaking out. You wanna know why?"

"Why?"

"Because there are no snakes in New Zealand."

"There aren't any in Iceland either," Dad adds.

A few minutes later, we exit the fern forest, and the ocean reappears. I can't wait for this hike to be over so I can get some ice cream. Just ahead, a steep wooden staircase leads down to the beach. I make my way down until my toes touch the sand. To the left, a gigantic limestone arch leads to another beach. Déjà vu! I've never been here, but I've seen this before. I run through the arch to the other beach where a massively famous white rock juts out of the ocean. My family catches up.

"This place is Insta-famous!" Delaney says.

"It was in the *Chronicles of Narnia* movie!" I say.

"I've done this virtual walk on the treadmill," Mom says.

"Welcome to Cathedral Cove," Dad announces in his tour guide voice. "Not all brown signs lead to boring."

"Why didn't we get a bigger car?" I cram my suitcase into the back of the tiny hatchback. Even though we don't have much stuff, we have to arrange our bags like puzzle pieces to make them fit.

"In Vietnam, they could get it all on a motorbike. No problem," Delaney says.

"Renting a car for a month in New Zealand is expensive," Mom says. "Would you rather have more space or more adventures?"

"More adventures," Del and I say.

"Speaking of adven—" I say.

"Don't go there. We're not bungee jumping," Mom says.

Bummer. I'm losing my touch. I'll compliment her first next time I try.

"If we're gonna spend a month in this car, then she needs a name. I think we should call her Pat," I say.

"Pat it is. Now, who's ready to visit Bilbo Baggins?" Dad asks. "Next stop is Matamata."

"If Hobbiton is half as cool as Hogwarts, this is gonna be a good day," I say.

J. R. R. Tolkien created Hobbiton like J. K. Rowling created Hogwarts. Even though we aren't *Lord of the Rings* superfans—like we are with Harry Potter—we did watch the movies before our trip. Since they are all filmed in New Zealand, it's a good way to see the country if you can't see it in person.

Two hours later, we step out of Pat and into The Shire, where we spend another two hours pretending to be Hobbits. I imagine myself living behind each brightly painted round door of the forty-four Hobbit Holes.

"This is like something out of a movie." I scan the Hobbit Holes, rolling hills, and green pastures that fill my views in every direction.

"It is the movie set. Duh," Delaney reminds me, sitting underneath the ginormous Party Tree.

And just like in the movie, a guy up the hillside begins running down the grassy slope.

"I'M GOING ON AN *AD-VEN-TURE*!" He jumps a wooden fence, nails the landing, and keeps running.

"That would've been hilarious if he'd busted," Delaney says.

We finish our Hobbiton tour at the Green Dragon Inn, where I find a rack of dress-up clothes. Jackpot! I handpick the perfect Hobbit outfit: a brown baggy jacket, a brown wool scarf, a beige straw hat, and a fancy pink lace umbrella with green tassels.

Sitting at a wooden table in the dark pub, Delaney says, "Thanks for bringing us here. It's really cool that we've gotten to see the movie sets from two of the most famous fantasy series ever written."

As we clink mugs of apple cider, Mom says, "Cheers to Tolkien and his famous words, 'not all who wander are lost.' I wouldn't want to wander this world with anyone else."

MATAMATA, NEW ZEALAND: Hobbit hole at Hobbiton

Delaney, 14

Social studies lesson

A *hangi* is a traditional Māori dinner where the food cooks in an underground earth oven. They dig an *umu* in the ground and line it with hot rocks. The Māori place baskets of food on the stones and cover the pit, where the food cooks for three to four hours.

"WHERE TO NEXT?" I climb into Pat's backseat.

"A hangi in Rotorua," Mom says. "It's less than an hour."

"What's up with all these weird names? Like Matamata? And Rotorua?" Riley asks.

"They aren't weird. It's the Māori language," I explain. "I was just reading about it."

"Fill us in, Del," Dad says, "so we'll know more before our dinner tonight."

"Well, the Māori are the original Kiwis. They came from Polynesia around 1300. They had The Land of the Long White Cloud—that's what they called New Zealand—all to themselves for centuries. The first White guys from Europe didn't show up 'til the 1600s. But when they did, they fought over the land."

"Doesn't that sound familiar?" Dad says.

"Yep. Most people speak English. But te reo Māori is the language of the indigenous people."

"That's interesting," Mom says.

"If you think that's interesting, would you believe there's a hill on the North Island that holds the Guinness World Record for the longest name? It has eighty-five letters."

TAUMATAWHAKATANGIHANGAKOAUAU

OTAMATEATURIPUKAKAPIKIMAUNGAH

ORONUKUPOKAIWHENUAKITANATAHU

"Try putting that in Google Maps," Riley says.

"No kidding. They call it Taumata for short. You know what else is super cool? New Zealand is the first country to name sign language as an official language."

I keep sharing tidbits about Māori culture from my book until we reach our dinner destination.

"Did you know that the Māori greeting is called *hongi*? Instead of shaking hands, the two people touch their foreheads and noses together, then breathe in at the same time."

"Ew. What if one has bad breath?" Ri says.

"You're so weird."

When we arrive, I climb out of Pat and follow a group of tourists down a dusty path through the woods. We reach the Wai-o-whiro stream, where trees and ferns stretch to the sky. People and tree trunks alternate along the dirt bank on both sides of the water. The moonlight slices through the trees, revealing the eerie fog rising above the river. Knowing there's no possibility of slithering snakes nearby helps me enjoy the moment.

Tribal chants cut through the forest sounds as a canoe cuts through the fog. Eight Māori men paddle the *waka*, with fiery torches projecting from its sides. They chant in unison, alternating strokes with over-the-head paddle claps. Intricate tattoos cover their faces. Brown loincloths, hanging from their large-but-soft bellies, reveal muscular legs. It reminds me of the Emberá Indians and the dugout canoes. But the Emberá didn't tattoo their faces, and their loincloths were much smaller.

After their dramatic entrance, we follow the dirt path to the dirt-floor theater. Māori men and women rest against tree trunks with scary faces carved into them. Flames dance in the rock circle firepit in the middle of the dirt stage. The women wear something resembling burlap, caveman-style across one shoulder. Their tattooed chins look like beards from a distance.

When the drums beat, the men and women line up. They chant like they've been sucker-punched in the stomach while stomping their feet, slapping their bodies, and making jarring arm motions. They move in unison. But the most fascinating part of the *haka* is when they make the faces. Their eyes bulge, their cheeks puff, and they stick out their tongues as far as they can.

ROTORUA, NEW ZEALAND–JAN 2014: Maori haka

"Is this supposed to be funny or scary?" Ri whispers to me.

"I'm not sure, but it's kinda both."

While we've been watching the haka, our dinner has been cooking in a Māori crockpot.

When the cultural performance is over, we join a hundred or so visitors in a large dining room. We share a table with two older couples from New Zealand and Australia.

"Kia ora koutou!" Our mic-holding-host, Anaru, welcomes us. "Is anyone here from England?" Four people raise their hands. "Hello, and welcome," he says. "How about France?" A few more hands go up. "Bonjour. What about China?" Hands shoot up from two tables. "Nǐ hǎo. And Brazil?" More hands. "Olá. Kenya, anyone?" One hand. "Jambo." Anaru randomly throws out country names until people raise their hands, then he greets them in their language. I've never heard of some of them.

"Holy cow. This is amazing," Mom whispers. Dad's jaw hangs open.

Country by country, Anaru makes his way around the room. And the world. When he has greeted visitors from most major and minor countries, he finally says, "And who's from Australia?" Half the hands in the room shoot up.

"G'day, mates!" Anaru belts out with a gigantic smile and teasing voice.

"AUSSIE, AUSSIE, AUSSIE! OI, OI, OI!" Half the room erupts in a raucous cheer. They repeat it several times with the same enthusiasm that people yell *ROLL TIDE!* or *WAR EAGLE!* at football games in Alabama. But this is so much cooler because it's a national cheer that unites *all* Australians. I wish the United States had something like that.

While we eat, Anaru shares more about the Māori culture. The best part is when he explains how their sports teams do the haka challenge before international games.

Back at our motel, we watch YouTubes of the New Zealand rugby teams performing the haka for their opponents before the World Cup. The two teams line up in the center of the field. Then the Kiwis break into an intimidating haka.

"It's like a dance-off, but the other team has no moves," Riley says.

"I love how the Kiwis have blended the indigenous culture into the mainstream. They didn't just put it in a box," I say.

"You're absolutely right. They've made it part of their national identity in a way that celebrates and integrates their diversity," Mom says.

I wish our country did that too.

"Y'ALL ARE CRAZY." Mom signs the Zorb paperwork. "Why would anyone want to roll down a hill in a giant hamster ball?"

"Because the Kiwis invented it, so it's gotta be fun." Dad turns to me. "How many rides should we do?"

You get a discount if you pay for two or more rides up front. We choose three rides each—one for each track: Straight, Mega, and Sidewinder. Next, we choose how we want to roll. Option one: strapped into a seat suspended in the middle of the ball. Or option two: sitting in a pool of water at the bottom of the ball. Dad and I choose one; Riley picks two.

Giant, translucent spheres balance at the edge of the steep green hill. A long gate arm keeps the balls from rolling forward. It reminds me of how parents extend their right arm over the passenger seat when they slam on the brakes. If the seatbelt doesn't work, what do they think their arm is gonna do?

Ri and I sprint up the hill chasing the same prize—the first Zorb ride. With my extra five inches and cross-country training, it's no contest. I climb into the translucent globe through the circular opening and hop into the suspended seat. The Zorber connects my straps and buckles as if he's launching a space shuttle.

"Have a great ride." He unlatches the gate and the arm swings away.

The ball starts rolling. One rotation. This. Is. Awesome! Another spin leads into another. I'm picking up speed now, somersaulting down the hill. But the awesomeness is wearing off. Fast. I lose count of the rolling-ralph-rocket rotations. Finally, the ball-of-misery slows near the end of the track. I climb out, holding my head, staggering around.

"How was it?" Mom asks.

"It was great," I say with fake enthusiasm. I can't give her the pleasure of being right.

"Aw, good. Looked awful to me. Your dad's about to go."

A few minutes later, Dad crawls out of his ball. He looks bad. Really bad. He clutches his stomach, stumbles to a nearby bean-bag, and falls into it. I sink into the beanbag next to his.

"I think I'm gonna throw up," he admits. What an amateur.

"What did you think was gonna happen after the barf ball?" Classic Mom offers no sympathy for our bad decisions.

We watch Riley's ball barrel down the slope. Water sloshes around like a washing machine. When it comes to a stop, water and Ri pour out the opening.

"That was a blast," she squeals. "Let's go again!"

"I'm good. I'll just watch," Dad says.

"Isn't that a brilliant pricing strategy?" Mom says. "I wonder how many people pay for two or more rides and then quit after the first one. I bet they make more money off the rides people skip than the ones they take."

Riley and I walk up the hill for round two. She can go first this time.

ROTORUA, NEW ZEALAND: *Delaney Zorbs down the hill in a giant hamster ball.*

Riley, 12

"WHY DO WE have to go to a sheep show?" I ask, opening Pat's back door. "Driving across New Zealand *is* a sheep show."

"I agree. But everyone says we have to go," Mom says. "Besides, you can't visit New Zealand without learning something about sheep."

"Did you know there are nine sheep for every person in New Zealand? I read that somewhere," the backseat bookworm says.

Over the past week, we've driven past thousands of sheep grazing in pastures. I don't know how you make a show out of that. They all look the same to me.

We stop at a light, and a dude driving a funky minivan pulls up next to us. Spray-paint psychedelic designs cover the van. Thick white letters scrawled across the back read:

> THERE ARE THREE KINDS OF PEOPLE
> THOSE WHO CAN COUNT,
> AND THOSE WHO CAN'T!

"Oh my gosh. That's hilarious." Mom digs for her camera.

"You'd never see that in Vestavia," I say.

The Kiwi nods his head, smiling at our reaction. A few minutes later, we park Pat in front of the Agrodome. We find four seats inside the barn-auditorium, where rows of wooden benches face the stage like an old church. Platform steps rise from one end of the stage to the middle peak, then go down again. The steps form an upside-down V. A shorter V sits in front of the other one, creating two rows on display. A sign hangs from each step—nineteen in all. The plaques display words like Suffolk, Corriedale, Texel, and Black Romney.

A bald cowboy named KJ leads a parade of nineteen sheep into the auditorium. The walking-wool-balls mosey to their designated spots and stand over their breed's name. The most important sheep—Merino—takes his place-of-honor on the peak of the back *V*. It's a sheep beauty pageant, and I can't decide which is my favorite.

The contestants range in color from dirty white, to beige, to gray, to faded black. Their toothpick legs poke out of their puffy, cotton-ball coats. Thick horns curl around the faces of Merino, Dorset Horn, and Drysdale. Merino's small, white face tries to escape the gray wool swallowing him. Drysdale's shaggy coat looks more sheepdog than sheep. Dreadlock curtains cover Cotswald's face. I was so wrong. Thinking all sheep are alike is as wrong as thinking all dogs are alike. KJ grabs his microphone and teaches me everything I never wanted to know about sheep.

Baa-baa sheep school!

Different sheep produce wool for various purposes. Sheep's wool is used for carpet, boots, and blankets. Merino wool—the most expensive of all—is used for fine clothing. Back in colonial times, wool was used to make wigs.

Grade A wool comes from the top of the sheep. It's soft, fluffy, and the most expensive.

Grade B wool comes from the belly, so it's usually full of grass and thorns.

By now, most of the sheep are snoozing on their platforms. They know this stuff already.

KJ turns and opens a wooden door. A frantic sheep darts out. The sheep-shearer snags the furball, plopping it on its rear between KJ's legs. He wiggles, trying to escape the humiliation of his public haircut. KJ grabs his shears and begins.

"The average shearer makes a dollar-eighty for each sheep he shears, and most can shear 280 to 350 sheep a day. The record number of sheep sheared in a nine-hour day is 723. The record time for shearing one sheep is 14.2 seconds."

Before we know it, the sheep is bald. Does he want to hide under a beach towel too? When KJ asks for volunteers, my hand shoots up like a rocket. So does my dad's. KJ chooses both of us. I speed-walk to the stage and bounce up the steps. Delaney would rather crawl under the bench than be on stage. KJ pulls out a milk-filled baby bottle (yay! I can't wait to feed something) and hands it to my dad. Bummer. He gets to feed a baby deer.

KJ points to the fat cow standing next to me. "Squat. You're gonna milk her."

I grab one of the finger-shaped things hanging from her rubbery udder. Ew. Ew. Ew. When I squeeze, a thin stream of milk shoots into the bucket. How did my Nanaw spend her childhood doing this? After squeezing out a spoonful of milk, I wipe my hands on my jeans and stand. KJ awards me a Certificate of Udderance.

After the show, we take pictures with our favorite sheep. We all choose the one with dreadlocks. Cheek-to-cheek with Cotswald, Dad covers his bald head with the sheep's blond dreads.

ROTORUA, NEW ZEALAND: Dale tries out dreadlocks.

"I need to go to the baa-baa shop," Dad says, doing his best sheep imitation.

"That was really baaaad." I crack up at my joke.

"Your jokes are lame by themselves. But together, they're udder-ly tragic." Mom jumps on our bad-joke train.

"I'm begging you. Either take me home, or shoot me now," Delaney says.

She's so dramatic.

ROTORUA, NEW ZEALAND: Agrodome Sheep Show

Delaney, 14

"WHO WOULD'VE THOUGHT a sheep show could be so much fun?" Riley buckles her seatbelt.

"Yeah, that was awesome. Where are we heading now?" I ask.

"Wai-O-Tapu. We just pulled onto the Thermal Explorer Highway. Why don't you give us some info about the area," Dad says.

I flip through the guidebook looking for some fun factoids.

Ring of Fire

The Thermal Explorer Highway connects New Zealand's geothermal playgrounds. New Zealand sits on the Ring of Fire, a horseshoe-shaped fault line that runs from New Zealand, up the east coast of Asia, down the west coast of the U.S., and ends at the bottom tip of South America. Fifteen countries around the Pacific Ocean sit along the Ring of Fire. Most of the world's volcanoes and earthquakes occur along this horseshoe.

"So basically, New Zealand is the southern hemisphere's version of Iceland—the Land of Fire and Ice—but with a ton of sheep roaming around," I say.

We pull into the Wai-O-Tapu lot and park next to another aerosol-art van, this one painted like a Jimi Hendrix album cover. Spray-painted lyrics cover the back. I don't know Jimi Hendrix or the song, *Purple Haze*, but my parents do. My dad sings it while playing air guitar.

Wai-O-Tapu means *sacred waters* in Māori. The boardwalk

around the geothermal park takes us from boiling mud baths, to colorful pools, to the Lady Knox geyser. Steam rises above Artist's Palette, a geothermal pond resembling melted yellow, orange, and green crayons. Devil's Bath is a crater waterhole the exact color of Shrek. Champagne Pool is the one people compare to Yellowstone. Oyster Pool's sea-glass-colored water makes me want to swim. But don't mistake the serene and psychedelic waters as places to take a dip. You would boil to death in some of these.

ROTORUA, New Zealand: Wai-O-Tapu Thermal Wonderland

We pile into Pat and head to our last stop on the North Island: Wellington. The most-southern-capital-city in the world is home to Wellington Zoo. And meerkat encounters. Riley's obsession with *Meerkat Manor* rivals my obsession with *Criminal Minds*. I have to admit, a meerkat encounter sounds much better than a serial killer encounter.

After Welly, we drive Pat onto the ferry and sail to the South

Island. Our first stop is Motueka. Like most people, we're here to tramp around Abel Tasman National Park. But we also find a great surprise. Wi-Fi! When the motel owner found out we are traveling long term and trying to homeschool, he gave us his network code. Jackpot! We've been disconnected for two weeks. Time to rejoin the world, even if that means online math lessons.

Ri and I sit at the small table in our living room. Laptops open. Earbuds in. Mom's on the sofa across from us, watching the flat-screen TV mounted over our heads. "Motel" in New Zealand is not the same as "motel" in the U.S. Motels in the U.S. are usually outdated rooms with two double beds covered with gross bedspreads. Motels in New Zealand are small apartments. Every New Zealand motel we've stayed in so far (except for the yurt) has been a two-bedroom apartment. The second bedroom always has twin beds or bunks. New Zealand is made for family travel.

When Riley sniffles, I look up from my Algebra lesson. Tears stream down her face. Math can't be that bad.

"What's wrong?"

"All my friends are being asked to the winter dance." Riley rechecks her phone.

"So?"

"So, I don't want to miss it." She wipes tears off her red cheeks.

"The winter dance is lame."

"Maybe because *you* were afraid Matthew might try to hold your hand. I want to go!"

"You know what's more important than the winter dance?" I lash back. "The eighth-grade banquet. And if we don't get home soon, the only guys without dates will be the ones who still tell fart jokes or pick their nose." I turn to Mom and cross my arms. "I *have* to be back by spring break. Everything good happens after that."

It's weird. For the past two weeks, I've barely thought about home. Now that we have Wi-Fi—and we're reconnected with the world—it's all I think about. What are my friends doing? Who's hanging out together? Do they miss me? Do they even remember me???

"Did y'all feel that?" Mom asks, ignoring my comment about spring break.

"What?"

"The floor just vibrated." She sits motionless. "There it goes again."

We turn on the news and learn that a 6.2 magnitude earthquake struck the southeast corner of the North Island near Wellington. People across the country felt the shocks. Welcome to the Ring of Fire.

FOR THE NEXT TWO WEEKS, we explore the South Island. We strap crampons to our shoes and hike on Fox Glacier. We marvel at Pancake Rocks, bizarre geologic formations that look like pancake mountains. We climb the World's Steepest Street in Dunedin and fall in love with its beautiful train station. We visit libraries. Not to check out books, but to mooch the free Wi-Fi.

We buy fruit from roadside honor stands, where farmers leave fruit baskets in wooden sheds perched on wagon wheels. The prices are scrawled on a chalkboard. We pick our favorite fruits and drop money in the metal containers. It's a great idea that could never work in most places.

We count lots of sheep and have even more conversations. Because that's what you do when trapped in a car for thousands of miles without online access.

"If you could have dinner with any living American, who would it be?" I ask.

"That's easy," Mom says. "Condoleezza Rice. She's from Birmingham and the first Black female Secretary of State."

"I agree. Condi is smart, musically talented, and loves sports. The trifecta," Dad says.

"I read that Dr. Rice speaks a bunch of languages, so I'll pick her too."

"What does the Secretary of State do?" Riley asks.

"They advise the president on foreign matters. They travel to countries around the world and meet with their leaders," Mom says.

"Then I'll pick her too. Lots of passport stamps mean lots of great stories."

We're cruising along the two-lane road between Dunedin and the Catlins when we pass through a tiny town. A few small houses with picket-fenced front yards sit along the quiet street. A homemade sign with DOLLYLAND stenciled across it hangs in front of one.

"Oh man, we gotta stop," Dad says, pulling Pat to the side of the road. We park behind a minivan masterpiece. Bold red spray paint shares classic Kiwi advice:

IF AT FIRST YOU DON'T SUCCEED,
SKYDIVING AIN'T FOR YOU!

"That's my favorite one yet." Mom pulls out her camera.

Mom, Ri, and I step onto the porch and ring the bell. A quiet man opens the door. "Come in," he whispers. When I step inside, the hairs prickle on the back of my neck. Hundreds of old baby dolls and Barbies line the walls. Plastic fairy dolls dangle from the ceiling.

What. The. Heck?! This could be the opening scene of a *Criminal Minds* episode. Mom and Ri have matching saucer eyes. After a quick picture, we skirt-skirt out of there.

Out front, Dad's talking to a couple and their teenage son, Ben.

"So, what'd you think of that?" Ben's dad nods toward the house.

"So creepy."

This family has been sailing around the world for five years. This is their last year before they return to California so Ben can start high school.

"I haven't sat in a classroom since third grade," the normal-seeming teen says.

This kid deserves a medal. He's spent five years trapped on a boat with his parents. Five months with my sister isn't so bad ... as long as I'm home by spring break.

DUNEDIN, NEW ZEALAND: The stunning Dunedin Railway Station

Riley, 12

I LOVE WANAKA (rhymes with Hanukkah)! Locals say it's how Queenstown was before the world discovered it.

We spent yesterday being confused at Puzzling World. It's a crazy place full of optical illusions, mind-benders, and a giant outdoor maze. The funniest was the room painted like an ancient Roman public bathroom. Real benches, with potty holes every three feet, run along the walls and "join" the virtual painted benches, creating the coolest illusion. Dad and Del smiled, but I gave a constipated grimace when Mom took our family potty shot with a bunch of Roman guys. Kiwi humor is the best.

I buckle my helmet and hop on the mountain bike.

"Be sure to stay on the family trail." The bike shop dude points to a line on the map Dad's holding.

"Will do." Dad stuffs the map in his backpack and hops on his bike.

WANAKA, NEW ZEALAND: The family-friendly bike path at Lake Wanaka.

"We haven't been on bikes since Lucca." Delaney pedals beside me on Lake Wanaka's paved path.

"Check out the lake." I turn toward Delaney. "It's sooo bl—"

Eeek! I veer off the path, heading straight for spikey bushes. My bike topples and I fall into sticker-mania.

"Ow! Ow! Ow!" Tiny needles poke out of my hands, feet (I'm wearing sandals), and handlebars. Mom helps me up, and we pull the stickers out of my hands and feet. But we can't get them out of the rubber grips. She kicks off her shoes and peels off her socks.

"Here." Mom hands me her warm socks. "Wrap these around your handles."

Ew. Not ideal, but better than gripping needles. Besides, I miss riding my bike. I'm not gonna let a few needles stabbing my hands steal my bike-riding joy. I drag my bike out of the bushes and hop back on. After cruising along the lake for a while, Dad turns off the wide, gravel path onto a mountain biking trail.

"The family trail goes this way," he says.

The course quickly turns from fun-dips-and-curves to narrow-steep-and-scary. On the right edge of the three-foot-wide path stands a rocky mountain wall. The left side of the track drops straight into the lake. Is this what Kiwis call family-friendly?! Rocks and roots jut out of the steep trail. I concentrate on the path, trying to avoid the stones that might launch me into the lake and the riders coming from the other direction.

I'm in front, then Mom, Del, and Dad. I pedal slowly. Since Kiwis drive on the left, I should ride on the left. But I hug the mountainside anyway, out of fear and habit. Shirtless guys blast past us. No one talks. We're too busy not dying. When the trail levels out, I stop. Mom and Delaney stop behind me. We lean on our bikes, one foot on the ground, waiting for Dad. We wait. And wait. What's taking him so long? He's the most experienced mountain biker of us all.

"This isn't a good sign." Mom glances at her watch.

A few minutes later, blood-and-dirt-covered Dad catches up. Bright red stains dot his ripped T-shirt. He's bleeding from his shoulder, elbow, hands, and shins.

"Are you okay?" Mom asks.

"I hit a rock and flipped over the front handlebars. Fortunately, the water bottles in the backpack cushioned my fall." He washes his wounds with lake water.

With no other options, we keep riding the gnarly trail trying to avoid death. I want to cry, but what's the point? Tears can't fix this. I pedal standing up, weaving between rocks and roots while avoiding the mountain wall and cliff. For an instant, I take my eyes off the ground and glance ahead.

"Look! It's an escape path!"

"Fabulous," Mom says, huffing and puffing.

A narrow path leads into a field. We push our bikes across the private property until we reach a fence with stairs.

"We obviously aren't the first people to need rescuing." Dad carries our bikes up and down the wooden steps, crossing the fence.

"It's the stairway to civilization," Delaney says when her bike is safely on the paved street. We pedal along the empty road for miles. When we reach an intersection close to town, I get off my bike. I'm exhausted. In the middle of the traffic-less street, I collapse. My bike crashes on top of me.

"Are you okay?" Mom hops off her bike.

A car stops, and the driver rolls down his window. "Do you need some plasters?"

"What?" Mom says, scrunching her eyebrows.

"She's bleeding. Do you need some plasters? I can run home and get you some."

"Ohhh. Band-Aids," Mom says. "Thank you, but we're almost back."

Legs locked so I won't bend my knees, I hobble back to town.

"You look like a zombie wearing a poopy diaper," Mom calls from behind.

I cry-laugh. Covered in dirt and blood, we survive the ten-mile family-friendly bike ride.

They don't call it the Adventure Capital of the World for nothing.

WANAKA, NEW ZEALAND: Puzzling World's Roman bath house illusion

MILFORD SOUND, NEW ZEALAND

Delaney, 14

"You've gotta work your magic," I tell Ri. "We're gonna be in Queenstown in a few days."

"I've tried guilt, tears, and compliments. Mom's not budging."

"Emotion won't work with her. We need to use logic. And competition."

Only a few more days until we reach the epicenter of the Adventure Capital. And I can't leave there without bungee jumping. But for now, I get to curl it up with Lilly and Moby, the house cats at our beach cottage on Curio Bay. We're spending a couple of days on the very southern tip of New Zealand. Nothing between here and Antarctica but the ocean. We're at the end of the Earth. And it feels like it.

The wood fireplace in the corner heats the cottage. The calico curls at my feet, and Riley pets the gray one lying next to her. There's nothing to do here but gaze at the rugged beach and read. I could stay here forever. A penguin couple lives under the house. They spend their days riding the waves and return to their nest beneath our beds each night. It's here that Mom gets the terrible news that her other Uncle Charles passed away. Two favorite uncles in less than two months. She's devastated, but I already know we won't be going home.

After a detour to postcard-perfect Milford Sound, we're finally here.

"Did you know Queenstown has over two hundred adventure activities?" I ask while we explore the cute downtown. Queenstown's super-blue lake is the exact shade of Mom's rain jacket.

"Sounds like the Fountain of Youth to me," Dad says.

"Sounds like the Fountain of Stupidity," Mom says.

I glance at Riley.

"You know bungee jumping in New Zealand is *the* traveler's badge of honor. Nothing else even comes close." Nice start, Ri.

I tag-team. "Not Zorbing, or luging, or jet-boating. Nothing."

"I can't think of anything cooler than bungee jumping off the bridge where it all started." Good one, Dad.

"Did you know more than two million people have successfully jumped off the Kawarau Bridge?" Riley pauses like a pro. "That's safer than scuba diving."

"Fine!" Mom says. "We can look into it."

Yes! Ri and I silently high-five behind Mom's back. Then Riley tops it off with a tiny celebration move. Since we happen to be standing in front of the AJ Hackett Bungy shop, we go inside and get the good-news-bad-news.

The good news: I book my bungee jump for tomorrow. The bad news: they reject Dad and Ri as jumpers. Dad because of his detached ACLs and Riley for the usual.

"Sorry, but the minimum weight is thirty-five kilos." The employee rubs his beard.

"What's that in pounds?" Riley asks with hopeful desperation.

His eyes scan a small chart. "Seventy-seven."

Even if Riley put on everything in her suitcase, she wouldn't weigh seventy.

"If I weigh enough by tomorrow, can I jump?" Riley pleads.

"Sure," the guy says, chuckling.

I'm hyped, but I play it cool because of Ri. We go to dinner, and Riley orders like she's a college football player. She eats it all, then orders ice cream. I hope she doesn't throw it all up. I can't share a room with that kind of disappointment.

IT's JUMP DAY. Riley gorges on a gigantic breakfast and lunch, then puts on her heaviest shoes. We drive to the bridge for my twelve-thirty jump. Riley runs inside the shop and steps on the scale. Seventy-one.

"IT'S NOT FAIR!" Tears pour down Riley's face. "Bungee jumping was *my* idea! I'm the one who wanted to do this!"

"I'm sorry, Ri. You can do it somewhere else when you're older." Mom tries to hug her, but Riley pushes her away.

"I HATE BEING SMALL!!! This is the one thing I wanted to do more than anything else on this whole trip!" Riley wipes snot from her nose. "The Riley Reinvention Project is a total failure, and I'm going home exactly the same!"

"I'm disappointed too," Dad says, trying not-to-cry.

We go to the observation deck and watch in silence as people jump, dive, and fling themselves off the bridge, with only a giant rubber band yanking them from death.

When it's my turn, Mom hugs me. "Don't die, or I'll kill you."

I sit on the two-foot-by-three-foot wooden platform, perched 141 feet over a swiftly moving river. A tattooed Kiwi straps my ankles together before I shuffle to the edge of the platform.

"Wave to the camera," he says.

I wave quickly, my body tingling. It's like I'm watching myself in a dream, doing something I'd never do in real life. A giddy-dizziness washes over me when I see the river below. Terror and exhilaration race through my body. I can't tell which is winning. I feel powerful. And I feel alive. Six months ago, I never would've done this. But I'm not that same person.

The jumpmaster counts down, "Three. Two. One."

I fall forward off the bridge, leaving the old Delaney behind.

As I plunge fourteen stories toward the river, terror loses to exhilaration. I beat my anxiety.

I. Can. Do. Anything.

QUEENSTOWN, NEW ZEALAND: *Delaney bungee jumps off the Kawarau bridge. Photo credit: AJ Hackett Bungy New Zealand.*

I stretch my arms toward the river. Just as I'm about to touch the water—*boing!*—the bungee yanks me back. I recoil, then I free fall again, over and over until my rope stops swinging. I'm dangling upside-down a few feet above the river. A guy in a nearby raft extends a long pole toward me. I grab it, and he pulls me into the boat. I lie on my back—my chest heaving—while a team quickly unstraps my ankles and paddles me to shore. My parents are waiting at the top of the steep gravel path.

"How was it?" Dad yells.

"IT WAS INCREDIBLE! There's no way to describe the rush." I lock eyes with Mom. "You have to do it."

"No, thank you."

"C'mon, Kel. Ri and I would give anything to do it, but we can't. You'll regret it if you don't," Dad says.

"I don't want to stand on the bridge, much less jump off it."

"Dad's right. You're gonna regret it if you don't do it," I say.

I walk my mom to the shop while she considers it. She hates regret more than heights.

"What if I get on the bridge and change my mind? Can I get my money back?" she asks the guy behind the counter.

"Nope. No refunds if you chicken out."

Bungee jumping costs over a hundred dollars. If she pays, she won't back out. She's more scared of losing money than jumping off a bridge. She signs the forms, exhaling deeply, then slides the money across the counter. He reaches for it. But Mom snatches it back.

"I don't know if I can do it," she whines like she's four, not forty-four.

"Yes, you can." I slide the cash toward the guy.

Just as he reaches for it, she yanks it back again.

"You're being ridiculous, Mom. Make a decision."

"Fine. I'm doing it." She pushes the money across the counter one last time.

Surrounded by people half her age, Mom waits on the bridge for her turn. Dad and I join Ri on the observation deck and make bets on whether she'll chicken out.

Twenty minutes later, Mom takes a seat on the step next to the platform. She's up. The tattooed Kiwi straps her ankles together and helps her stand. She shuffles to the edge of the tiny wooden square. She looks across the canyon at us. Channeling her inner Katniss, my mom touches three fingers to her lips and gives us a *Hunger Games* salute. But she doesn't jump.

She launches into an Olympic-medal-worthy swan dive.

It. Is. Epic.

QUEENSTOWN, NEW ZEALAND: *Kellie bungee jumps off the Kawarau bridge. Photo credit: AJ Hackett Bungy New Zealand.*

PASSPORT LESSON #10:

If you give in to your fears,

you'll miss out on life's greatest moments.

NEW ZEALAND
High-Low Report Card

	🙂	🙁
Delaney	Bungee jumping	Lack of Wi-Fi
Riley	Meerkat encounter	Not bungee jumping
Mom	Bungee jumping	Sold out tix at Cinema Paradiso in Wanaka
Dad	Stunning natural beauty	Not bungee jumping

Bali
INDONESIA

Languages:
Balinese &
Indonesian

Currency:
rupiah

ASIA

ISLAND
OF BALI

JAVA SEA

barf boat

spiritual
capital

Amed .

giant sarcophagus

Ubud

cemetery
with
snacks

Seminyak

Bali
belly

Trash
surfing

INDIAN OCEAN

18.

A Cultural Onion

February 4–18

You can't have a narrow mind and a thick passport.

— PAULINE FROMMER

Delaney, 14

"That's interesting." Riley motions to the opposite side of the street, where three women stroll with baskets on their heads.

"We're definitely not in Oz anymore," I say, not referring to the *Wizard of Oz* but the nickname for Australia.

We walk carefully, trying not to step on the tiny flower baskets that litter the sidewalks. A blue laundry basket filled with clothes rests on the woman's head in front of us. Her left arm carries a large shopping tote while her right arm dangles freely.

"I wish I could do that. It'd be like having a third hand," Mom says.

We just arrived in Bali, and we're trying to find our guesthouse in Ubud. Our suitcases clack-clack behind us.

"I don't care where we stay. It just better have air-conditioning," Riley says, as tiny beads of sweat form above her lip.

"And Wi-Fi," I add. "This could be hotter than Port Douglas."

"If you could only have one—A/C or Wi-Fi—which would you choose?" Dad asks.

"In New Zealand, definitely Wi-Fi. But here? I gotta go with air-conditioning," Mom says.

We all agree. A few minutes later, we find the entrance to our guesthouse. Two statues sitting in lotus positions flank the entrance. Hot pink flowers rest in the statues' laps. We step over the mini flower basket lying on the sidewalk and push open the wooden door in the towering stone entrance.

"Whoa," I say, scanning the lush compound.

UBUD, BALI: Carefully placed flower blooms decorate the outdoors.

Tropical trees form a canopy in the walled yard. Stone paths criss-cross the green lawn connecting the guesthouses. The chirping birds and trickling water give off a seriously Zen vibe. Flower blooms decorate the walls, steps, and paths. Water runs down the face of the goddess fountain while stone gods and goddesses, covered in moss and flower blooms, guard this oasis.

"Om swasti-astu." An older woman greets us, her palms pressed together in front of her chest. "You must be Kellie and family. I am Wayan. Come with me."

Dressed like all the Balinese women we've seen, she wears an ankle-length skirt and a long-sleeved top with a thick sash tied around her waist. Her silver-streaked hair sags in a low bun. I tug at my shorts, trying to make them longer. New culture. New dress code. How do they stand this heat with every inch of skin covered?

We follow Wayan to the open-air lobby. She hands us colorful drinks with paper umbrellas poking out. I know I should sip it, to be polite. But I drink it in three gulps. After checking our passports, Wayan leads us to our guesthouse across the compound. Exotic furniture, books, and artwork fill the living room. But it may as well be ugly and empty. Without A/C, we won't be spending any time there. Ri and I find our bedroom. It has twin beds. Yay. The other good news? The air-conditioning is ice cold. The bad news? The network only connects in the living room. It's the real-life version of *Would You Rather?*

Since we didn't know we were coming to Bali until a few weeks ago, I don't have any required reading for here. So I grab a Bali guidebook from the living room and flop on my bed. Even though I finally have Wi-Fi, I can't talk to anyone back home. It may be six in the evening in Bali, but it's three in the morning there. While I learn about Bali's history, Riley researches fun things to do. We stay in our air-conditioned paradise until dinner time.

UBUD, BALI: *Local women carry offering baskets on their head.*

WHEN THE SUN and heat go down, we walk a few blocks to Murnis' Warung—the first restaurant in Ubud. It's legendary among locals and travelers. Ri and I order a banana *lassi* (fruit and yogurt smoothie) and chicken satay. My parents order beef cooked in coconut milk. When I taste their *beef rendang,* I regret playing it safe.

"So, what did you learn this afternoon?" Mom asks.

"There are tons of spas, and they are super cheap! That would be so fun. Can we go?" Riley jumps in. She loves being pampered.

"We'll see. Did you *learn* anything?" Mom tries again.

"Did you know Indonesia's made up of over seventeen thousand islands? And Bali is the only one that isn't Muslim. Bali is mainly Hindu. And not just regular Hindu like we've seen in other places, but *Balinese Hindu,*" I start.

"That's interesting," Dad says. "How is it different?"

"Before Hinduism made its way to Bali around the ninth century, the Balinese practiced *animism.* So Balinese Hinduism combines the two."

> Animism is the belief that everything has a spirit. Rocks, trees, animals, everything. And people can communicate with those spirits— the good ones and the bad ones.

"So that explains why we can eat beef," Mom says, taking another bite.

"And also the fantasy creatures around the temples," Riley says.

She's right. Standing all around Ubud—in front of houses, along the streets, and carved into the temples—are monster statues. They are funny-scary, like fairytale monsters with fangs, potbellies, buckteeth, sagging boobs, and bulging eyes. With their mouths open and teeth bared, I can't tell if they're laughing or screaming. Riley and I pose next to our favorite animal-monster mashups and mimic the facial expression.

"Exactly. And the women with the round baskets on their heads? They were carrying offerings to the spirits. You carry them on your head because it's the most sacred part of the body," I explain.

"Thank you, Del, for the social studies lesson. Bali could be the most interesting place yet." Mom turns to Riley. "Now, tell us about the spas."

UBUD, BALI: A typical Balinese-Hindu statue.

WE GET AN EARLY START exploring Ubud. We're trying to beat the heat, and Riley wants to find the Putri Bali Spa.

"Oooh, look," Riley says. "One, two, three, four, five, six, *seven* girls our age!"

Just ahead of us, a pack of school-bound girls fills the sidewalk. They wear knee-length khaki skirts, knee-high white socks, and white blouses with khaki ties. A pair of dark brown ponytails or braids dangle below their shoulders. When they spot us, they turn to each other and giggle. Then, they smile and wave. The squad stops walking so we can catch up.

"Hel-lo," the bravest girl says.

"Hello," we say. We can't remember any Balinese words, but that's okay. They want to speak English. The teenage girls take turns practicing their foreign language with us. When they ask where we're from, we tell them the truth. They aren't trying to rip us off. After a few minutes, Mom takes a group picture, and the girls continue on.

"In just a few weeks, that'll be you. Back to school," Mom says.

"These four months have flown by," Dad says.

It's hard to admit, but he's right. We continue along the main road in Ubud, stepping over miniature flower baskets along the way.

"I know the litter is bad in Bali, but that's ridiculous." Dad nods toward the graveyard we're passing.

"Seriously. That cemetery is the only place in Bali that *isn't* covered in flowers," Mom says. "But it should be."

Soda cans, drink boxes, fruit, and cookie wrappers litter the graves. It looks like a convenience store exploded, and everything landed in the cemetery.

"Remember when we used to play opposite day?" I ask Ri. "That's what Bali reminds me of." Back home, flowers fill our cemeteries, and litter (if there is any) is on the street. But here, flowers are on the roads, and garbage fills the cemetery.

"If you let my grave get trashy, I'll come back and haunt you," Mom says.

We keep walking along the road in this strange, new place, wondering what our next surprise will be. It doesn't take long to find it.

What are they making? Right next to the road, a Balinese guy stands on top of a wooden ladder. Two buddies assist him from the ground. The three men add the finishing touches to what appears to be a larger-than-life bull piñata.

"What is it?" I ask, hoping they understand English.

"We make for burn." The guy on the ladder flashes a gigantic smile.

"Huh?"

"For cremation. Man die. Body go here," the piñata-maker explains in his limited English, which is superior to my non-existent Balinese.

"Ohhhh, it's a sarcophagus. So the body goes inside, then

you cremate it?" (*Sarcophagus* sounds so much better than piñata.)

He smiles and nods, obviously pleased that we understand his explanation.

"I thought a sarcophagus was just something from ancient Egypt," Ri says. "I didn't know it was still a thing."

The gigantic bull stands about ten feet high. Gold designs accent the black material stretched around it. The torso is large enough to hold a human corpse. Mom asks more detailed questions about the cemetery and cremation, but the conversation is too complex for our language barrier. We take a picture of the trio and their cremation creation and continue our journey in this fascinating place.

UBUD, BALI–FEB 2013: *Balinese men make a cremation sarcophagus.*

Riley, 12

I'M SO HYPED. Ubud is a spa-seeker's paradise. Spa days aren't really my mom's thing, but she said we could do it here. She loves a good bargain. I researched them all and chose Putri Bali. For the same price as getting a gel manicure at home, we get a five-hour spa package that includes a mani, pedi, massage, facial, milk bath, and hair conditioner. I'm even getting my legs waxed. Yay. No more shaving.

Dad and Del sign up for the $8 one-hour massage. I don't know why she's passing up the five-hour package, but she is. What a dummy.

"Enjoy your spa day," Dad says as they leave.

"Good luck with your legs. Can't wait to hear about *that*," Delaney says, smirking.

Mom and I spend our first hour getting side-by-side massages. When that is over, Wayan (my attendant for the day) leads me to a private room with a tub. Good. That would be weird to share a tub with my mom. I soak in the flower-filled milk bath, sipping hot tea while Zen music and incense fill the room. Red and white petals float on the surface, swishing around in kaleidoscope patterns. This is the best day ever!

When bath time is over, Wayan hands me a sarong to wrap around my body and a towel to wrap around my hair. I sit in a chair while she smears something on my face. It smells good enough to eat. Wayan massages something else through my hair. She leads me to another room with two cushion-covered tables. Mom is already on one. I lie down on the other. Wayan paints my fingernails and toenails while the hair and face masks work their magic.

I feel like a princess.

"Wax legs?" Mom's attendant, Ketut, asks her.

"No, thank you."

"Wax legs?" Wayan asks.

"Yes."

"You sure about that?" Mom's eyes go wide.

"Yes, my friends have done it and said it's fine."

"Okaaay."

The attendants each take a leg, smearing a section of my calves with hot wax that feels like peanut butter. They press a strip of material into the gooey mess. Mom reaches for her camera. Yank!

"AGGGHH!" I scream just as Mom takes my picture. "THAT KILLS!"

The attendants giggle. I bet they love torturing tourists.

"Do you want them to keep going? Or not?" Mom asks.

"Keep going," I say, through gritted teeth.

Wayan, Ketut, and I continue the smear-press-rip-scream-laugh cycle until my legs are as smooth as my dad's head. I can't wait to show Delaney. And I will never, ever, tell her how much it hurt.

UBUD, BALI: Riley and Delaney stroll through a rice paddy.

Delaney, 14

"How was it?" I look up from my book when Ri walks in.

"It was awesome. Feel my legs." Riley rubs her hand up and down her shin.

A few minutes later, we leave for dinner. Guesthouse-host Wayan (not spa Wayan) crosses the courtyard with an empty basket on her head. She's just left her evening offering of fruit and flowers to the spirits. My parents try to greet her in Balinese, but they mess up.

"How was your day exploring Ubud?" Wayan asks.

"It was great. We met some guys building a sarcophagus, and we also saw the cemetery. I have a million questions. Do you have time to talk?" Mom asks.

We totally forget our hunger when Wayan begins sharing the Balinese's beliefs about death and the afterlife.

"One of the core beliefs of Balinese Hinduism is reincarnation. For reincarnation to occur, the spirit must be released from the body. That only happens during cremation. So, the most important duty for adult children is to make sure their parents are properly cremated. If they don't, their parents will not complete the cycle of reincarnation."

"That sounds like a lot of pressure on the kids. What if they're losers?" Riley asks.

"The major challenge is not irresponsible children. It's money. Cremation ceremonies cost around twenty-five thousand dollars. Only the wealthy can afford them. The typical worker makes less than two hundred dollars a month. As a solution, many villages host mass cremation ceremonies every five years. This only costs around five hundred dollars per person being cremated."

"If it's only every five years, what do you do with the bodies in the meantime?" I ask.

"We bury them. Since the spirit is still in the body, it's important to keep them happy. So family members leave food and drink offerings on the graves for years. The spirit consumes the *essence* of the offering."

Wow. That wasn't litter on grandma's grave. It was a snack. Boy, did we misjudge that!

Wayan continues with our reincarnation lesson.

When cremation day arrives, it's a huge celebration. They dig up the bodies and place them in the sarcophagi. Firewood is stacked under the bellies of the animal-coffins and lit. While they burn, a high priest conducts a ceremony to release the souls.

Important! The family members must act happy because displays of grief inhibit the reincarnation process. When the burning is over, family members collect the ash and bone and throw it into the river or sea.

More important! A person's deeds in one life determine if they will reincarnate into something nasty, like a rat—or something wonderful, like a grandchild—in their next life.

I should stop torturing Riley with my hairballs in case my afterlife depends on it.

UBUD, BALI: Local women shop in Ubud.

THE DRIVER LOADS OUR BAGS into his car for the two-hour drive to Amed. When we all get settled, he turns to the back and flashes a big Balinese smile. "Howdy. My name is Wayan. But my friends call me Cowboy."

"Why does it seem like everyone is named Wayan?" I ask.

"Because most people are." He grins. "There are basically only four Balinese names: Wayan, Made, Nyoman, and Ketut. And they are given based on birth order. Wayan is the name for first-borns, so it is the most common."

"But what if you have more than four kids?" I ask.

"Then you start over. So the fifth-born would also be Wayan. But sometimes, the parents add *Balik* after it. That means repeat. That's why a lot of Balinese pick a personal name. Like Cowboy."

"That's so cool," Riley says. "So Delaney's *Wayan*. Mom and I are *Made*. And Dad is *Nyoman*."

Bali is a cultural onion. Each layer we pull off reveals another fascinating lesson.

Bali's baby names

First-borns: Wayan (or Putu, Gede, or Ni Luh)
Second-borns: Made (or Made, Kadek, or Nengah)
Third-borns: Nyoman or Komang
Fourth-borns: Ketut

Riley, 12

SEMINYAK, HERE WE COME! After three days of chillin' on Amed's black sand beaches, we are heading to our last stop in Bali. Amed was beautiful—and boring. We tried to snorkel from the beach, but the water was murky. So, we hired a guy to take us out on his *jukung,* a traditional Indonesian fishing canoe that looks like a giant spider. We bounced over the waves until we got far enough out to snorkel. As soon as we got in the water, both of my parents puked everywhere. Dad was on one side of the canoe. Mom was on the other. I dove straight back into the boat to avoid their floating barf, although it did attract some fish. Ew!

I'm mainly excited about two things in Seminyak: surf lessons and Waterbom. Waterbom is the best water park in Asia. Not the best on the island or in the country. The best on the entire continent. It's gonna be epic.

Cowboy drives us through the tropical mountains with rice paddies stair-stepping down the slopes in front of a palm tree backdrop. From a distance, the rice paddies look like Kermit-green-patchwork lawns. But when you get closer, you realize that the rice isn't in blades like grass. It's in plugs, like Barbie hair. Cowboy turns off the main road into a parking lot.

"This is Tirta Gangga. It's a water palace you must explore," Cowboy says. "Tirta Gangga means holy water of the Ganges, the most sacred Hindu river. Those who bathe in the waters under a full moon will be blessed with lasting youth and healing."

"Fountain of youth? I'm in." Mom opens her door. "Ri, grab your baton. This could be a great spot for your video."

The water palace isn't a building. It's more like a football-field-sized water garden. Ornate fountains and statues appear to stand on the water's surface. Stop-sign-shaped stepping stones create paths across the deep water. Lily pads and giant fish circle the stones.

"I feel like a token on a giant board game." I carefully step from pedestal to pedestal, making my way to the center.

"For real. And if we move off our square, we'll fall into the water," Del says. "This would be a cool place for your video."

"No way am I twirling it out here." I grip my baton as I balance on the water stone. "I'd either drop it in the water, or smack a statue god in the face and get a lifetime of bad luck. No thanks. I'll wait until I'm on solid ground."

Next to the stepping-stone-path main pool is the bathing pool. Fully clothed people float around the holy waters hoping for a facelift or healing. Since I don't need either, I don't get in.

KARANGASEM, BALI: The water at Tirta Gangga palace, named after the sacred Hindu river Ganges, is believed to be holy by the Balinese-Hindu.

"I FINISHED HOMESCHOOL!" I yell, running down the steps. The blue-laptop screen (I can't believe it still works) proves I just finished my science curriculum. I finished math yesterday. I bust into some awesome dance moves.

"You still owe me a Bali post. Then you're done," Mom reminds me.

I've written sixteen blog posts so far about new things I've done or learned. My last one will be about surfing in Bali.

"How are you sitting out here? It's four million degrees," I ask.

Mom's sitting in the living room, which is really an outdoor patio. Bali houses are bizarre. In Seminyak, long walls run down the streets like hallways. Doors in the walls lead to small, private compounds. Shrines stand outside each entrance where the Balinese leave their daily offerings to the spirits.

Inside our compound, a small swimming pool fills the left side. On the right is a covered patio with a small kitchen, a table and chairs, two uncomfortable wooden sofas, and one dinky ceiling fan. The master bedroom is upstairs, and the other bedroom sits behind the swimming pool. The only thing that matters about the bedrooms is they have air-conditioning. Even the swimming pool isn't refreshing. It's a hot tub without the jets.

"Family meeting everyone," Mom calls so Dad and Del can hear from the bedrooms.

After they join us in the outdoor sauna, a.k.a. the living room, Mom makes the announcement.

"It's time to book our last flights—to China and then home."

"For real?! What day are we going home?" Delaney jumps up, clapping. She's smiling so big her face might crack.

"In ten days. The twenty-second. We'll be here a week, then we'll do the seventy-two-hour stopover in Beijing. Then home. I've been looking at flights, and there aren't any non-stops between Bali and Beijing. We can either fly through Kuala Lumpur or Shanghai. Which do you want to do?"

"Not KL. I hate that airport," I say.

"Shanghai has to have a better food court," Delaney says, and we all agree. "It'll be our first taste of China."

Even though Delaney's thrilled we're going home soon, I'm not. Unless there's a growth-spurt-miracle in the next two weeks, Riley 1.5 will be on the last flight home.

"SURF'S UP, FOLKS. Time to G-O," I yell to the fam. Time for lessons at Double Six Beach. We grab our towels and sunscreen and begin the five-minute walk.

"Race ya!" I say when we can see the water. Del and I sprint down the sidewalk, careful not to trample the offerings in front of each store.

"What. The. Heck," Delaney says when we reach the sand.

"Ew, that's nasty." I scan the trash-covered beach.

"This is not what Bali looks like on social media," Mom says when she catches up.

It looks like a Dumpster exploded on the beach. A Corgi, clenching a plastic bottle in his mouth, runs by. A giant tractor creeps down the coast, scooping up trash.

"Oh. Lovely." Dad points at the blue Bombay Sapphire bottle lying in the sand.

We clear a spot and wait for our instructor to arrive. I'm watching the cute Corgi retrieve trash when I see something blinding. It kills my eyes, but I can't look away.

"Delaney! I need a *huge* root beer at three o'clock." We haven't played Root Beer since we were the root beer in Sri Lanka.

Delaney bolts up for the alert. "O. M. G. That's not a root beer. That's a crime."

An old White guy—with leathery skin and a potbelly—strolls down the beach. His teeny-tiny thong is giving him a great-big wedgie.

"Ew! Ew! Ew!" I smack my hand against my head, trying to undo the damage.

"I think I'm gonna get one of those." Dad glances from his swim trunks to the gray-haired-ponytail-thong guy.

"Stop it, Dad! Not funny." I would die if my dad went out in public like that.

"You must be the McIntyres." A Balinese guy wearing knee-length board shorts walks up. Dark curls hang to his shoulders, and a grin stretches across his face. "I'm Gede. Your surf instructor."

When Gede (pronounced like Aussies say G'day) turns to my parents, Delaney mouths, "He's cute." Mom raises her eyebrows and nods.

"Hi, Gede. You're the oldest child, aren't you?" Dad says, pleased that he remembered the birth order names.

Gede explains that it's *trash season*. Between December and March, strong currents send trash from the ocean onto Bali's beaches, especially Seminyak and Kuta. The beaches look more like landfills than paradise. Unfortunately, if you're a beginner surfer and want nice beginner waves, then Seminyak is the place to be.

"What's a little trash when your instructor looks like that?" Delaney whispers.

We wade into the trashy water for our lesson with Gede and his assistant, Made. Every time a wrapper or bag brushes against my legs, I freak out. Gede teaches us how to lie on our stomachs and wait for the perfect wave. Then how to paddle and pop-up at just the right time. They alternate helping the four of us. We all fall on our first two attempts.

"Woo-hoo!" Delaney rides the wave all the way on her third try.

I *have* to make it up this time. I ignore the trash floating around and wait for the perfect wave. Here it comes. I paddle like a maniac and pop-up, balancing my weight perfectly. I ride the wave until my fin sticks in the sand.

"Way to go, Ri," Dad says. I swim my board out and go again. And again. I get better with each ride, making tiny turns and finally dragging my hand in the water like I'm a pro. Ride. Repeat.

"I'm done. My knees are bleeding." Delaney drags her board onto the sand.

What a wimp. Even when red streams start trickling from mine, I don't quit. This is the best day ever!

"MOMMM! DELANEY HAS BALI BELLY!!"

I hear her barf splat-splat-splatting against the hardwood floor as I run down the steps. Mom passes me at the bottom and sprints up the stairs, two at a time. I'm not going up there any time soon. When Mom opens our bedroom door, her head jerks back, and she gags. The combination of heat and vomit is toxic. Mom leans back, takes a deep breath, pinches her nose, and barges into the barfroom. A few seconds later, she runs halfway down the steps and stops. Mom leans against the wall and breathes like a doctor has a stethoscope pressed against her back.

"That's bad. What happened?" Mom asks in between breaths.

"We were just watching TV, and she said she didn't feel well. And two seconds later, splat!"

"I've never seen so much vomit in my life. The floor isn't level, and the puke puddle is running under the bed. It's on the walls. It's everywhere. I don't know how I'm gonna clean that up. At least there isn't carpet."

"I guess I'll go into y'alls room." I'm not about to volunteer for vomit duty. Moms have the worst jobs. "It's too hot to sit out here."

"You don't wanna go in our room. Dad has Bali belly too. Out the other end. But at least he made it to the toilet."

After Mom finishes her puke patrol, she asks if I want to go to the grocery for Sprite and crackers. I'll go anywhere that has air-conditioning. Plus, I need deodorant. When we leave our guesthouse, our next-door-neighbor opens his gate.

The shirtless man wears a white sarong wrapped around his brown waist. He kneels down, removes the *canang sari* from his tray, and places the small flower basket in front of his gate. He nods and smiles before going inside. I turn and check both directions, inspecting the hallway-street. Our entrance is the only one without an offering.

SEMINYAK, BALI: A local man leaves a canang sari outside his gate.

"Maybe if we'd put out an offering to the spirits, they wouldn't have Bali belly," I say.

"Maybe we should move his canang sari in front of our gate." Mom nods toward our neighbor's flower offering.

I can't tell if she's kidding or not.

"NO! DON'T! We'd probably get the plague if we put out a stolen offering. That's worse than no offering at all."

We pass hundreds of tiny flower baskets on our walk to the store. In front of shrines and shops, people pile their canang saris. When the flower towers get too high, they topple over, spilling blooms onto the sidewalks and streets.

"So I guess we're not going to Waterbom?"

"No. Sorry. I'm bummed, too."

Ugh. Another epic adventure down the drain. And splattered against the wall.

"I have a great idea for Delaney," I say as we pass a souvenir shop. "How 'bout a T-shirt that says I YAKKED IN SEMINYAK."

"Great idea. And we could get your dad a matching one that says I HAD A CRAPPY TIME IN BALI."

"Can I at least get a fish pedicure?" I ask when I see the doctor-fish tank in the pharmacy. It tickles like crazy when the tiny fish suck the dead skin off your feet, but it's so fun.

"Sure. But first, we need to take the Sprite and crackers back."

We step into the store next door. While Mom gets the groceries, I search for deodorant. I find the right aisle, but I'm so confused by my choices. Mom finds me staring at shelves full of

SEMINYAK, BALI: Garra rufa nibble the dead skin off Riley's feet.

skin-whitening-and-lightening deodorants, lotions, and face creams.

"Why do all of their beauty products have lighteners in them?" I ask.

"Why do you and your friends lay out and use self-tanners?"

"Because my skin is pale. The Balinese have a beautiful skin color."

"And they might think you have a beautiful skin color."

"Huh." A new question spins around my head, then sinks in, deep and heavy. "Do you think anyone is happy with how they look?"

But I don't wait for an answer. Instead, I grab a deodorant. And a new attitude. I may hate being pale and small, but that's what makes me, me. Besides, I'm not even small in some parts of the world. I was wrong about the Riley Reinvention Project. It wasn't a failure. Just the opposite. I may still look the same on the outside, but I'm not the same person at all.

The fun in traveling is meeting people who don't look the same, dress the same, or believe the same. If we were all the same, the world would be the most boring place of all.

PASSPORT LESSON #11:
Every time you leave your bubble, you enter someone else's.
The best thing to do is ask questions.
Then close your mouth and open your mind.

BALI
High–Low Report Card

	🙂	🙁
Delaney	Trash surfing	Bali belly
Riley	Trash surfing	The smell of Bali belly
Mom	Warm people & fascinating culture	Cleaning up Bali belly
Dad	Trash surfing	Bali belly

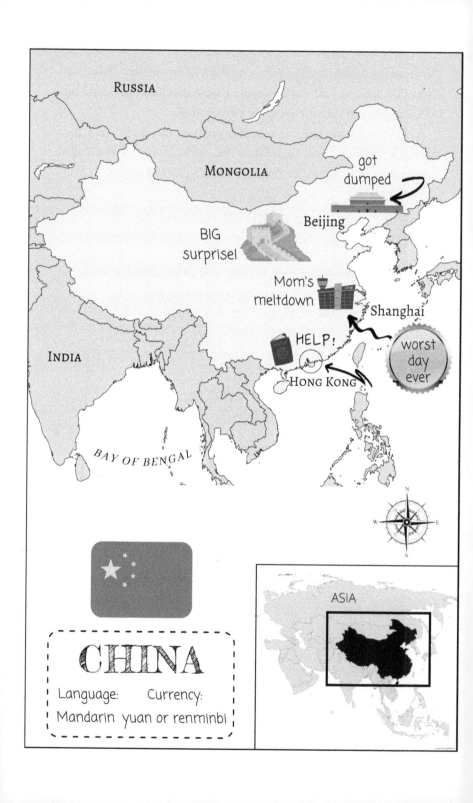

19.

The Final Challenge

February 19–22

It is easy to take liberty for granted when you have never had it taken from you.

— Dick Cheney, 46th Vice President of the United States

Delaney, 14

I hate waking up at four in the morning for early flights, but this one is worth it. There's only one tiny thing standing between me and the eighth grade. The Great Wall of China. It's the final challenge of our 'round-the-world quest. And the best news of all? I'll be home just in time for the high school open house on the twenty-fourth.

Life. Is. Good.

For me, anyway. Riley woke up sick. But at least it's not Bali belly.

We quickly make it through the his-n-hers airport security lines, as required in Muslim nations. (Even though the island of Bali is mainly Hindu, it is part of Indonesia, which is an Islamic country.) But now, we've been waiting to check-in for an hour-

and-a-half. With at least a hundred passengers in line with us—most of them sitting on the floor—there's no way Abysmal Air can check us in on time. Mom feels Riley's forehead, then pulls two white pills out of the medicine bag. After the Case of the Missing Backpack in Sri Lanka, she won't let anyone else be in charge of it.

"Go lie on one of those." Mom points to empty benches along the wall.

Finally, an Abysmal Air agent shows up and rushes through the line collecting passports. She scurries off, carrying a rainbow stack of passports. Twenty minutes later, the agent reappears, handing out passports and boarding passes.

"That's so weird," Mom says, inspecting our boarding passes.

"What is?" I ask.

"She didn't ask for our visa information or proof of onward travel. And she only gave us our boarding passes to Shanghai, not Beijing."

"This is the most clueless airline yet."

"No doubt. Do you realize we've been traveling over four months without a single hiccup? Not a missed connection, not a goofed-up hotel reservation, not a single visa issue. Nothing has gone wrong. It's been flawless," Mom gushes with pride.

We finally board and settle in. For once, Riley falls right to sleep. Mom and Dad sit in the row across from us. Our flight departed an hour late, and Mom checks her watch every few minutes. When the flight attendant brings drinks, Mom tries to ask her a question about our connection. But the flight attendant's English is limited to the snack menu. And our Mandarin is limited to *nǐ hǎo* (hello). Way later than scheduled, we land in Shanghai.

"Move fast and stick together," Dad says when we enter the jetway. "Our connection is very tight."

We speed-walk through the crowd—like sixth-graders

learning to switch classes—until we reach Immigration. We approach an immigration window and hand over our passports.

"Visa?" the officer asks.

"Yes. Seventy-two hours," Mom says.

"Onward flight confirmation?" My mom shows her our flight confirmation from Beijing to Chicago three days later.

"This is from Beijing." Her face shows no expression.

"Yes, I know. Our tickets are to Beijing, not Shanghai," Mom says, her voice going up an octave. "It's one reservation. Bali to Beijing. Please look." She hands over our itinerary.

The officer's face changes. And not in a good way. She gets the attention of another officer and waves him over. He looks reasonably friendly, as immigration officers go. Again, Mom explains the scenario: We have tickets *to* Beijing. We are flying home *from* Beijing. Our flights connect in Shanghai.

And, *bam!* Before we can count to *san*, he snatches our passports and turns us over to a not-so-friendly Chinese immigration officer.

"Excuse me, sir—" Dad begins.

Immigration-officer-number-three narrows his eyes and screams something in Mandarin. Mom's face turns white as Dad's turns red. I don't have to speak the language to know this guy is on a serious power trip looking for a place to happen.

We're about to be that place.

Without another word, the Chinese official herds us into a corner of Immigration and turns us over to a guard. Holy crap! Confiscated passport. Guard. Communist country. We're starring in our very own episode of *Locked Up Abroad*. While my parents whisper to each other, Riley and I assess our "holding cell." I've never been sent to detention in school, much less a foreign country. This is not good. Not good at all. We've only been with the guard for a few minutes when another officer escorts three twenty-ish-year-old guys to join us.

"Our tickets are to Beijing!" one guy yells. "We were told it was okay to get off the plane. We didn't even know we were stopping here!" Their pale faces are tinged with anger. The smug officer refuses to listen. He smirks and struts away.

We swap stories, and theirs is identical to ours. They have tickets from Japan to Beijing, and from Beijing to Australia three days later, using the seventy-two-hour tourist visa. We're just getting acquainted when another immigration officer brings a Russian woman to join our detention party. When the officer learns she has no visa and no onward ticket, she's escorted away. We never see her again.

Three nationalities. Three itineraries. The only thing we have in common is Abysmal Air.

A long hallway extends from our corner of Immigration to an employee entrance. Freezing, polluted air pours into the building each time the door opens. The security employees working in this area wear coats and masks *inside* the building to protect them from the cold and pollution. We huddle together on the floor, shivering in our Bali-weather clothes. The guard refuses to let us get our coats from our suitcases. We tuck our faces into our shirts to filter the indoor pollution. And wait. For what? I have no clue.

Dad asks the guard, "Can we please get some water. We've been here for hours."

Almost an hour later, the water arrives—two mini-bottles for the seven of us. The size that parents pack in their preschooler's lunch. Our family takes one.

"Don't let it touch your lips," I tell Ri when she takes a sip. I don't want what she has.

My parents are always telling us to look for the silver lining in bad situations. Fortunately, I don't have to look that far. There are three blond ones in front of me. Cute, cuter, and cutest. Meanwhile, the conversation with our detention buddies goes like this:

Them: Where are you from?

Mom: We're from the United States.

Them: You'll be fine, then. We're from Sweden. It won't be good for us.

Dad: Are you kidding? Everyone hates America. No one hates Sweden. You'll be fine. We're hosed.

And just like that, I start laughing. It is the kind of laughing when you know you shouldn't, like at a funeral. And the more you try not to laugh, the harder you do. It's not my fault that I don't know how to act. "What to Do When You're Detained in a Communist Country" isn't a chapter in any of the guidebooks.

"This isn't funny," Dad whisper-scolds. His usual pink face is unusually pale.

He's right. It's not funny. It's absurd. My life is absurd. Two days ago, I just wanted to survive Bali belly. Now I'm being held in a communist country. Is being a normal eighth grader too much to ask?!

After three hours, Mr. Power Trip and an Abysmal Air rep approach our group. They lock eyes with the Swedish guys and announce, "It is all straightened out. We talked to your embassy. You will be on the next flight to Beijing."

Mom untucks her face from her shirt. "What about us?"

"Oh no. *Not you.* Just the Swedes."

Seriously? We're a family with a couple of underweight, athletically-challenged girls, a dad with bad knees, and a mom who's only scary when she's hangry. And we're a bigger threat than three single guys in their twenties???

Then we're given the "American" options. Option one: pay $2,800 and immediately fly home from Shanghai. Or option two: ~~depart~~ deport China and fly to Hong Kong at Abysmal Air's expense. Then, pay another $1,400 to fly to Beijing, so we can catch our already-booked-and-paid-for flight home.

"That's absolutely asinine! We already *have* tickets to Beijing!" Mom's disgust hangs in the air.

Riley leans over so only I can hear her. "They must think we have money shooting out our butts like a bad case of Bali belly."

"Those. Are. Your. Only. Options." Mr. Superiority Complex narrows his eyes, obviously enjoying his dominance. He slaps our stack of passports against his hand, teasing us with his power. Each slap reminds us we have none.

After my parents "choose" option two, the immigration dictator turns us over to the Abysmal Air agent. We are officially his problem now. He's required to get us out of China as quickly as possible. After another two-and-a-half hours, our airline chaperone informs us we have seats on the 5:05 p.m. flight to Hong Kong. Hallelujah! We're finally getting out of airport lockup.

At six o'clock, we're still in detainment. Alone. Our flight to freedom left an hour ago. The Abysmal Air bonehead returns, and now he's trying to force us on the 9:45 p.m. flight, arriving in Hong Kong after midnight.

"No! We've been up since four o'clock this morning. We're *not* leaving at nine forty-five," Mom says, throwing her hands in the air. After hours of talking in circles with Chinese Immigration and Abysmal Air, my parents are cracking.

"This is ridiculous! We should've been on the five o'clock flight," Dad lashes out. "Don't you care how you treat your customers?!"

"No, sir." The Abysmal Air rep sticks out his jaw and slowly shakes his head. "I. Do. Not."

And, *bam!* Mom does something I've only seen one other time in my life.

She cries.

And not just a few tears rolling down her cheeks. But a full-on I-think-Mom's-having-a-breakdown sobbing episode. Ri and I wipe away Mom's tears—in a weird role reversal—assuring her it will be okay. But will it? Does she know something that we don't? In the middle of the Shanghai International Airport, the four of us embrace in a *Hallmark*-channel group hug. Other travelers stare as they walk by, careful not to get too close.

Six hours and $1,400 later, we have confirmed seats to Hong Kong tomorrow morning. And then to Beijing. There's a word for this kind of idiocracy. But I'd be grounded forever if I used it. Our Abysmal Air babysitter escorts us to the airport hotel with strict orders not to leave and to check-in for our flight first thing in the morning.

As if we'd miss it.

The hotel only offers rooms with twin beds, but my parents refuse for us to separate. So Ri and I share a twin, and so do my parents. No one complains.

"I need to let my parents know what's going on." Mom opens the door. "There's Wi-Fi in the lobby."

"Be careful what you say. They're probably monitoring our communications," Dad warns.

"Do y'all remember when we thought getting kicked out of that souvenir shop in Italy was bad?" I ask.

"Who can forget that?" Riley says. "I really wanted that scarf."

"Those were the good ol' days—back when I didn't know you could get kicked out of a country."

Ri and I lay our heads on the same pillow—we're positive it's filled with rice—and settle in for an unsettling night.

Riley, 12

THE PEOPLE in the Hong Kong airport are so nice. The employees smile and everything. And they aren't rude to the janitors like in Shanghai.

"Whoa. It has two floors." I step into the ginormous plane. Unfortunately, the upstairs is only for business class, so I don't get to see it. I plop into my cheap seat for our flight to Beijing. Take two.

Halfway through our flight, Mom leans over and feels my forehead. My face must be red. She does the same to my dad, then gives us some pills. He woke up feeling awful, too. Two hours later, we land in Beijing.

"Alright folks, let's hope this goes better than yesterday," Mom says, walking into the airport from the jetway.

Dad stops in his tracks. "You've got to be kidding me." He stares ahead at the passengers walking through something that looks like a high-tech soccer goal.

"What is it?" I ask.

"A thermal scanner," he says, "to detect people with fevers."

"And what happens to people with fevers?"

"They're detained." Mom shakes her head.

I scan the terminal for other options, but we have no choice. We have to walk straight into the mouth of the thermal monster. Like going under water, I instinctively hold my breath as I walk through the fever detector. As if that will change my temperature. I brace for flashing lights, blaring sirens, and another trip to airport lockup. But we get silence. It's the most beautiful sound I never heard. We hold our breaths again as we go through immigration. We majorly exhale when the officer stamps our passports, admitting us into China. Yay.

I think.

I spot the exit for taxis and roll my bag through the doors.

Bam! Pollution smacks me in the face. I cough, my body rejecting the toxic air. How can humans live in this?! I bet I'm losing one year of life for every hour I'm here. When my hacking fit dies, I pull my coat over my mouth and nose and drag my suitcase to an empty taxi.

"Nǐ hǎo," Mom says after she stops coughing. She hands the driver a slip of paper with our hotel name and address in Mandarin.

He holds up two fingers and points to his car. Then points to the empty cab next to his. Dad shakes his head, holds up four fingers, gestures to us, and points to the taxi. The guy shakes his head, holds up two fingers and points back and forth between the two taxis.

Tired of the first cabbie's treatment, my dad looks at the other taxi driver and puts up four fingers. Dad uses hand-and-eyebrow motions to ask the driver if he'll take us. The second taxi driver crosses his arms and shakes his head. I don't know what their problem is. Those taxis are limos compared to Pat.

We're getting nowhere quickly when a Chinese woman appears out of the pollution. She marches to the first driver and snatches the paper out of his hand, shaking her finger and yelling at both of them. She's been watching our losing game of Mandarin charades with the drivers. I may not speak Mandarin, but I know what she said. She hands our hotel information to a third taxi driver and gives him instructions. He nods his head rapidly and puts our bags in his car.

The stranger turns to us and smiles. In perfect English, she says, "I'm sorry they were so rude. I hope you enjoy your stay in Beijing."

It's about time our guardian angel showed up.

I'M TRIPLY HAPPY when we arrive at the Double Happiness Courtyard Hotel. Lion statues guard both sides of the red gate leading into the 250-year-old Chinese hotel. Round, red lanterns trimmed in gold hang in perfect rows along the *hutong*, old Beijing's ancient alleyways.

"I feel like I'm in *Mulan*," I say.

"Please. Follow me." Li Na's voice is barely more than a whisper. We follow her through the courtyard maze, her slippers clop-clopping along the red carpet. I feel underdressed in my jeans and sweatshirt, but they're the warmest clothes I have. She opens the door to our room and steps aside.

"Whoa, that's awesome." I kick off my shoes and step inside. "I wanna sleep in there."

"That is a traditional Chinese wedding bed," Li Na says.

The bed reminds me of a princess play fort that rich dynasty kids would make. The way Del and I used to make forts out of sheets and blankets draped over furniture. This bed-fort is made from carved wood with red fabric walls and ceiling. I climb through the red curtains pulled to the sides of the footboard, and sprawl across the dragons-and-flowers embroidered gold bedspread. Shimmery, beaded pillows line the back of the biggest, fanciest bed I've ever seen.

"Y'all sleep there. I'll take the twin." Dad coughs, pulling the blanket tighter around his shivering body.

"What's up with the Wi-Fi?" I ask. "I thought it would be good here."

"For real. Instagram won't load." Delaney tosses her device on the bed.

"Well, shoot. I wanted to upload Riley's trash-surfing post. But our website won't load either," Mom says, staring at her laptop.

"What do you mean? The Wi-Fi is great," Dad says. "I just checked the weather. The high tomorrow is only forty."

"This place is amazing. It feels like a Chinese palace."

Delaney moves through the room, examining every inch of the decor. "Now, the only thing standing between me and eighth grade is the Great Wall." Before she can hide it, a smile sneaks across her face.

BEIJING, CHINA: Riley kicks back on a Chinese wedding bed at the Double Happiness Hotel.

OUR DRIVER, John Wayne, picks us up at 7:00 a.m. Since he makes a living driving English-speaking tourists, he uses a fake name that's easy to say and remember. Our final day of world school includes a field trip to Beijing's top sights: Tiananmen Square, Forbidden City, and drum roll please, The Great Wall.

"Can we stop at a pharmacy first?" Dad's cough shakes the car. Even though he's really sick, he refuses to miss out.

"Yes. I will go in with you. Nothing will be in English, and no one will help you."

No joke. China is the only country we've visited that's basically impossible for non-Mandarin Chinese speakers to manage. We've gotten by everywhere with only English plus a few local phrases. Except here. But there's no language barrier big enough to keep me from my favorite hobby.

While Dad stayed in bed yesterday, Mom, Del, and I figured out how to take the subway from our hutong to *Hongqiao* (the Pearl Market). Nearly five months of wearing the same five outfits, plus five floors of name-brand knock-offs, equals shopping paradise.

"Oooh, I love this color." I shoved my foot into a seafoam athletic shoe.

"I've gotta get this," Mom said, inspecting a leather clutch with a gold emblem.

"I'm having a Fuggs flashback." Delaney pulled on black rain boots. "But this is awesome!"

We filled our shopping bags with Funter rain boots, Fike running shoes, and Fake Spade handbags. They look exactly like the real deal. I wish we had malls like that at home.

"Is the pollution always this bad?" I ask as we drive to our first stop. A thick gray-brown fog fills the city.

"Almost always. It is so bad that the school children no longer have recess," he says.

"No recess?" Recess is the best part of elementary school. It was always such a bummer when recess got canceled on rainy days. I'd hate living in a place where you could never play outside.

Our first social studies lesson—on my last day of world school—is visiting Tiananmen Square.

"Did y'all know it's the largest public square in the world? It can hold one million people," Delaney reads from her guidebook. "The Ming dynasty built this 'Gate of Heavenly Peace' in the 1400s."

"Well, that's ironic," Dad says, "because Tiananmen Square is most famous for its not-so-peaceful events."

"You're exactly right." John Wayne meets our eyes in the rearview and shares the awful story.

Tiananmen Square Massacre

China calls it the "June Fourth Incident," but the rest of the world calls it the Tiananmen Square Massacre. In the spring of 1989, college students began protesting for democracy, freedom of speech, and freedom of the press. The number of protesters grew daily between April and June. The government feared a political uprising and wanted the protests to end. On June 4th, Chinese troops opened fire on the demonstrators, killing thousands. Most of them were students.

"I was in college and their age. I remember watching the horror of it on TV. The whole world watched." Mom turns her gaze from the window to us. "I couldn't believe their bravery, and wondered if I would have the same courage if I were in their shoes. They died fighting for something that I enjoyed every day. That I did nothing to deserve. Freedom and democracy."

"I'll never forget the tank man. As the tanks rolled into Tiananmen Square, he stood his ground. One man faced down a long row of military tanks. He eventually climbed onto one. We need to look it up on YouTube," Dad says.

"China blocks YouTube. They block most social media," John Wayne says. "They don't permit anything that would allow people to organize themselves outside of the government's control. They even block Google."

Holy guacamole. That explains our technical issues.

"At least I won't have to see all the pictures of the Valentine's dance I missed," I say.

"And I won't be updating our blog," Mom says.

"So almost thirty years after those students were killed for wanting freedom of speech and press, they still don't have it?" Delaney asks.

"That is correct," John Wayne says as sadness steals his smile.

As we walk to Forbidden City, a single question spins around my head. Would I be brave enough to die for the freedoms I already have? The things I didn't even realize were freedoms, like social media and freedom of speech?

Forbidden City fun facts!

Forbidden City isn't actually a city. It is the world's largest ancient palace. For 500 years, twenty-four emperors from the Ming and Qing dynasties lived there. During that time, it was forbidden for commoners to visit. In 1911, a revolution overthrew the Qing dynasty and created the Republic of China.

Now, the Forbidden City isn't forbidden. Regular people can visit the 980-red-building palace with yellow tiled rooftops.

"Why is everything red and gold in China?" I ask.

"Red symbolizes happiness and good luck. That's what Chinese brides wear. And yellow is the imperial color. It represents power and royalty." John Wayne continues, "Forbidden City is believed to have 9,999.5 rooms. Emperor Chengzu, who built the palace, said only the God of Heaven may have ten thousand rooms."

We're wandering around taking pictures when a pack of teenagers surrounds Del and me. If we'd never been to Asia before, we might freak out. But we know exactly what they want. And we give it to them.

"I think the entire continent is on a secret scavenger hunt." Delaney smiles for a picture with a stranger. "And one item to check off is Take a Selfie with a Foreigner."

"I feel like a movie star," I say, smiling while the other girls flash peace signs.

One minute, Del and I have a line of fans waiting for selfies. And the next minute, *poof*, they're gone.

"What happened?" I ask as my selfie-seekers scurry off in the same direction.

"We just got dumped," Delaney says, spotting Forbidden City's newest visitors.

Before the two basketball-tall, Black guys can open their tourist brochures, a fan club (three times the size of ours) surrounds them, begging for selfies.

BEIJING, CHINA: Delaney and Riley's bright jackets stand out against the choking pollution at Forbidden City.

Great Wall of China !!

Construction on the Great Wall began in the 7th century B.C. and lasted two thousand years. At 13,000 miles long, it is the longest manmade structure in human history. That's more than halfway around the world!

 The Ming Dynasty (1368-1644 A.D.) was the last to rebuild part of the wall. The Ming section, which most people visit, is 5,500 miles long. That is the same as driving from California to New York and back!

ON THE DRIVE to the Great Wall, John Wayne squeezes over 2,700 years' worth of history into ninety minutes. That's my kind of history lesson. He's taking us to the Mutianyu (MEW-shen-yu) section. In addition to forts and watchtowers, this section has a twenty-first-century, kid-friendly update: a mile-long speed-slide from the wall down to the entrance!

"Grab your baton." Dad opens his door. "This is your grand finale."

"I can't believe we are finally here." Del leaps out of the car.

We pass souvenir stalls as we hike up a long hill toward the ticket gate. We have three choices for getting up the mountain to the wall: hike, cable car, or chairlift. Dad's sick, and it's freezing. So, we choose to take the chairlift up and the toboggan down.

The chairlift carries us up the mountain and drops us at watchtower number six. We're standing on top of the longest building on Earth. And we're alone. Everyone else must know it's too cold to come here in February. We hike from tower to tower in the frigid, filthy air.

THE GREAT WALL OF CHINA: Riley, Delaney, and Dale
hike to a watchtower.

"I want to know who started the rumor about being able to see the Great Wall from space. We can barely see it from here." I squint, trying to spot the next watchtower through the thick smog.

"Another social media lie," Mom says. "Let's get your video, buy a T-shirt, and call it a day."

I pull off my gloves, but my frozen fingers refuse to cooperate. After missing my first few tosses, my fingers warm up. Standing atop one of the Seven Wonders of the World, I launch my final 'round-the-world toss. It is epic.

[vimeo.com / 90537008]

"Time to bounce," Del announces, heading for the speed-slide entrance.

"This is one way to get kids interested in history." I hop on my toboggan and fly down the mountain's curvy metal slide. I don't pull the brake until I reach the bottom.

We trek down the hill, stopping to buy T-shirts dancing in the windy stalls. At the bottom of the hill, strolling toward us, three figures emerge from the haze. In a city of a bazillion people, I cannot believe my eyes.

"It's the guys from the airport!" I squeal.

"HEY!!!" we scream and wave, running to them. Mom hugs them like her sons have returned from war. I've read stories about the bonds strangers form during traumatic experiences, like war or hostage situations. Being detained in a communist country by a dude on a power trip ranks pretty high on the travelers' trauma list. When you've always lived in freedom, you take it for granted, because you don't know there's another way. Trust me. There is. And you don't want to find out for yourself.

"We never thought we'd see you again." Dad smiles, shaking their hands.

"We wondered what happened to you," the swoopy-haired one says.

"We've been talking about you for two days," the cutest one says.

I'm ninety-nine percent sure they're a Swedish boy band, but I play it cool. Mom hands her camera to a stranger to take the exclamation-point picture of our 'round-the-world journey. Then the seven survivors of Abysmal Air and China's seventy-two-hour visa hug one more time. We gush goodbyes to our Swedish detention buddies—the people I spent the scariest hours of my life with.

And we don't even know their names.

*MUTIANYU, GREAT WALL, CHINA–FEB 2013:The McIntyres and their
Swedish buddies from Chinese Immigration detention.*

PASSPORT LESSON #12:

Freedom is like oxygen.

You don't realize how important it is until it is gone.

	☺	☹
CHINA High-Low Report Card		
Delaney	Reunion with detention buddies	Detention and deportation
Riley	Shopping at the Pearl Market	Detention and deportation
Mom	Reunion with detention buddies	Detention and deportation
Dad	Reunion with detention buddies	Detention and deportation

20.

'Bama Bound

February 23

No one realizes how beautiful it is to travel until he comes home and rests his head on his old, familiar pillow.

— LIN YUTANG, CHINESE PHILOSOPHER

Delaney, 14

"Welcome aboard." A plastic smile stretches across the flight attendant's face.

"Thank you!" A genuine grin beams from mine.

I practically skip to the back of the economy section. I feel no jealousy as I pass through business class. Those people are probably going on, or returning from, a work trip. I'm going home, and not even a cramped seat on an overnight flight can ruin my mood.

We figured out about five countries ago that if we book window and aisle seats in the back of the plane, the middle seat will usually remain empty. Only a desperate traveler would book a middle seat in economy class, sitting between two strangers on a thirteen-hour flight. So we reserve aisle and window seats and hope the gamble pays off.

I find our row and slide next to the window. I shove my back-pack under the seat in front of me and my knee-high Funters under the middle seat. They aren't the most practical shoes for twenty hours of travel, but it's the only way to get them home.

"We did it." I turn to Riley as she settles into her beloved aisle seat. Our new seat strategy has eliminated the middle seat argument. "Can you believe the next beds we sleep in will be ours?"

"I can't wait. You know what I can't believe? We just spent twenty-four-seven as a family for almost five months. We didn't kill them. They didn't kill us. And we didn't kill each other." Then, she adds in her goofy voice, "It's a Christmas miracle."

"I wouldn't have made it without you, Ri. You made me laugh when I wanted to die."

"Same." She rips the plastic covering from the airline blanket, stuffs it in the seat-back pocket, then turns to me. "Just think of the stories we're gonna tell our kids one day."

"They won't believe half of them." I adjust the air overhead. "What's the first thing you're gonna do when we get home?"

"Shower. And then bed. I can't wait for my pillow. But the next day? You wanna build a bonfire with these clothes and roast marshmallows over them? I'm never wearing them again."

"I'm in."

I watch our battered bags creep up the conveyor belt into the belly of the plane. Each scuff is evidence of their own global journey. If all goes as planned, we'll make it back just in time to attend the high school open house. It's a lot to process. One day I'm trapped in Chinese Immigration begging for my coat and water. A couple days later I'm deciding between Honors and AP World History. Talk about cultural whiplash!

Only two people besides our grandparents know we're coming home. Since our friends surprised us with a going-away party, we're going to surprise them with our return. Two of our family's favorite friends, Pam and Margaret Ann, are picking us up from the airport tomorrow night. We know our secret is safe with them. Under the cover of darkness, we'll sneak into our house and hope the neighbors don't notice. The next day, we'll show up in the school cafeteria at lunchtime. I can't wait to see everyone's faces.

Eighth grade, here I come.

III. The Difference

difference
noun dif·fer·ence | \ ˈdif(ə)rəns \

: a point or way in which people or things are not the same.

Oxford Languages via Google.com. 2022.

21.

Malaysia Airlines Flight 370

March 8

There is nothing like returning to a place that remains unchanged to find the ways in which you yourself have altered.

— Nelson Mandela, *A Long Walk to Freedom*

Delaney, 14

Our eyes are glued to the family room TV. I click from station to station, watching coverage of the missing international flight mystery. Malaysia Airlines flight 370[1]—the flight from Kuala Lumpur to Beijing that we chose not to take two weeks ago—has disappeared over the ocean with 239 people on board. Three of them are Americans. A decision that we made based on bad food court experiences plus two weeks' time equals the only reasons there aren't seven Americans on that plane.

"I'm sick." Mom covers her mouth with both hands.

"How horrific. We were literally just there," Dad says, watching hysterical families waiting for updates in the Beijing airport.

"It's morbidly ironic. If we had taken that flight, we wouldn't

have been deported. If we'd taken that flight two weeks later ..."
Mom's voice trails off.

"Our guardian angel deserves a raise," Riley says quietly.

Feelings of horror, sadness, and relief simultaneously race through my body in a dead heat. Six months ago, I wouldn't have spent more than thirty seconds thinking about this. It would've been another random disaster in some random part of the world. Today, this tragedy feels as personal as if a plane full of my neighbors disappeared. For the past five months, the world was my community.

And those were my neighbors.

22.

Perspective

Spring of Senior Year

Sometimes not getting what you want is a wonderful stroke of luck.

— DALAI LAMA XIV

Delaney, 18

"I'm home!" I kick off my shoes in the laundry room. Riley and I are supposed to train our friends to leave theirs at the back door, too. That's one of the long-term results of spending so much time in Asia. Mom even mops the floors after parties now, instead of before. Sometimes—if my parents aren't home—Ri and I sneak and wear them inside anyway. If that's the worst of our teenage rebellion, they shouldn't complain.

In just a few months, I'll be leaving for college. I was a hardcore University of Alabama football fan (*Roll Tide!*) growing up. But when it came time to apply to colleges, I only applied to one: Auburn University (*War Eagle!*). I'm counting down the days 'til I move to The Loveliest Village on the Plains in August.

"How was your day?" Mom spins around in her chair. She's working at her desk in the kitchen.

"It was good. How was yours?"

"Really good. The PTO president for the middle school called. They're planning an International Day, like the one when you were in elementary school. I've been asked to be one of the keynote speakers."

"That's awesome. Are you gonna do it?"

"I am. But you know what would be *really* awesome?" She scribbles something on a sticky note and adds it to the collection on her monitor. "If you did it with me. The students would love to hear what you have to say. You could share your leadership talk."

My Youth Leadership II class requires each student to write a TED-type speech. Mine is about how traveling has made me a better American.

"Sure. I'll do it," I say, after considering it for a few seconds.

"Really? Thank you. I thought you'd make me work a little harder for it." Mom grins. "They've asked someone really important to give the opening speech. It depends on whether that person is available that'll determine if we do the opening or closing. I don't know who it is. I just know it's a big deal."

Mom, Dad, and I squeeze into the middle school conference room. Even after spending three years at this school, I've never been in this room. A table fills most of it. Around the walls, school officials, teachers, and a handful of parents and their children wait. Buzzing energy fills the room. The excited whispers remind me of starstruck kids waiting in line for an autograph from their favorite sports player or pop star. An office worker rushes in.

"She's here. Remember, quick handshakes and photos. She's on a tight schedule."

My jaw drops when "she" walks into the room. The person my entire family agreed would be our dinner-guest-of-choice as we drove across New Zealand four years ago. The person my mom and I will follow as keynote speakers today. Former Secretary of State, Dr. Condoleezza Rice!

VESTAVIA HILLS, ALABAMA–MAY 15, 2018: Dale, Kellie, and Delaney McIntyre with Dr. Condoleezza Rice.

Dr. Rice's speech this morning was incredible. How am I supposed to follow that? My only advantage is that I'm relatable. Dr. Rice was once one of the most powerful people in the world. I'm just a girl from the neighborhood. Their neighborhood. And I spent my middle school years sitting in those same bleachers, listening to inspiring talks.

Almost five hundred kids file into the gym, heading to their designated sections: sixth on the left, seventh in the middle, and eighth on the right. Some walk in packs. Others walk alone. Middle school is still middle school. I'm glad that's behind me.

The three most memorable speakers that I've listened to in this gym are:

1. a concentration camp survivor from the Holocaust,
2. a woman with brittle-bone disease who climbed Mt. Kilimanjaro, the highest mountain in Africa, and
3. our nation's former Secretary of State, Dr. Rice.

No. Pressure. At. All.

My heart pounds as the students clomp up the bleachers. Thanks to the famous Iceland-locker-room lesson, I know I won't die from embarrassment. At least I'm not naked.

When the students get settled, the principal introduces my mom and me. I'm going first, then Mom. The irony of the situation is comical. Four years ago, I literally bawled my way out of this building because of my parents' crazy dream. Today, I'm going to tell them how that crazy dream changed my life. I take a deep breath, squeeze my boyfriend's hand, and walk to the podium:

"Travel is fatal to prejudice, bigotry, and narrow-mindedness, and many of our people need it sorely on these accounts. Broad, wholesome, charitable views of men and things cannot be acquired by vegetating in one little corner of the Earth all one's lifetime."

These are the words of Mark Twain. My parents firmly hold this to be true, which is why—in my eighth-grade year—my parents pulled me and my seventh-grade sister out of school for eighteen weeks. After years of fantasizing, they booked one-way tickets and decided to plan the rest along the way. This would not be a five-month vacation in fancy, all-inclusive resorts, but authentic travel featuring public transportation, hostels, and street food. So I spent half of my eighth-grade year world-schooling on a cheap laptop wherever I could find free Wi-Fi. I crammed entire chapters of math and science into one day after avoiding my school work for weeks. Looking back, I can't recall any of my online lessons. I even repeated Algebra I my freshman year. But it is my real-world education that I'll never forget.

I learned that there is no perfect country. Each is great and not-so-great in different ways. Today, I'm going to share how I learned what is great about the United States of America.

I learned that If I lived in Thailand, I'd probably be in prison; China, I would lose all of my online friends and followers; and Germany, I would have failed eighth grade.

And I also learned that Americans take so much for granted. In our country—where so many people are divided over racial and socioeconomic issues—we often overlook the privileges *all* Americans possess. If you've never traveled beyond our country's borders, or your travel has been limited to resort destinations, it is easy to focus on what is wrong with our nation. However, even with our issues—and we definitely have them—the United States provides more freedoms and liberties than most other countries. Let me share a few examples.

Thailand and China taught me what freedom of speech really means. In China, we couldn't get on our social media or our personal website, because the government blocks it. In Thailand, insulting the king can land you a spot on the next episode of *Locked Up Abroad*. Coming from a country where bashing the president (no matter who is in office) is our nation's favorite sport, I now understand the magnitude of freedom of speech.

Fashion. Americans are accustomed to dressing however we want. Sometimes we have to follow dress-code rules in school, but the rest of the time is a fashion-free-for-all. But just because it's normal to wear shorts or strappy dresses here, doesn't mean it's okay in other places. In many countries, we wore long pants and modest tops because of religious and cultural norms—no matter how hot it was. As travelers, it's important to respect the local customs, even if that means not wearing our favorite fashions.

Education. I was fortunate that through homeschooling, I could continue my eighth-grade education while exploring the world. But some countries, like Germany, do not allow homeschooling. Americans view European countries as having all the same freedoms we have, but that's not always the case.

Furthermore, many countries do not provide free education for the children. If the parents cannot afford to pay the school fees, the kids don't attend school. Without education, these children cannot break the cycle of poverty in which they are trapped.

Traveling has taught me far more than just about the places I have visited. I can pack enough clothing for any climate in a carry-on suitcase. I have learned how to sleep sitting up for sixteen hours. I have learned to hope for the best and brace for the worst—because sometimes you can't predict being deported. Even when we think we are living our worst nightmare, Americans still have more liberties and privileges than most of the world.

I understand that my parents have given me the biggest blessing —the opportunity to have my eyes opened—and I also understand that most people won't have the same opportunity. But you don't have to leave the country to leave your bubble. You can drive across town, open a book—or maybe—just walk across the room and invite someone to sit at your lunch table.

I challenge each of you to do two things to become better Americans: One, seek opportunities to connect with people who are different from you. Your life will be enriched in ways you cannot imagine. And two, never forget what it really means to live in the land of the free.

Thank you.

As the students clap, I take my seat on the front bleacher. I rub my damp palms across my yellow dress. My heart is still racing when Mom begins. As she shares lessons we've learned from traveling the world, I think back to a conversation we had almost five years ago. Back when I blamed my parents for ruining my life.

The most valuable souvenir that I've brought back from my travels wasn't the Funter rain boots. It's so much bigger than that. Country by country—continent by continent—I picked up bits and pieces along the way. And I brought home the very thing I was missing.

Perspective.

23.

Full Circle

Spring of Junior Year

I was not born for one corner. The whole world is my native land.

— SENECA THE YOUNGER, PHILOSOPHER

Riley, 17

The first thing we did after returning home was downsize our house. Not one time did we miss it. We missed our pillows, sheets that didn't smell like B.O., and clothing options, but not all the extra stuff. In fact, it felt ridiculous returning to a house with more toilets than people. The only time we'd even need four toilets is if we all got Birmingham belly at the same time. And that's never happened.

After our big trip, I felt like Dorothy from the *Wizard of Oz* when she woke up in her bed. Everything was black and white again. It's hard to return to ordinary when you've experienced extraordinary. Travel is a lot like the yellow brick road. The farther you go from your bubble, the brighter the colors get. I'll be chasing those colors for the rest of my life.

I inherited a double-dose of my parents' wanderlust genes. It turns out my love for adventure really may be a part of my

DNA. My mom claims to be distantly related to Meriwether Lewis of the famous Lewis & Clark expedition team. I'm not sure if that's true, but it's far more likely than her being related to Betty Crocker or Gordon Ramsay.

We met our six-continent goal early. And I love Africa as much as I love Asia. I've been back to Europe, and it's growing on me. I think you have to be older to appreciate it. One day I might even give Italy a second chance. But, in my opinion, Africa and Asia are the best out-of-the-bubble experiences for kids. As for me, the top items on my bucket list are:

- Bungee jumping. (Thanks to the eventual completion of the Riley Reinvention Project, I weigh enough now.)
- Antarctica. Why stop at six continents when there are seven? (Mom and Dad tell me I'll have to fund that one myself.)

Every year since the big trip, my parents ask if we'll ditch school for another extended adventure. Their world is brightest out of the bubble too. Our answers are always the same: *Yes!* from me. *No!!* from Delaney.

The thing about travel is the more you see, the more you realize what you haven't seen. So far, I've visited thirty countries. Which sounds like a lot, until you remember there are 195. The world is full of fascinating people and places—and I want to experience everything I can while my parents are footing the bill. As I told that scammer in Italy, Genovians aren't dummies.

So, I'm cooking up a plan. While middle school is the best time to travel long term with kids, there is another window that can work: spring of senior year. It's the lame-duck semester of high school. By that point, all of the critical academic stuff is done, like ACT/SATs, GPA, college admission, and scholarships. You could miss a chunk of that semester, and it really wouldn't matter. Even the best schools can't teach the lessons that come from the real world. Which is why my passport is the best teacher I've ever had. Next year, Delaney will be away at college. I just have to convince my parents of the plan. Which shouldn't be too hard.

After all, they created this monster.

It's funny how life comes full circle. I traveled around the world to learn what I already knew when I was seven, that I painted on a canvas one summer day:

EVERYBODY IS THE SAME WHEREVER THEY GO.
IN THEIR HEART, THEY ARE THE SAME.

Passport Lessons

I. You won't die from humiliation if you try something new when you leave your bubble.

II. While all travel transforms, the most life-changing transformation occurs when you're farthest from your bubble.

III. If you insist on doing things your way in a different culture, things could get nasty.

IV. Visitors will love or hate your school, your community, and your country based on the people they meet. Don't be a jerk.

V. People are like presents. Some come in fancy wrappings and others in plain bags, but the best part is what's inside.

VI. Life's most memorable lessons don't come from textbooks.

VII. Our country, culture, and interests bond us as humans— not our skin color.

VIII. There are two sides to every story. Especially war. Most people only know the version their country tells. But there are two weapons more powerful than hate: love and forgiveness.

IX. In a sea of strangers, it only takes one friend to feel at home. Be that friend.

X. If you give in to your fears, you'll miss out on life's greatest moments.

XI. Every time you leave your bubble, you enter someone else's. The best thing you can do is ask questions. Then, close your mouth and open your mind.

XII. Freedom is like oxygen. You don't realize how important it is until it is gone.

PLEASE
Leave a Review!

Thank you for reading our story. If you enjoyed it, would you pretty-please-with-sugar-on-top leave a review at Goodreads or the online retailer of your choice? It's the best way to let the author and world know that you enjoyed it (other than buying a gazillion copies for your friends and family).

Thank you for giving me your time. I hope it was worthwhile.

Discussion Questions

1. If your parents announced you would be going on a world-wide trip, would you be thrilled (like Riley) or upset (like Delaney)? Which sister do you identify with more and why?
2. What would be the maximum amount of time you would be willing to go? Three months? Six months? A year?
3. Who or what would you miss most while you are gone?
4. Would you rather spend all of your time in one part of the world and learn about it in depth? Or skip around and visit lots of different places? Why?
5. Delaney and Riley's parents prioritize experiences over material things, like the latest clothes/toys/electronics. Which do you prefer? Why?

PART TWO: THE WORLD

Iceland:

6. How would you feel about sharing a house with strangers?
7. Before going to the community pool, the McIntyres had to shower in a room full of people. Are you a modest person? Would you have been freaked out by the locker room rules? If so,

would you go through with the pre-swimming ritual? Or miss out on the swimming experience altogether?

England:

8. Adults keep telling the sisters that they are learning more by traveling than sitting in a classroom. Do you agree or disagree with this statement? Why or why not?

Italy:

9. The McIntyres experience a series of unfortunate interactions with the locals. How do the people we meet influence how we feel about an experience or place? Why is it important to not judge an entire group of people based on our interactions with a few?

Sri Lanka:

10. The sisters feel very self-conscious in their yoga pants when all of the other females are wearing saris or burkas. Have you ever been judged by the clothes you wear? How did it make you feel?
11. Have you ever judged others based on how they were dressed?
12. Have you ever been in the minority due to race, religion, or economic differences? How did it make you feel?

Thailand:

13. Do you think all humans are connected in one way or another? Why or why not?
14. Were you surprised to learn that some countries imprison their citizens for making negative comments about the presi-

dent/leader/government? What would the United States be like without freedom of speech?

Malaysia:

15. When the McIntyres want to talk with "our people" after the church service, did you think they were referring to the White family with daughters? Or the Black couple? Who did they have more in common with? Why?

Vietnam

16. Were you surprised to learn that the swastika was an ancient symbol for good luck before it became associated with evil?

Australia

17. How do you think it made the McIntyres feel to visit the family they met in Vietnam at their home in Australia? Have you ever been homesick? How did you deal with it?

New Zealand

18. Were you surprised when Delaney and Riley's mom bungee jumps? Would you bungee jump?
19. Have you ever allowed fear to hold you back from taking a risk? Do you regret that decision?
20. What does Delaney's bungee jump represent?

Bali, Indonesia

21. What is your Balinese name? What do you think about Bali's naming tradition?

22. What are some interesting things you've learned about other religions through Delaney and Riley's experiences?

23. Is it possible to be friends with people whose spiritual beliefs differ from yours? What can you learn from each other?

24. What does Riley realize when she's shopping for deodorant? How is it significant?

China

25. Were you surprised to learn that each country makes its own rules about who is allowed to enter and the paperwork required? What are the pros and cons of this?

26. When the McIntyres don't have the right visa due to their flight's itinerary, they are detained at the airport. How did you feel reading about the McIntyres' detainment and deportation? Was it fair? Or unfair?

27. When the McIntyres are detained in a communist country, it is their first experience with loss of freedom. How do they each react? Why?

28. Have you ever lost your freedom? Can you imagine living in a country or world without it?

Part Three: The Difference

29. What does it mean to "live in a bubble?" Do you? Why or why not? Why is it important to get out of your bubble?

30. What are some ways to get out of your bubble in your own city?

31. Which of the countries that you learned about would you most want to visit? Why?

32. Which was the scariest situation? The most unusual? The most exciting? The most humiliating? The most heartwarming?

33. How did Delaney and Riley change over the course of the journey?

Acknowledgements

For the past year, Dale has repeatedly asked, "If you'd known it would be this much work to write a book, would you still do it?"

I'll let you know the final answer in a few months. The reality is that I had no idea what I was getting into when I started *The Passport Project*. But I do know that I wouldn't be here, typing the final words of my first book, if not for the support and encouragement of countless people.

The first person I confessed my book secret to was my dear friend and book club leader, Carrie Wertheimer. Her enthusiasm landed her the job as my first alpha reader. Chapter by chapter, Carrie's spot-on feedback helped shape this book from draft one.

Thank you to my other alphas, Eleanor Mahlow and Robin Mahlow. With Eleanor's middle-school perspective, Robin's homeschool perspective, and both of their wise editorial suggestions, I hit the jackpot when they read my raw first draft.

Thank you, Carlin Gregory and Diana Goldstein, for choosing the beta version of *The Passport Project* for your niece-aunt book club. Your feedback was invaluable in refining the manuscript.

Thank you, Holly Meadows, attorney extraordinaire, for helping me sleep better at night. You are the best.

Thank you to my middle-grade editors, Erin Arcand and Sara Schonfeld, and my travel editor, Barbara Noe Kennedy, for not telling me my manuscript was perfect when that is what I wanted to hear.

Thank you, Victoria Scott, for creating the perfect book cover. I'm embarrassed by the number of revisions I requested and grateful for your patience and professionalism. You are a gem!

Thank you to the Mackintosh, Mahlow, and Shropshire family focus groups for never tiring of my requests for cover feedback.

Thank you, Captain Bob Loewer and Agnes Patel-Purohit, for your historical and cultural feedback.

Thank you, Rachel Macy Stafford, for encouraging me to jump on the author train. From neighborhood mom to multi-NYT-best-selling author, you are an inspiration.

Thank you, Rachael Brooks, for suggesting I include maps. They only added an extra hundred hours of work, but their inclusion makes the book.

Thank you to my beta readers for your encouragement and feedback: Nora Arcand, Lori Baerg, Erin Brooks, Anika Schurman, and Peggy Walker.

Thank you, Kelli Eshleman, for inviting Delaney and me to speak at Liberty Park Middle School's International Day. We didn't know it at the time, but you gave us the perfect exclamation point for Delaney's character arc.

Thank you to the entire AuthorTube community for my creative writing degree, including, but not limited to: Abbie Emmons, Alessandra Torre, Alexa Donne, Bethany Atazadeh, Book Launchers, iWriterly, Jenna Moreci, M.K. Williams, Reedsy, Shaelin Writes, and The Creative Penn. I haven't been alone in my car or walking the dog in over a year. One of you is always riding shotgun.

Thank you, Charles and Mary Welden, for sparking our initial fascination with, and subsequent love for, Southeast Asia.

Thank you, Melissa, Rich, Taylor, and Sydney Baum. From our first trip to Akumal when the kids were in preschool, to the epic road trip around Namibia when they were in high school, and all the ones in between, we cherish our four-continent McBaum adventures.

Thank you, Cora Passman for the going-away party and Chris and Allison Morhard for fostering Molly.

Thank you, Vestavia Hills City Schools, for valuing experiential learning and graciously accommodating our world-schooling stints without undue bureaucracy.

Thank you, Ken Coleman, for helping me identify my talents, my mission, and my passion. *The Passport Project* is the outcome of bingeing *The Ken Coleman Show* during a pandemic.

Thank you, Mom, for your spirit of adventure, and Dad, for your gift of storytelling. You made genetic contributions to the book. As always, thanks for keeping the pets.

Thank you, Dale, for insisting I continue writing as I neglected all of my responsibilities. I am blessed to have you as my husband and companion. I'm grateful to be married to a man who would rather fly across the world to eat fifty-cent street food than drive across town for a fifty-dollar steak.

Thank you, Delaney and Riley, for allowing me to share our story. We're blessed to have made memories together across the globe, and I hope one day you'll ruin your kids' lives, too.

Finally, I thank God for creating a world that is filled with interesting people and places. If He wanted us to stay home, everyone and everywhere would be the same.

Endnotes

CHAPTER 5: PANAMA: COCKROACHES IN PARADISE

EPIGRAPH
Vidor, King, Victor Fleming, George Cukor, Richard
Thorpe, Norman Taurog, and Mervyn LeRoy. 1939. The
Wizard of Oz. United States: Metro-Goldwyn-Mayer
(MGM).

PART II: THE WORLD

EPIGRAPH
Holiday magazine, March 1956, pp. 40-51.

CHAPTER 14. MALAYSIA: FINDING OUR PEOPLE

EPIGRAPH
Jones, Shirley A. *Simply Living: The Spirit of the Indigenous
People*. Novato, California: New World Library, 1999.

CHAPTER 15. VIETNAM: THE GIRL IN THE PHOTO

1. Former POW and U.S. Senator John McCain passed
   away on August 25, 2018.

Chapter 19: China: The Final Challenge

1. China has updated its transit visa exemptions since 2013. Please confirm the current visa requirements before traveling to China or any other country.

Chapter 21. Malaysia Airlines Flight 370

1. Extensive investigation concluded that flight MH370 ended in the southern Indian Ocean. There were no survivors.

About the Author

Kellie McIntyre is a Southern girl with a passion for the world. Her quest for culture and adventure has taken her to nearly 50 countries across six continents. In 2013, Kellie and her family traded their suburban bubble for a journey around the world.

Now, she's on a mission to help other families travel boldly.

Kellie holds a BA from Western Kentucky University and a Master of Public Health from the University of Alabama at Birmingham, but her worn passport has provided her most valuable education. She shares tips for planning and surviving global family (mis)adventures at 4WornPassports.com.

Kellie lives in Vestavia Hills, Alabama. *The Passport Project* is her first book.

KellieMcIntyre.com | 4WornPassports.com

facebook.com/4WornPassports
twitter.com/4WornPassports
instagram.com/4WornPassports

CPSIA information can be obtained
at www.ICGtesting.com
Printed in the USA
LVHW010124230222
711737LV00004B/102